IMAGES
of America

RICEVILLE

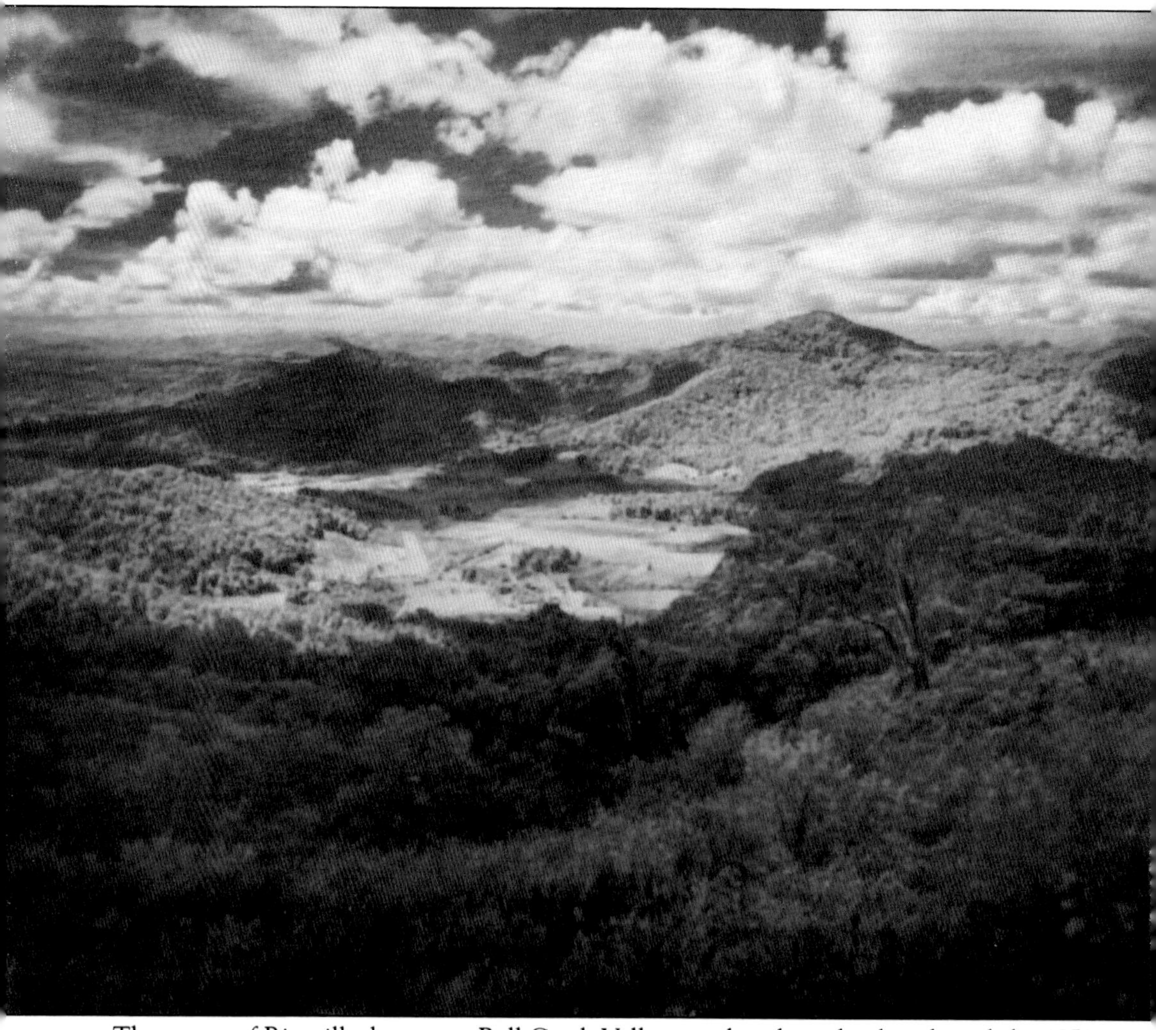

The center of Riceville, known as Bull Creek Valley, was largely undeveloped until the 1950s when land began to be subdivided. Before this time, land was cleared primarily for farming and grazing. (Courtesy of Cobb Hughey.)

On the Cover: Students at the Riceville School in 1917 are, from left to right, (first row) Margarite Rice, Ruth Shope, Vivian Shope, Della Cordell, Mary Lyle Whistenhunt, Connie Shope, Carolyn Shope, Nidra Shope, Violet Allison, and Arlene Alexander; (second row) Thad Gregg, Lynol Gregg, Harold Cordell, Douglas Allison, Thurman Lunsford, Stanley Lunsford, Billie Shope, Ladd Joyner, Leonard Cordell, Raymon Parker, Grady Shope, Neil Alexandra, Richard Hughey, Jonas Hughey, Thalous Shope, Junior Allison, Wayne Stephenson, Clyde Hall, Howard Creasman, Rhubin Clark, and Bill Allison; (third row) teacher Barney Edwards, Emmit Clark, Earnest Jones, Leonard Clark, Gayle Keacher, Mae Hughey, Evelyn Joyner, teacher Roberta Shufford, Pauline Rice, Hazel Shope, Bertha Gregg, Lucy Gregg, Eppie Shope, Thelma Gregg, Ethel Shope, Lucille Rice, Pearl Stephenson, Halmenton Slagle, Tom Creasman, and Talmadge Shope. (Courtesy of Sara Sawyer and Mr. and Mrs. Robin Gregg.)

IMAGES
of America

RICEVILLE

Anne E. Chesky

ARCADIA
PUBLISHING

Copyright © 2011 by Anne E. Chesky
ISBN 978-0-7385-8791-2

Published by Arcadia Publishing
Charleston, South Carolina

Printed in the United States of America

Library of Congress Control Number: 2011925223

For all general information, please contact Arcadia Publishing:
Telephone 843-853-2070
Fax 843-853-0044
E-mail sales@arcadiapublishing.com
For customer service and orders:
Toll-Free 1-888-313-2665

Visit us on the Internet at www.arcadiapublishing.com

To the Riceville community, for sharing its photographs and memories

CONTENTS

ACKNOWLEDGMENTS

Thanks to all who contributed to putting this book together. It would not have been possible without the many stories and photographs shared with me by the Riceville community. Special thanks especially to Sybil Fox, Robin and Wendi Gregg, Cobb Hughey, Butch and Judy Reed, Rafe Rice Jr., Tip and Sara Sawyer, John Weakly, and Nancy Wrenn. Thanks also to the Scenic Riceville Advocates, Pat Beaver, and Sandy Ballard for their support during the initial stages of this project. And, finally, thanks to Mom and John, who kept me fed, and Grandmother, who piqued my interest in local history.

INTRODUCTION

Located seven miles northeast of Asheville, North Carolina, Riceville boasts some of the most undeveloped land in Buncombe County. In these wild spaces exists incredibly high biodiversity of flora and fauna. Oak, maple, hickory, birch, pine, ash, beech, buckeye, sourwood, and poplar are only a few of the tree species found here. In some spots, which were too difficult for loggers to reach, a few old-growth species remain, and some trees may be more than 300 years old. These forests are also home to many species of wildlife. Salamanders, turtles, and fish inhabit Riceville's lakes and ponds. The forests provide nesting grounds for a variety of migrating birds. Mammals such as black bears, coyotes, bobcats, raccoons, foxes, opossums, squirrels, and chipmunks roam Riceville's forests and are often seen taking shortcuts through the neighborhoods.

Riceville's vast expanses of farmland are also a unique and valued part of this valley. Some cattle still remain here, although farms in Riceville are becoming fewer and farther between. Land has been divided up and more houses have been built, but Riceville is still blessed with large areas of green space.

When residents think about the valley today, they must first consider the people that lived here before them: the ancestors of the Cherokee. Long before Joseph Marion Rice—Riceville's namesake—settled here, the early ancestors of the Cherokee had villages around the Asheville area for thousands of years, and they used the Riceville and Swannanoa Valleys as hunting grounds. Warren Wilson College's archaeology program has unearthed artifacts ranging from projectile points and pot handles to jewelry and pottery, which indicate that nomadic tribes of the Early Archaic tradition established semipermanent camps in the valley more than 10,000 years ago.

While few of Riceville's residents mention interactions with the Cherokee in their family histories, many artifacts similar to those found in Swannanoa have been found in Riceville. Based on the number of artifacts found in the valley and the abundance of land and water, many residents suspect that Cherokees may have built settlements in Riceville. The Smithsonian and the University of North Carolina at Chapel Hill have surveyed and recorded the presence of Native American artifacts on the land between Parker and Bull Creek Roads. Family stories about finding Indian gravesites also exist within the Riceville valley.

During the 1700s, conflicts over land between Native Americans and European settlers were common, and though both often attempted peaceful resolution of land disputes, there was still much misunderstanding and bloodshed between the two groups. Thus, the transition of western North Carolina from Cherokee to European hands was not without conflict. In 1783, the State of North Carolina signed a treaty with the Cherokee Indians to allow for some early European settlement, and by 1784, the Swannanoa Valley was occupied by white settlers.

Unlike many settlers, Joseph Marion Rice, the first white settler in the valley, reportedly had a friendly relationship with the Native Americans. In the spring of 1782, Rice came to Riceville. He brought goods to trade with the Indians, and according to Helen Whittemore, before he obtained his own land, Rice stayed with a band of nomadic Shawnee Indians who were camped at a lake at the head of Bull Creek.

Family stories report that the Indians "granted [him] a sum of land . . . that he could walk around and stake between sun-up and sundown," which amounted to around 200 acres. In the late 1780s, Rice pitched his tent at the headwaters of Bull Creek, built a cabin, and then brought his wife, Margaret, his horse, and his gun, which he called "Bacon Betsy," to settle. Rice is perhaps most infamously known for shooting the last buffalo seen in western North Carolina. Whether this is true or not is still debated today.

According to Nancy Wrenn, after settling, Rice impounded part of the creek and began to charge a fee to the drovers taking livestock over the mountains to South Carolina markets. A three- to five-acre, spring-fed lake nearby supplied water, but because of an earthquake in the early 1800s, the lake disappeared and is now referred to as the Dry Pond. While living in Riceville, Joseph and his wife had three sons—Joseph Jr., William, and a third whose name is unknown—and one daughter, Elizabeth. It is from William and Elizabeth Rice that many of Riceville's current residents are descended.

Another landowner in the early Riceville area was John Craig, the first treasurer of Buncombe County. Craig owned more than 100 acres in Riceville that is still called Craigsfield Farm today and is still owned by his descendants. He built a home on Bull Creek, operated a mill there, and raised nine children with his wife, Hannah Davis. While little else is recorded about Craig's life, much more is known about his death because of its suspicious circumstances. On March 31, 1808, the *Raleigh Minerva* reported the following:

"About 4 o'clock in the afternoon, Mr. Craig, being at his mill alone, heard his dogs barking—he turned with an intention of crossing the stream, but coming within 20 or 30 yards of the noise, a gun was discharged from the thicket, and a leaden ball entered his body a little below his ribs, and lodged just within the skin of his back. Mr. Craig survived this unhappy circumstance about three hours; manifested a firm mind, and retained his senses to the last moment of his life; said he saw the man, who he supposed shot him, run off from the thicket, and fully believed the man to be Henry West, who lived within a small distance of the mill."

On April 10, West was convicted of murder and sentenced to death by hanging. A set of footprints—one shallow and one deep—were found at the murder scene. This evidence was used against West, who had a deformed leg allegedly from being attacked by a shark in Charleston, South Carolina.

After the trial, however, evidence was found that implicated another man, Thomas Rogers, in Craig's death. Rogers and Craig had been quarreling for a long time. West, on the other hand, was not known to own a rifle and was engaged to marry one of Craig's daughters. In light of this evidence, West's execution was delayed. James Patton and Jane Erwin, Patton's sister, were political opponents of Craig and sought to secure a pardon from the governor for West. At noon on the appointed day, while awaiting Erwin to return with the pardon, Patton convinced Buncombe County sheriff James Hughey (who is also an ancestor of folks in Riceville today) that his watch was wrong, and the execution was delayed again. While West was waiting for his execution, he agreed to give Philip Creasman, the burying man, a tract of land on Lower Grassy Branch Road in exchange for a proper burial. After they made the deal, and just as the hangman was ready to throw the trap, a horseman galloped over a hill with West's pardon from the governor. When West was pardoned, Creasman refused to return the land deed and replied that he would still bury West when the time came.

Several decades later, the close-knit Riceville community was divided by the Civil War. One Swannanoa church, led by a Northern minister, even split over the issue of slavery. Many of Riceville's men, even those opposed to the war, were mustered into the Confederate army.

After the Civil War, with the formation of a school, several churches, and a post office, Riceville was quickly becoming a more organized community. In the later part of the 1800s, the Presbyterian church sent missionaries to the Blue Ridge Mountains to educate the "poor white mountaineers." Although most teachers came from outside the region, western North Carolina–born A.M. Penland founded schools across the Asheville area. On September 15, 1873, he founded and became the first principal of the Montanic Institute, which was located on the hill adjacent to

Riceville Presbyterian Church. The school was the center of the Riceville community during the late 19th and early 20th century. It was advertised as, "a public day school, free from sectarianism, open to all classes of (white) boys and girls."

One of the teachers who came to the region was Frances Louisa Goodrich, of Allanstand Cottage Industries fame. She came to Riceville in the autumn of 1890 when the teacher Evangeline Gorbold requested help from the Board of Home Missions. Goodrich described the school and her surroundings: "Imagine a valley shut in on all sides by mountains covered with a thick growth of oak and walnut and pine. A few cabins and farm houses scattered along the road, which runs through the center; not enough dwellings in sight to account for the 90 or more children said to be within reach of the proposed school, though a crowd of little faces peeps at you from every cabin door."

After the Montanic Institute, three schools operated in this location: Vaughn Academy, the Peabody School, and College Hill School. Another school for local children, known as the Brush Hill School, was located on Old Farm School Road. And many of Riceville's boys would go on to attend the Asheville Farm School—now known as Warren Wilson College.

Now, Riceville was blooming as a community. From around 1873 to 1923, mail was delivered to a post office located in Riceville. Riceville was actually home to two post offices—one that served the community while Democrats were in county office and the other while Republicans governed.

Infrastructure—a school, post office, and roads—was necessary, as most of Riceville's residents made their living within the community, and transportation out of the valley was difficult and time-consuming. The 1883 *Buncombe Gazetteer* listed Riceville's prominent residents, their occupations, acreage, and the distance of their property from the post office: G.W. Burnett sold general merchandise at a local store, J.C. Clark operated a sawmill and gristmill, and J.A. Reed was a gunsmith. Other listed residents—S.W. Glass, C.P. Gragg, Samuel Hughey, A.J. Rice, W.R. Shope, B.G. Shope, J.M. Shope, S.A. Stroup, S.F. Stroup, and D.C. Stephenson—all owned around 100 acres in the area and made their living farming. There was also a blacksmith shop that operated at the end of Jones Cove.

Building and maintaining roads into and around the valley was important in its development as a community. The ancient buffalo track over the mountain was known as Bull Gap, and the road that ran down to Riceville became known as Bull Creek Road. The first public road in this part of the county, though only a dirt path, Bull Gap was the main passageway at that time for people passing from the Riceville side of the mountain over to Weaverville and on west to Unicoi County, Tennessee, or farther. It was a major route, used by farmers, in places like Tennessee or Kentucky, who made the annual trip south to bring their livestock to sell in South Carolina. These drovers moved hogs, turkeys, and cattle in huge herds or flocks, taking a month or longer to make the trip. They stayed at inns or stock stands along the way, such as that operated by Joseph Rice.

Religion and worship were also very important to the Riceville community during its formation. Between 1850 and 1950, four churches were organized in Riceville. These churches became the center of social life in the community, and congregation members often came together for community events.

Berea Baptist Church is Riceville's oldest church. Located on Riceville Road, south of Bull Creek, Berea Baptist Church was organized in 1853. The first pastor of the church was Thomas Stradley, from the First Baptist Church of Asheville. About a mile past Berea Baptist, is Riceville Presbyterian Church, which was established in the spring of 1876 and met at the home of Samuel and Margaret Hughey on Bull Creek. The first church building was built in the late 1800s, and until 1953, was known as College Hill Church and School. On the other side of Riceville is Bethel Methodist Church. In 1886 and early 1887, the Reverend E.H. Reynolds encouraged Methodists to build a church on a section of what is now Riceville Road. The church building was constructed in 1888, by mostly volunteer labor, on land donated by Joseph and Hannah Glass. The building was dedicated in 1890, and services were held once a month by circuit riders. In 1923, the first church building burned, but was rebuilt by 1925. The fourth and youngest church in Riceville,

Grassy Branch Baptist and was organized in the fall of 1949. It outgrew its original building twice and currently meets in the new sanctuary, which was built in 1986. These four organized churches continue to hold weekly services and promote various programs for their members—and all are open to the public.

By the 1950s, Riceville's post offices and schools had closed, but residents were still able to purchase many of their everyday necessities in the community at one of many country stores. Near the Parkway tunnel was Padgett's Garage, owned and operated by Bill Padgett, one of the members of Riceville's Board of Directors. Between Grassy Branch and Bethel Methodist Church was Elmer Reed's Grocery. Reed sold gas, oil, and groceries to the community. The building has since been renovated into a home. Farther down Riceville Road was Dooley Clark's workshop, which had previously been a factory that manufactured metal spiral staircases. This garage was also used as the fire station for four years. The brick-front building near the current fire station was Tal Shope's store, which carried a variety of goods. And, finally, just before the intersection of Bull Creek Road and Riceville Road was M.J. Carter's Grocery. At the time, his was the youngest of the Riceville stores. The store was later converted into an apartment building and is currently used by Don Cordell as a tractor barn. Just northwest of Carter's grocery was an old gristmill where residents brought their corn to be ground. Cordell can still remember taking the corn to the mill and picking up a warm sack of meal when he was a little boy. In 2011, though there are no stores open in central Riceville, many residents still operate businesses within the community.

In the 1950s, the Riceville Community Development Council helped coordinate and organize the community's existing organizations by supporting the development of the Riceville Community Center. They helped the Riceville Men's Club purchase eight acres on Parker Road for the original community center and later helped open the current community center and fire station. Money for the original center was raised by the men's club as well as by a Home Demonstration Club bake sale, a Bethel Church supper, and a turkey shoot. The center was built in 1957. Money donated by the owner of Beacon Blankets in Swannanoa helped purchase and construct the current center and fire department 10 years later. The Riceville community was also vital in raising money to fund the purchase of several fire engines and ambulances for use by the Riceville Fire Department.

Today, just like in the 1950s, Riceville's residents need to know how they are working together. And they need to ask, "How can we continue to support the Riceville community?" There are already many institutions within Riceville with missions to support the community, such as the Riceville Community Center, the Riceville Fire Department, the area's churches, the neighborhood associations, and the Scenic Riceville Advocates. These organizations are helping to create a sustainable future for the Riceville valley, to keep its history alive.

One

THE EARLY YEARS

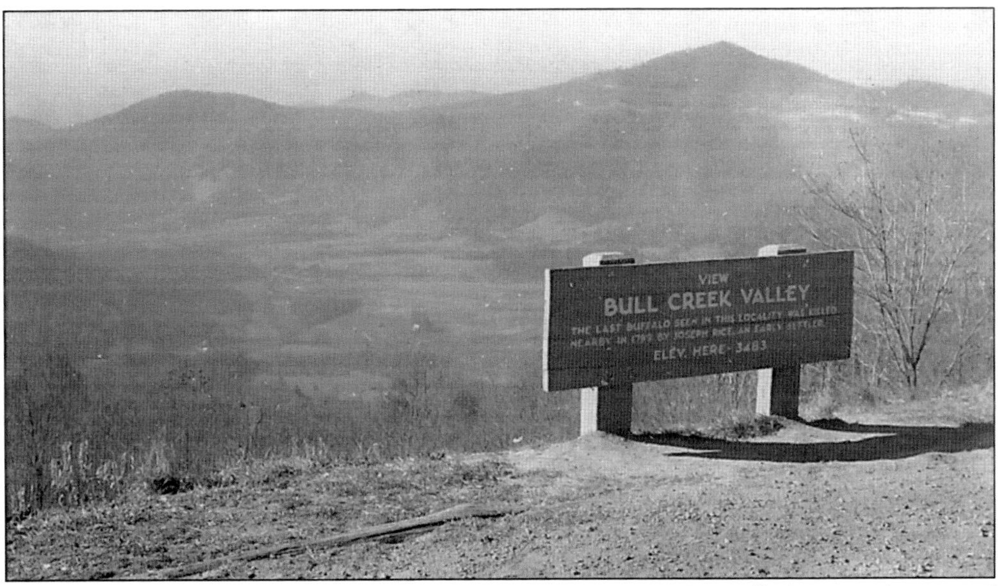

Near milepost 374 on the Blue Ridge Parkway, visitors can view Riceville from an elevation of 3,483 feet. The historical marker at the site reads, "Bull Creek Valley, the last buffalo seen in this locality was killed nearby in 1799 by Joseph Rice, an early settler." Whether Rice truly killed the last buffalo is still debated today. This photograph was taken in the 1940s, just after completion of the parkway. Many of Riceville's residents found jobs building the Blue Ridge Parkway in the 1930s. (Courtesy of Rafe Rice Jr.)

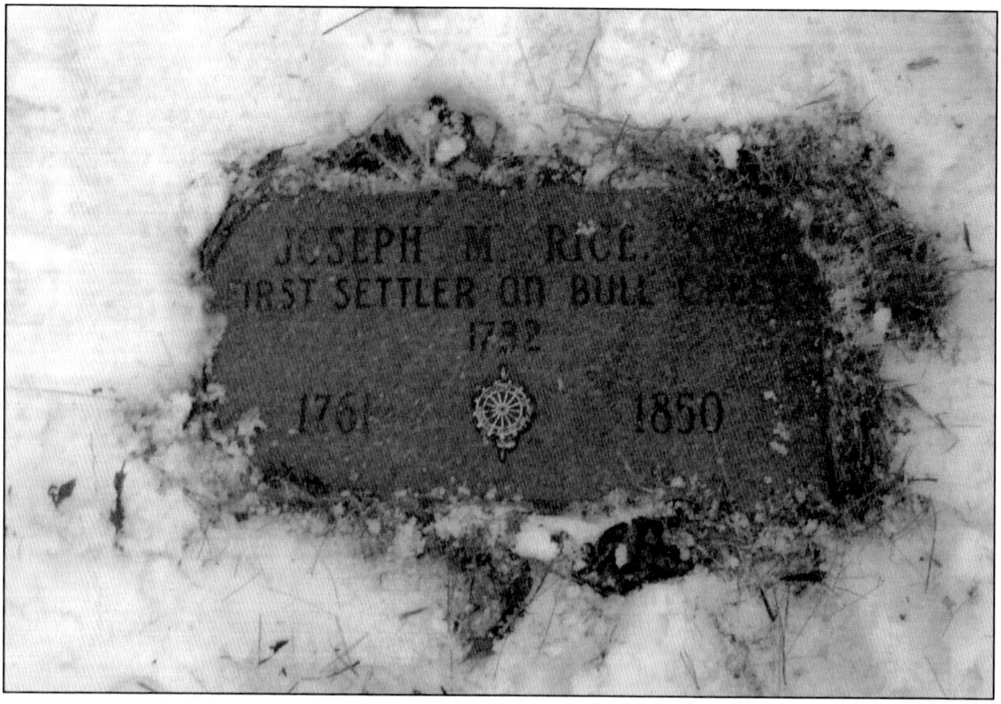

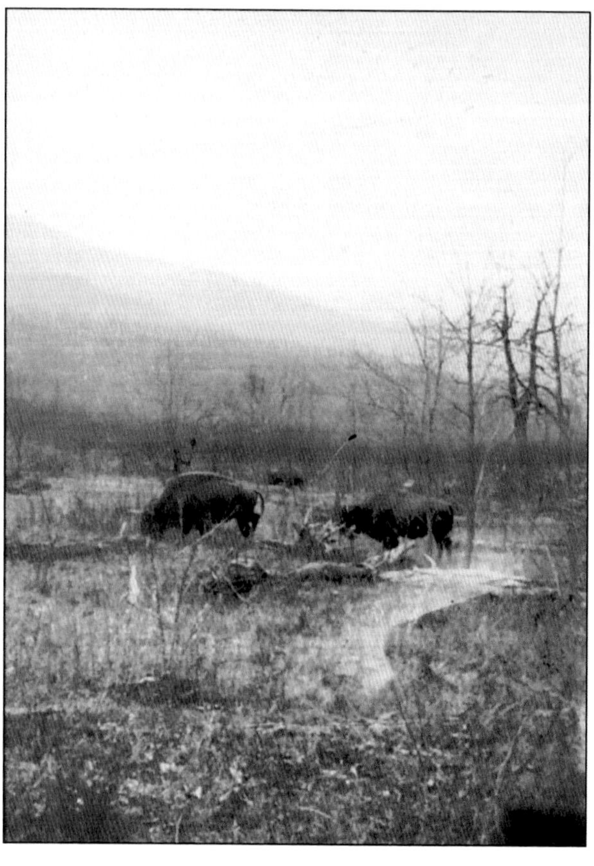

After settling, Joseph Marion Rice impounded the creek and began to charge a fee to drovers taking livestock to market. He cleared a place for the livestock to rest, fed them some fodder, and began collecting money. The Daughters of the American Revolution placed a marker honoring Rice in the Rice-Hughey cemetery—almost directly across the street from where it is believed Joseph Rice operated his stock stand. (Courtesy of the author.)

Three buffalo graze in a field in the 1920s with the Blue Ridge Mountains behind them. Buffalo were once prevalent in the Bull Creek Valley, and many present-day roads follow the old buffalo trails. Though buffalo were not present in Riceville after 1800, perhaps there was an attempt in the 1920s to reintroduce them. (Courtesy of Rafe Rice Jr.)

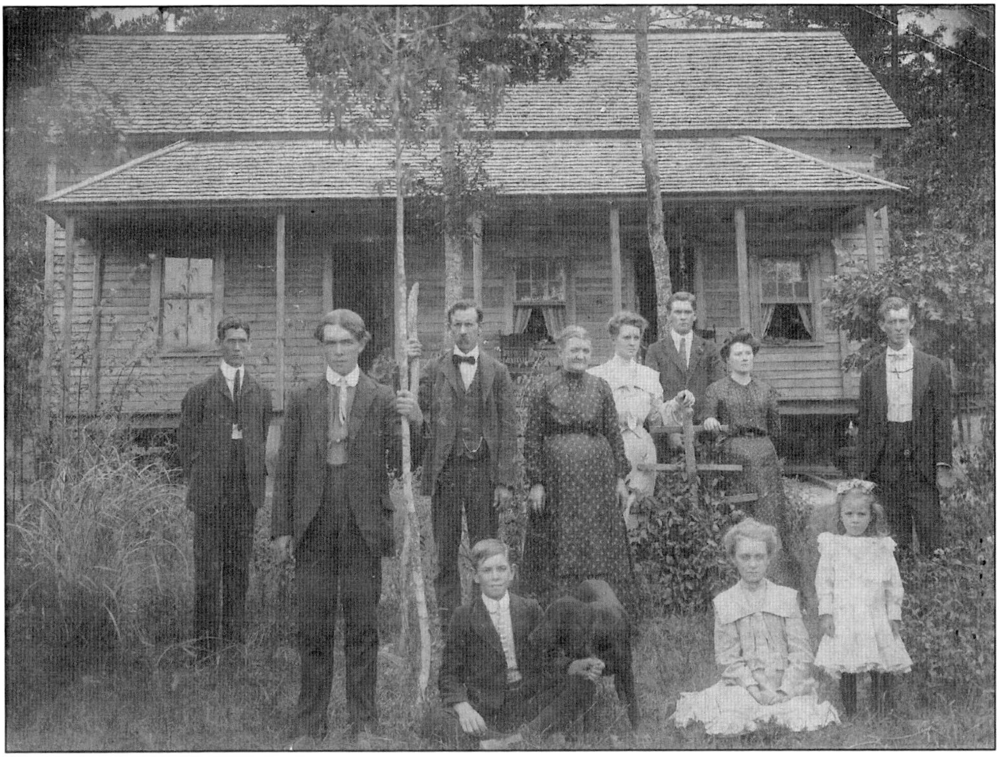

In 1900, the old Rice family home place was located off Old Farm School Road. Pictured are Raphael Rice Sr. (sitting by dog), Jack Rice (with walking stick), Florence Rice (girl standing), May Rice (woman standing in white dress), Josie Rice (woman in far back), and Frank Rice (man in far back). The others are unidentified. (Courtesy of Rafe Rice Jr.)

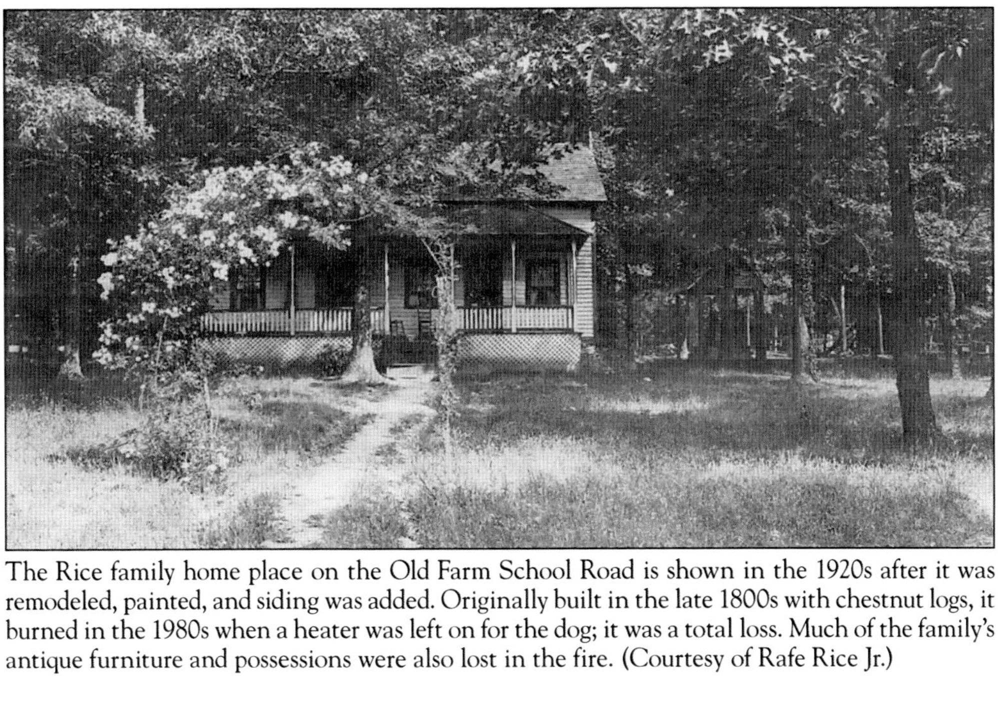

The Rice family home place on the Old Farm School Road is shown in the 1920s after it was remodeled, painted, and siding was added. Originally built in the late 1800s with chestnut logs, it burned in the 1980s when a heater was left on for the dog; it was a total loss. Much of the family's antique furniture and possessions were also lost in the fire. (Courtesy of Rafe Rice Jr.)

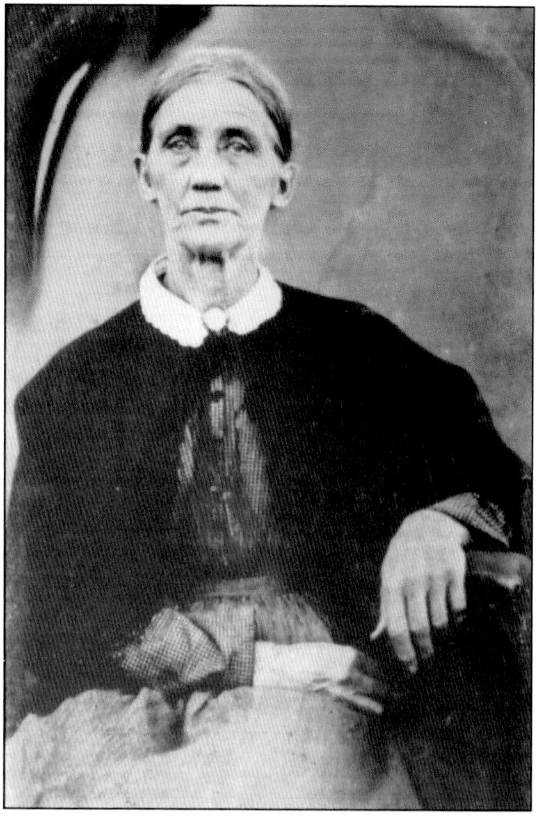

Born in 1824, Martha Roseanne Stephenson Rice married John Longmire Rice, son of William and Martha Longmire Rice. They had three sons, Rev. William "Billy" Francis, Alfred, and John Winslow. John Longmire opposed the Civil War but was put in charge of the horses in Will Thomas's legion. He got sick and was sent home during Christmas 1864, suffering from malnutrition so serious he could not be fed. (Courtesy of Sybil Fox.)

The Martha Roseanne Stephenson Rice cabin, referred to locally as the "Roseanne Cabin," was located on Rice property off Bull Creek Road. Roseanne was the daughter of Abraham Stephenson and Martha Craig and the granddaughter of John Craig, the first treasurer of Buncombe County, who was murdered in Riceville. (Courtesy of Sybil Fox.)

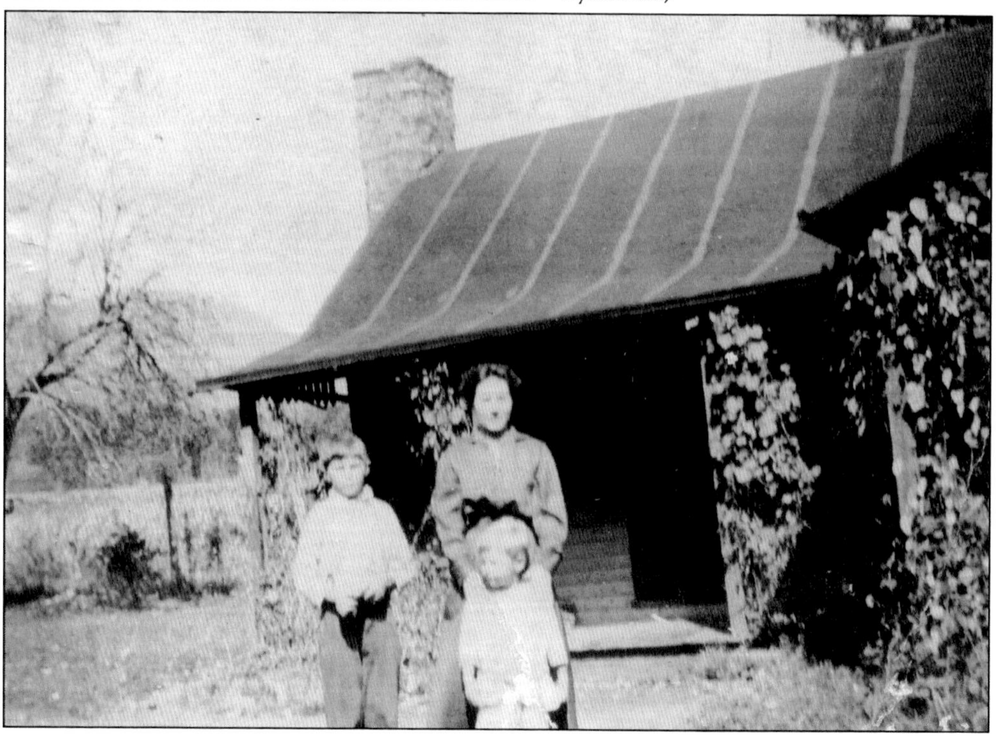

Rev. William "Billy" Francis Rice was born to Martha Roseanne Stephenson and John Longmire Rice on October 1, 1847. Billy was going to town one day and stopped over in Haw Creek to water his horses. He met a pretty young girl by the name of Margaret Henryetta Lindsay, the daughter of a devout Episcopalian family. He married Margaret and became a lay reader in the Episcopal Church. (Courtesy of Sybil Fox.)

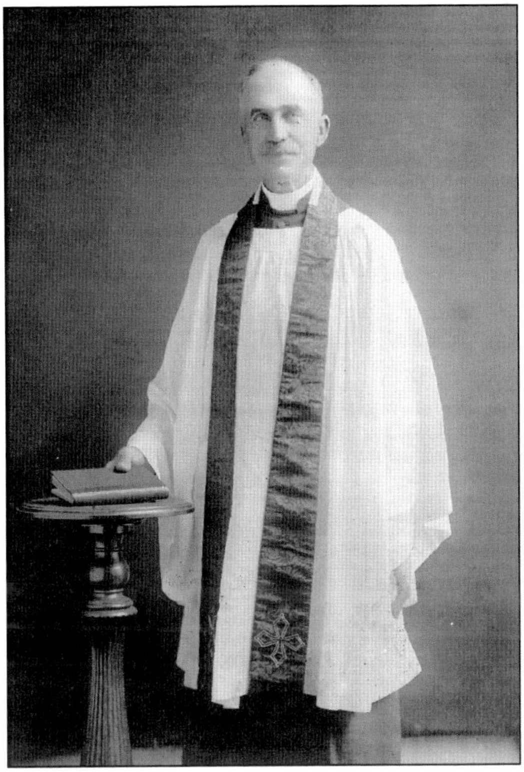

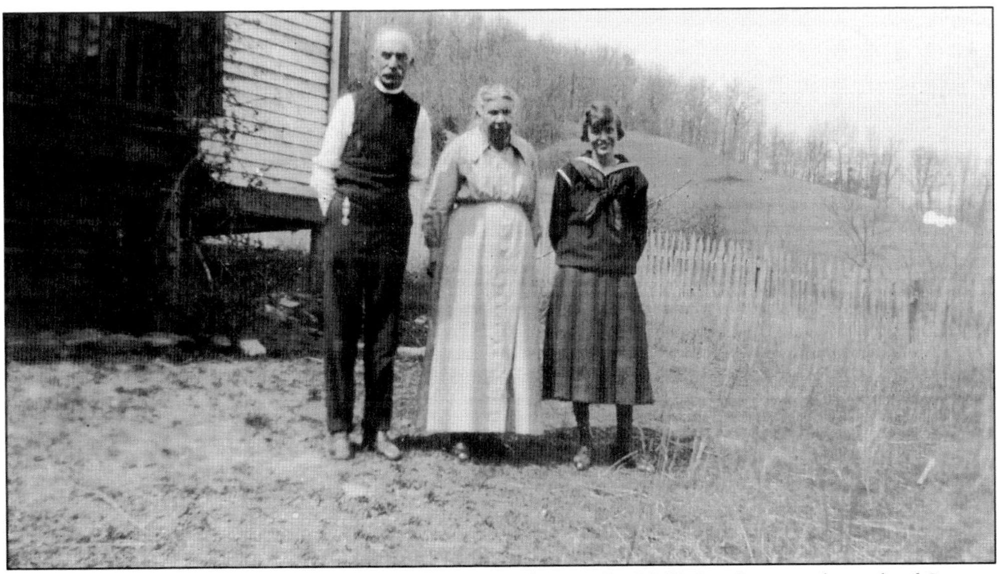

Rev. Billy Rice stands next to his wife, Margaret, and Cornelia McDebitt Joyner, the wife of George Clarence "Mug" Joyner, on the side of the Joyner home place. Just over the hill behind them is the current location of Jewell Acres. After Billy was ordained, he helped build the Grace Church in North Asheville. When digging out the foundation of the church, they found the skeletons of two children. The men who were working for him refused to continue digging, so Billy had to finish the foundation himself. The bones are still underneath the chancel of the present-day church. (Courtesy of Sybil Fox.)

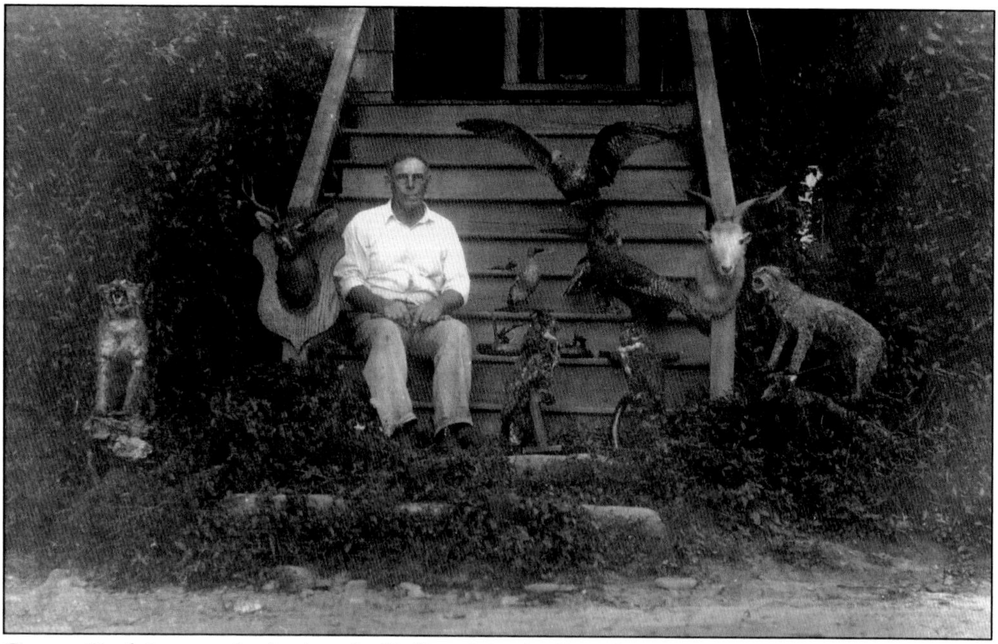

George Croft Joyner, the husband of Lillian Martha Rice Joyner, is pictured with many of his taxidermy creations on the porch of their house in Black Mountain a few years before he died in 1939. The couple moved from Riceville for the convenience of George's taxidermy business. Many of the animals in the photograph, however, may have come from the forests in the Riceville valley. (Courtesy of Sybil Fox.)

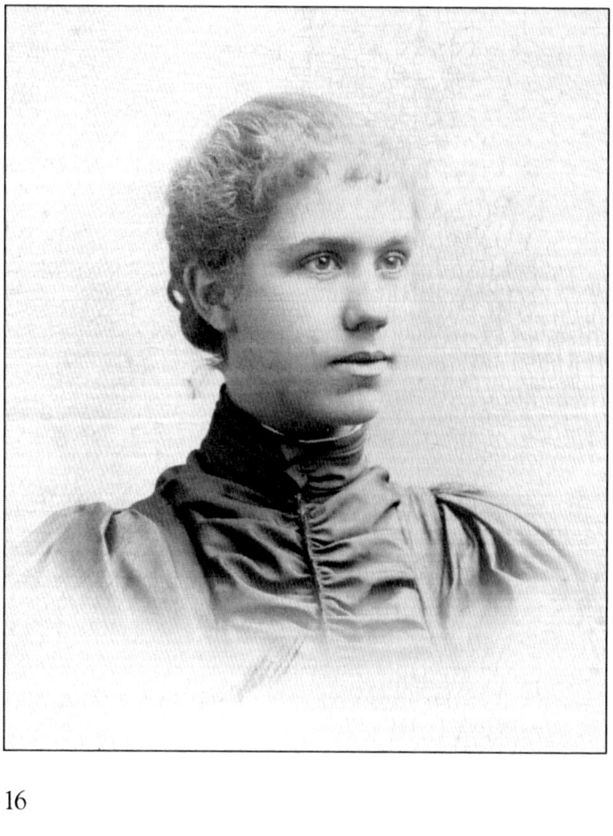

Lillian Martha Rice Joyner, one of Rev. Billy Rice and Margaret Henryetta Lindsay's children, is pictured in February 1894. Lillie was the oldest of Billy's children and inherited the Joyner house and 15 acres. She married George Joyner, a well-known taxidermist, who also gathered and sold timber rattlesnakes. (Courtesy of Sybil Fox.)

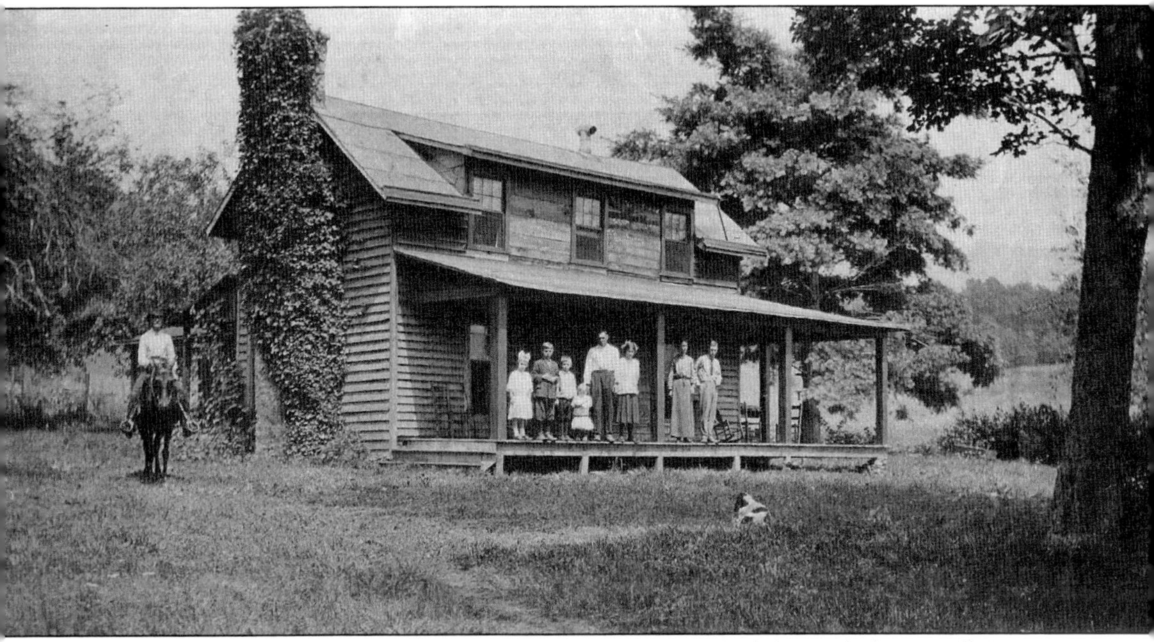

The original Joyner home place still stands on Parker Road on the left, just before Jewell Acres. Standing on the porch are, from left to right, Evelyn Joyner Moore, Frank Joyner, Fred Joyner, Ladd Joyner, George Croft Joyner Sr., Margaret Joyner, Lillian Rice Joyner, and Clarence Joyner. Reverend Billy (on horse) and his family lived at another home on this property while the children were young. The home was located near the top of present-day Jewell Acres and has since been remodeled. There were four houses on the property, one of which was the Roseanne Cabin. Another was called the "Jim Cabin" and was home to one of the farm laborers. Reverend Billy also operated a sawmill on the property at one time. He rented shares of his land to support his family. He later became the minister at the Episcopal Church in Black Mountain and would commute back and forth to Riceville during the summer. (Courtesy of Sybil Fox.)

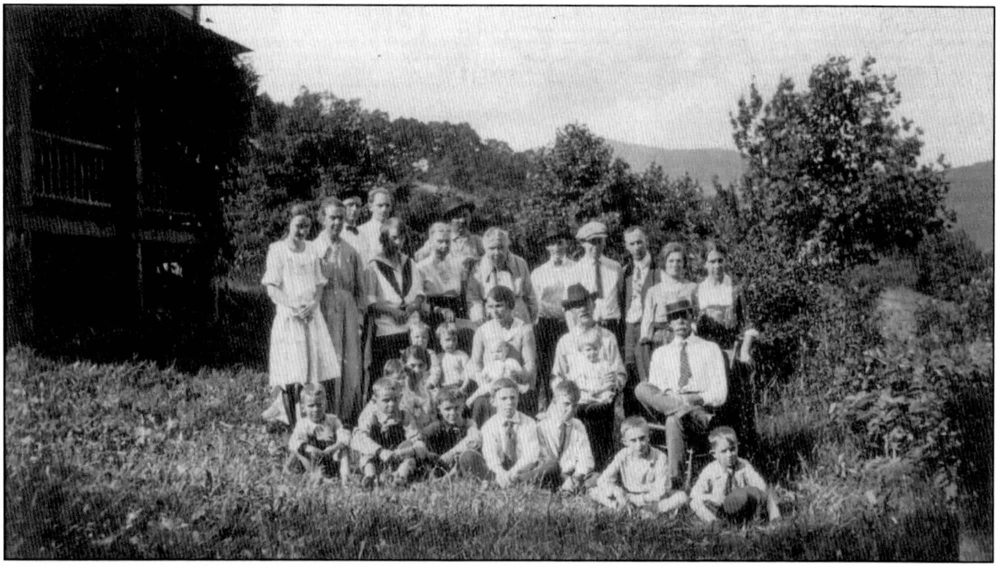

The Joyners gather for a family reunion outside the old home place in Riceville during the early 1920s. Standing in the back (on the left side) are Frank Roberson (in hat and bow tie) and George Clarence Joyner; in the middle are William Sawyer (center with bow tie) and Thomas Patton Rice (standing with hat and mustache). Standing in front of the men, are from left to right, two unidentified women, Evelyn Joyner (in sailor outfit), Nan Rice, Margaret Lindsay Rice, George Croft Joyner, Tom P. Rice, Peggy Rice, and Lillie Rice Joyner. The adults sitting in the next row are Margaret Joyner Sawyer, William F. Rice, and an unidentified man. (Courtesy of Sybil Fox.)

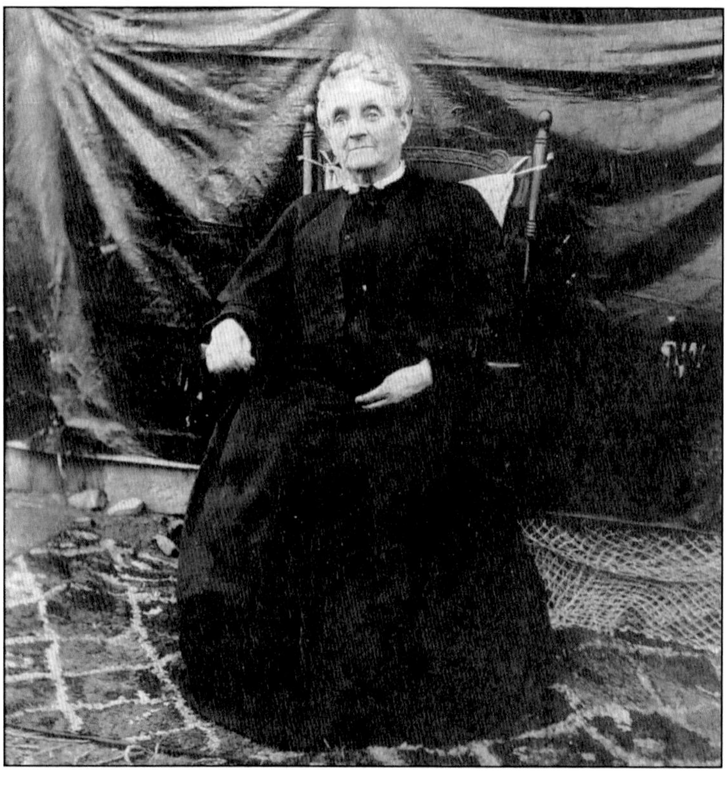

Eveline Virginia McBoom Joyner was born around 1832, to Elkannah McBroom and Roseannah Saltz, and died on December 12, 1915. She married Rev. Henry Edison Joyner, the father of George Croft Joyner, who operated a taxidermy shop from 1921 until his death in 1939. Henry was the pastor at Alexander Methodist Church, near Weaverville, North Carolina. (Courtesy of Sybil Fox.)

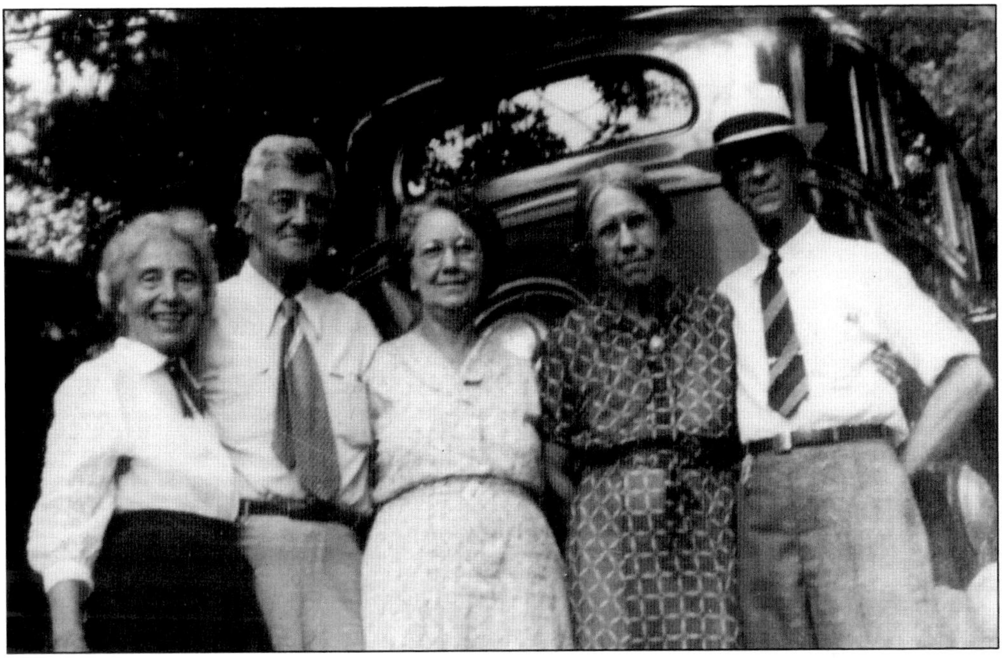

Pictured are, from left to right, Elsie and John Campbell, Babe Rice Roberson, Lillian Martha Rice Joyner, and Thomas Rice. Elsie was first married to Ernest Rice, another child of Rev. Billy Rice. Ernest was the headmaster of the Bingham Military Academy in Asheville. During his tenure there, he often challenged difficult students to fist fights after school to gain their respect. (Courtesy of Sybil Fox.)

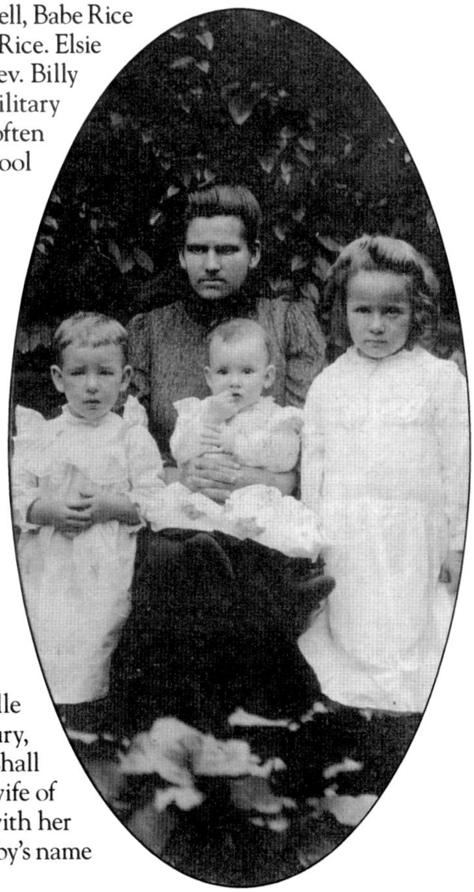

One of the few Cherokee members of the Riceville community after the beginning of the 19th century, Lissa Stephens Fox was the daughter of William Marshall and Matilda Two Horse Stevens. She was the first wife of William Arthur Fox (1882–1964). She is pictured with her two older children, Jerry Paul and Jessie Fox. The baby's name is unknown. (Courtesy of Sybil Fox.)

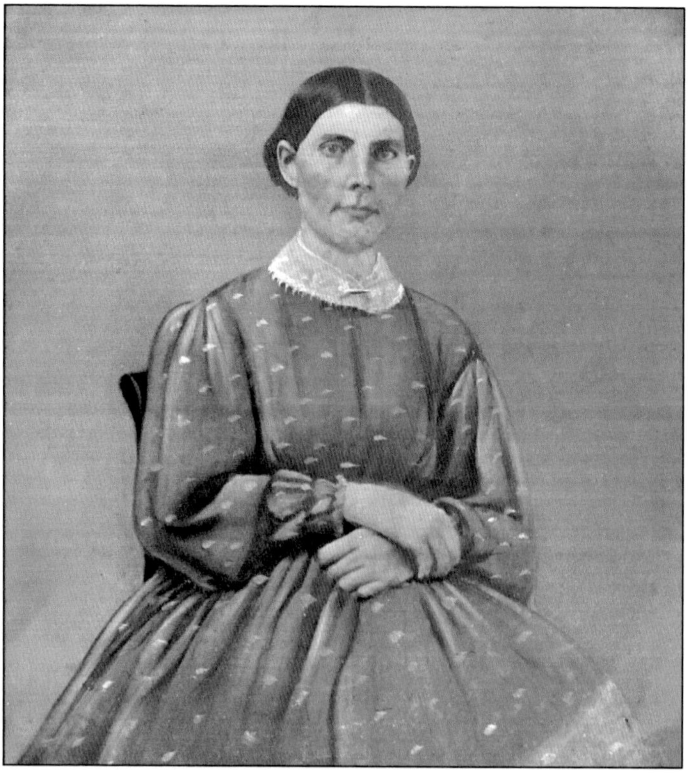

Rosannah "Rhoda" Ray Rice married Jackson Rice, another son of William and Martha Longmire Rice, who was born in the 1820s. After Jackson Rice died in Tennessee, Rosannah and their son, Joseph Hasque Rice, returned to Jones Cove and lived with her father, Archibald Ray. According to some records, Archibald tried to get guardianship of Joseph Hasque when he was about six years old. Rhoda died around 1900. (Courtesy of Rafe Rice Jr.)

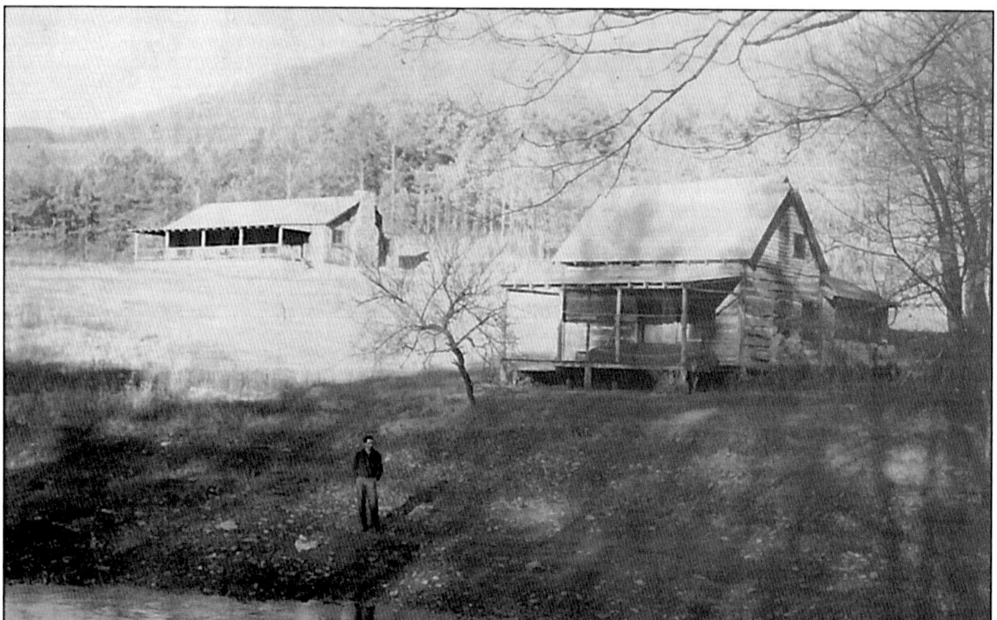

The Joseph Hasque Rice cabin, owned by Rhoda and Jackson's son, sits by the lake on what is now Nancy Wrenn's property. It is in this house that all 11 of Joseph's children were raised. The living room was downstairs, next to a very long, narrow kitchen. All the children slept upstairs in the loft, which was accessed by a spiral staircase. (Courtesy of Rafe Rice Jr.)

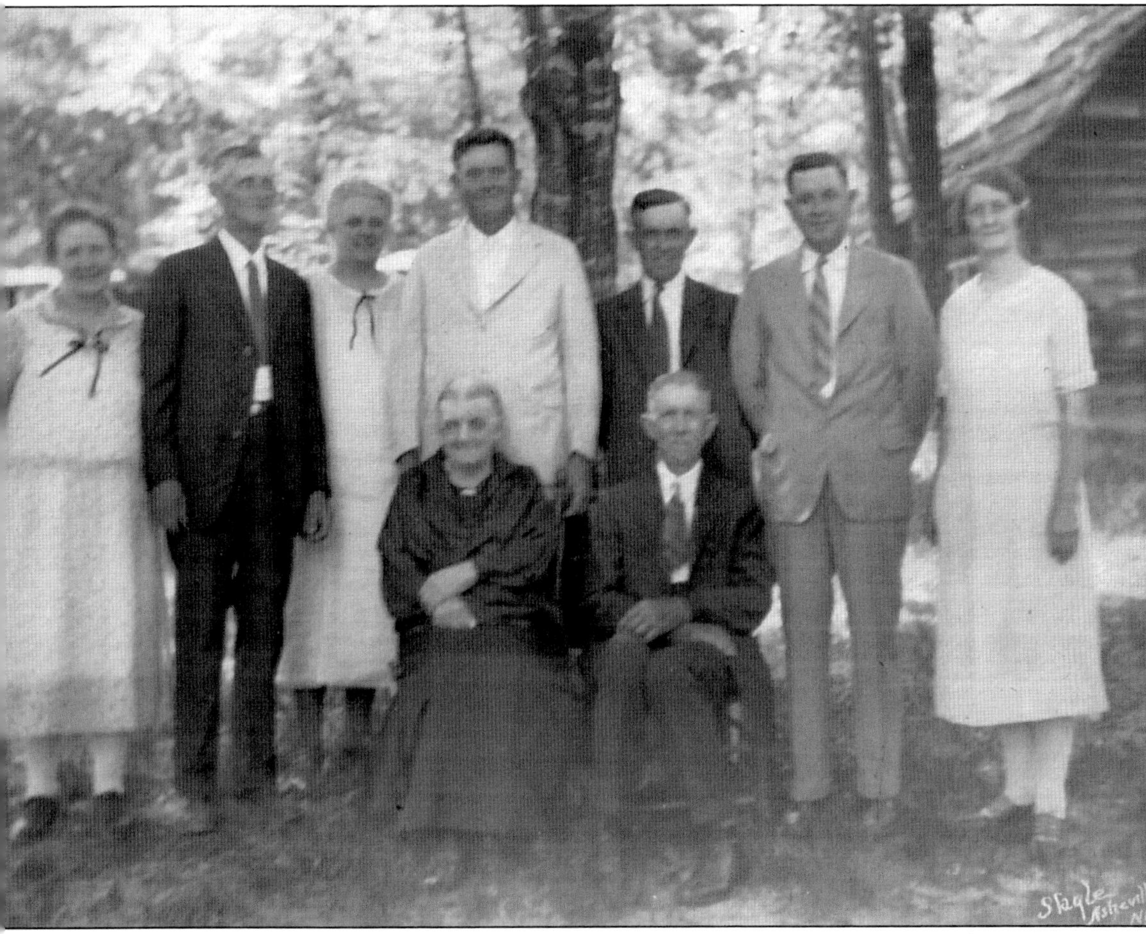

Joseph Hasque, the only son of Jackson Rice and Rosannah Ray, is a great-grandson of Joseph Marion Rice. He married Rhoda Carolina Shope. Joseph Hasque inherited a good deal of land from the original grants held by Joseph Marion Rice. He is credited with selling 1,000 acres of land to Dr. Chase P. Ambler for Rattlesnake Lodge. Rice also donated the land for the Brush Hill School and supplied them with water from his well. He also gave land for the Rice-Hughey cemetery, off Bull Creek Road and still had land to parcel out to his children. Pictured are, from left to right, Rosannah and Joseph (sitting in front) and seven of their children, Minnie E., Joseph Frank, Hattie May, Arthur Ray, Elmer "Jack" Alexander, Raphael Monroe, and Florence Gertrude. The family moved out of the cabin in 1900, but Joseph would still come back to tend the orchard in the hollow behind the house until 1916, when a flood caused a large landslide. (Courtesy of Rafe Rice Jr.)

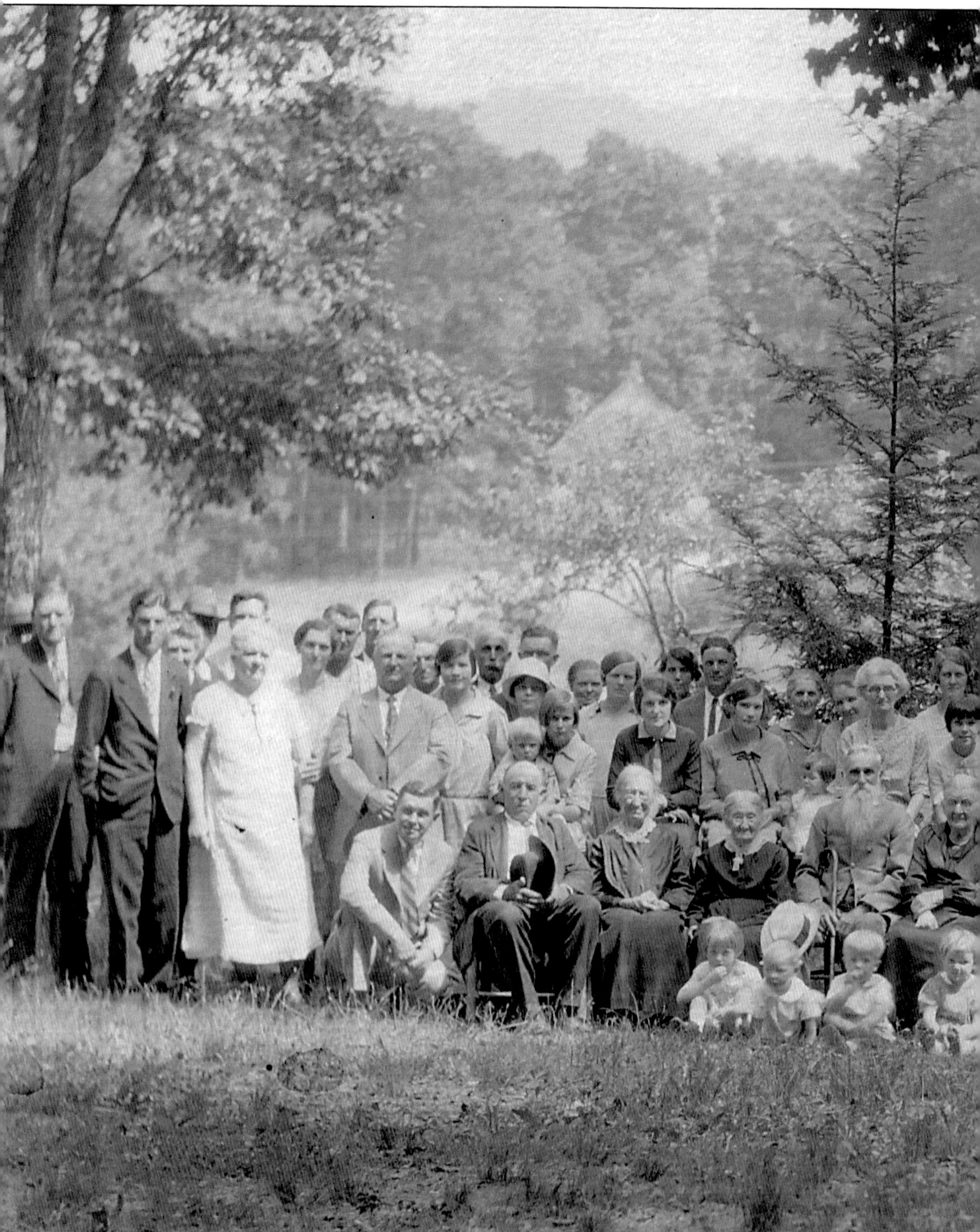

Pictured is the Rice family reunion at the old Rice home place in July 1921. The photograph was taken looking out toward Old Farm School Road. Every summer, the family would get together and hike the trail from Rattlesnake Lodge up to Mount Mitchell. They would camp for three nights

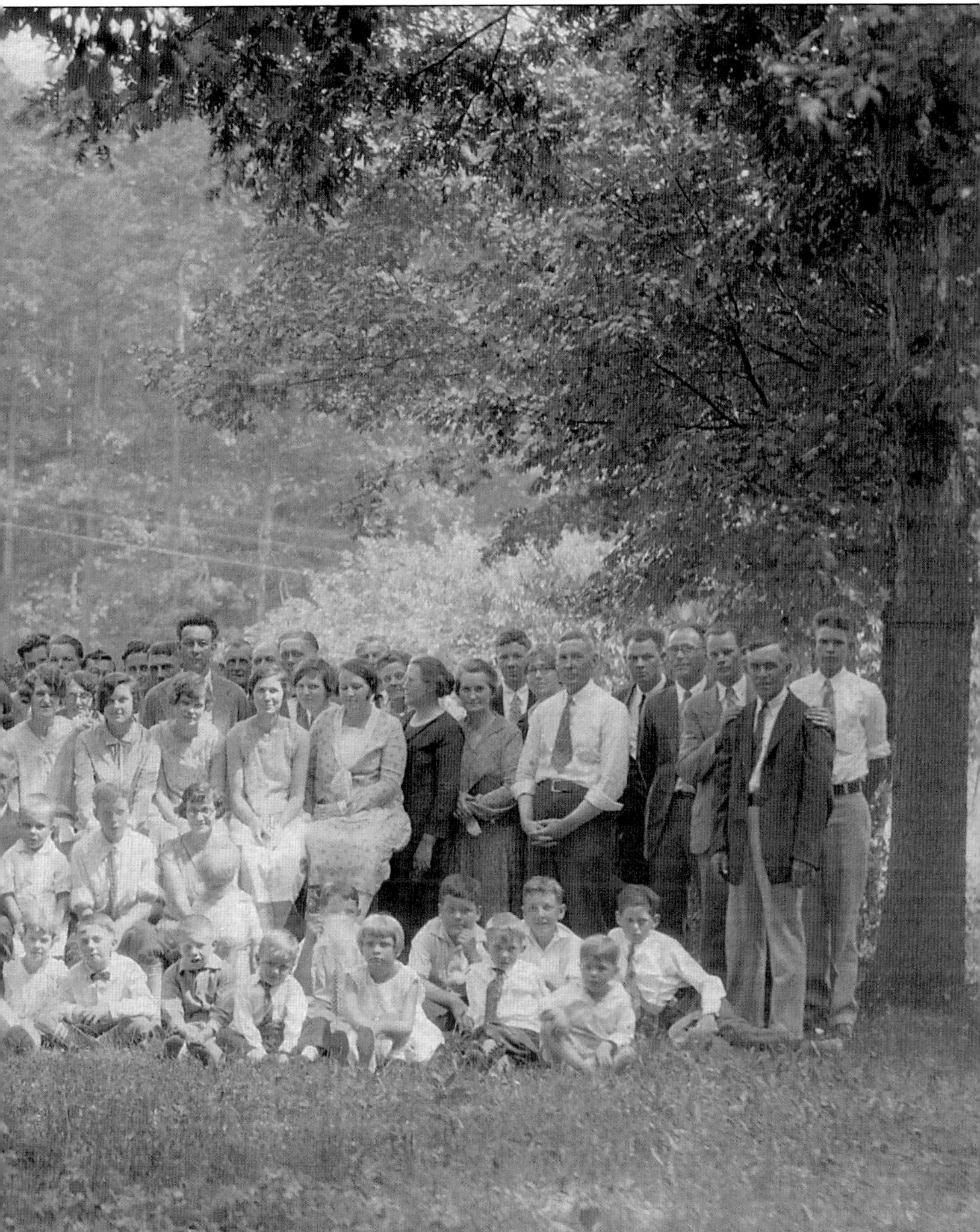

and then take the log train back down to Black Mountain. Almost all of the original families in Riceville can trace their family trees back to Joseph Marion Rice, Riceville's first settler, either through bloodlines or marriage. (Courtesy of Rafe Rice Jr.)

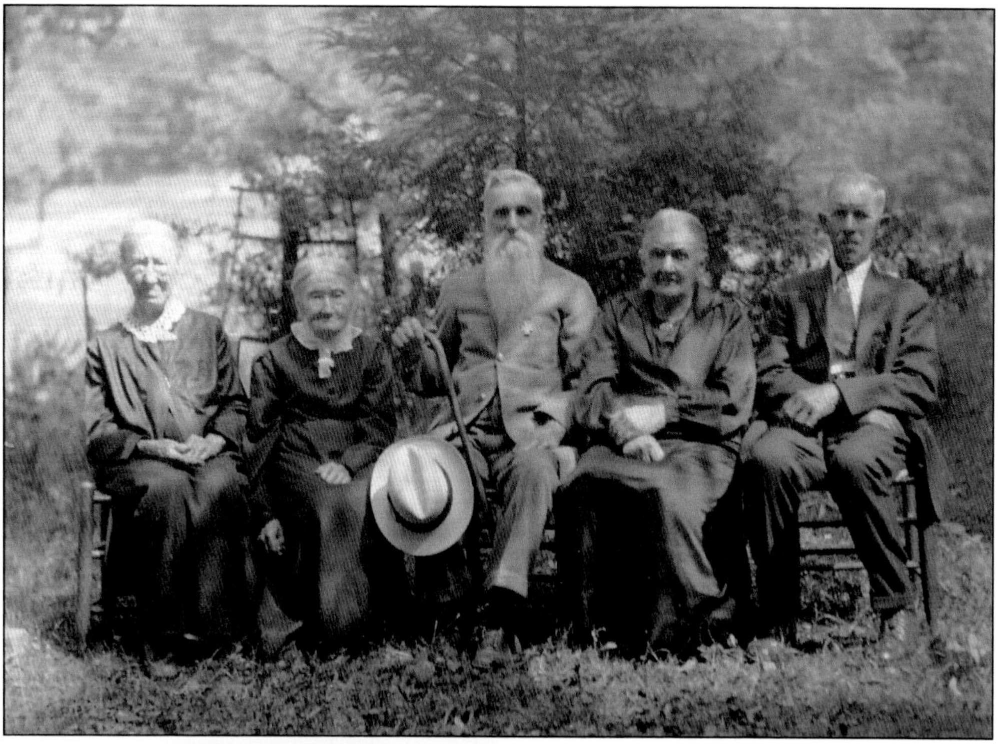

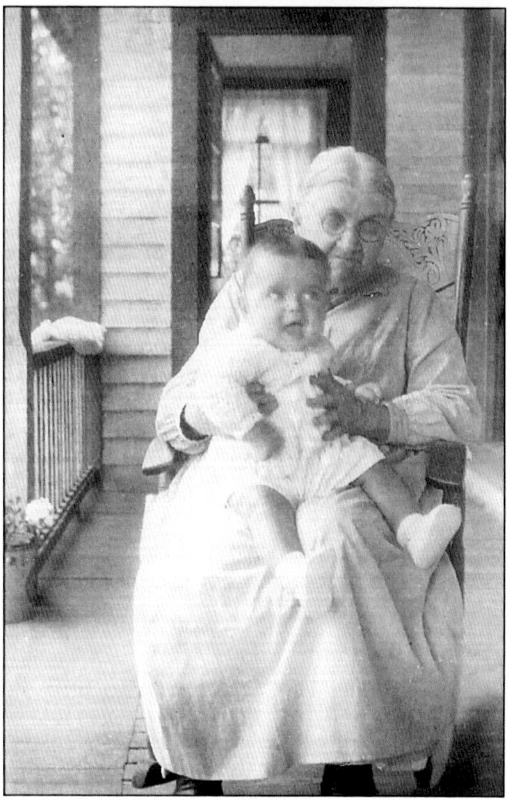

Neil Sales (middle with beard) was called "Santa" by many of his relatives. Neil served in the Confederate army, and after the war, he walked home from Charlotte. On Neil's right are Rhoda and Bud Rice, and on his left are the Scottish Creighton sisters, who settled on a large farm on the land that is now Botany Woods. (Courtesy of Rafe Rice Jr.)

Rhoda Ray Rice, the mother of Joseph Hasque Rice, holds her grandson Raphael Rice Jr. on the front porch of the Rice home place. Raphael Jr., born on January 30, 1930, grew up in Riceville and is the great-great-grandson of Joseph Marion Rice. He is the current inheritor of Joseph Rice's gun, Bacon Betsy, which allegedly shot the last buffalo in the area. (Courtesy of Rafe Rice Jr.)

Raphael Monroe Rice, the grandson of Joseph Hasque Rice, built this log cabin for his family in 1934. His brother Frank helped with the log work. All the logs used in the house were cut on the property. Raphael's brother-in-law Hal Reed, one of the best rock masons in the area, built the chimney. Raphael Rice Jr. currently resides in the home. (Courtesy of Rafe Rice Jr.)

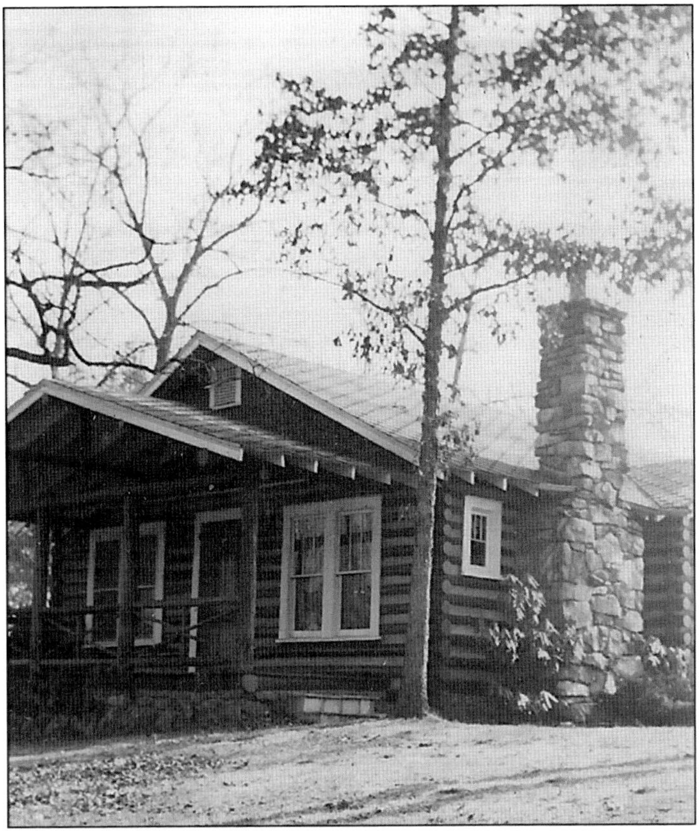

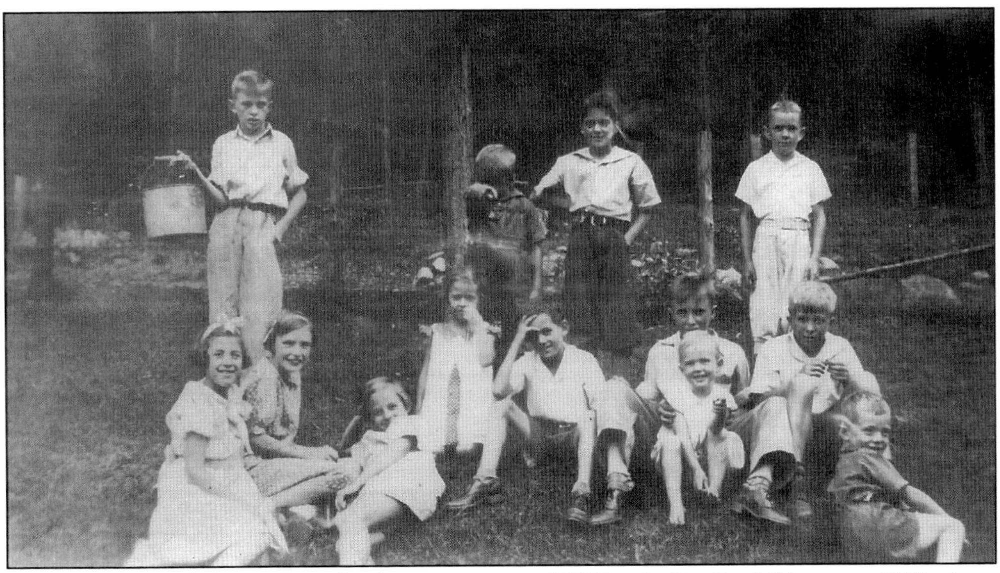

Children relax and play at a Rice family reunion around 1935 at the Jay Cordell house on Dillingham Circle. Pictured are, from left to right, (first row, sitting) Mildred Creasman Tipton, Elizabeth Cordell Marlowe, Sara Shope Sawyer, Barbara Creasman Whitt, James Creasman, Don Cordell, Christine Cordell Chapman, Paul Shope, and Cecil Cordell; (second row, standing) Arnold Cordell, Bobby Bugg, Calvin Creasman, and Carl Cordell. (Courtesy of Sara Sawyer.)

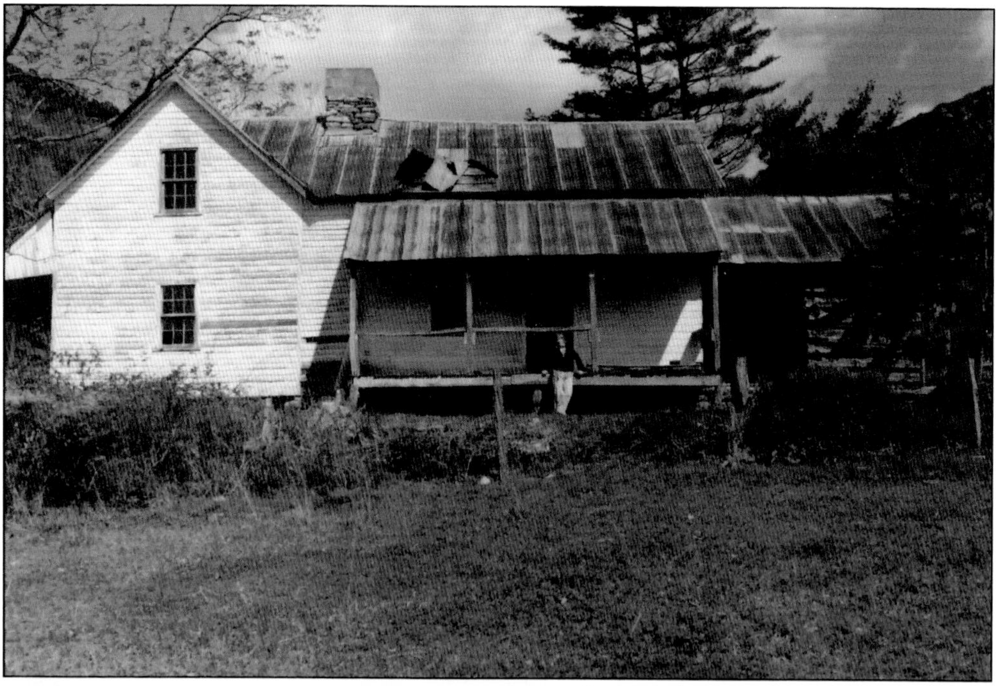

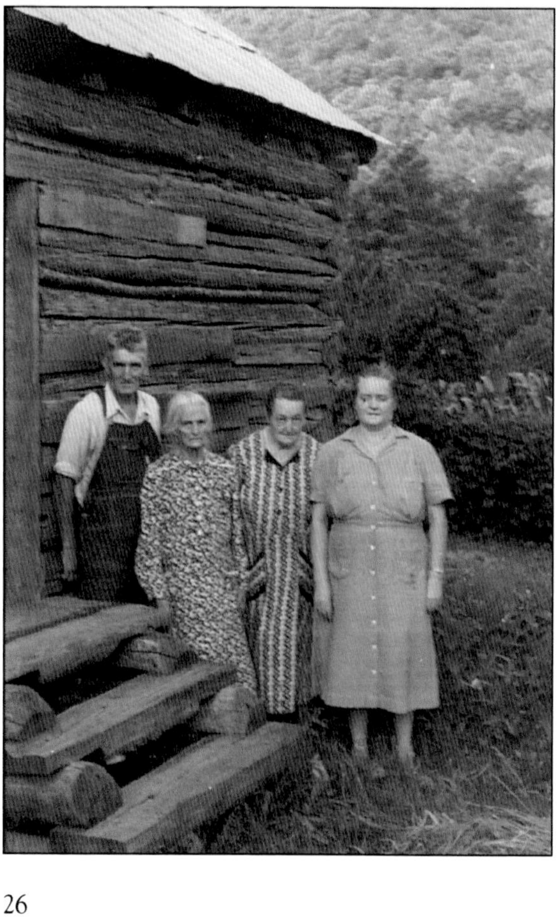

Pictured before it was modernized and the original two log-cabin portions of the house were taken down is the Jones family farmhouse, located at the end of Jones Cove Road. It is the oldest surviving log cabin in the area, built in the mid-1800s. The two-story frame house was added in the late 1800s by Thomas J. Jones. An old log barn across the driveway from the house is older than the original building. (Courtesy of Starr Cash.)

Pictured from left to right, Marcus Bearden Jones stands beside his mother, Sarah E. Moffitt Jones, and his sisters Mary Jones Godfrey and Ellen E. Jones, next to the original Jones cabin. Neither Bearden nor Ellen ever married, and they continued to live in the family home place with their mother, Sarah, who died in 1953. Bearden passed away in 1958 and Ellen lived there alone until her death in 1974. (Courtesy of Starr Cash.)

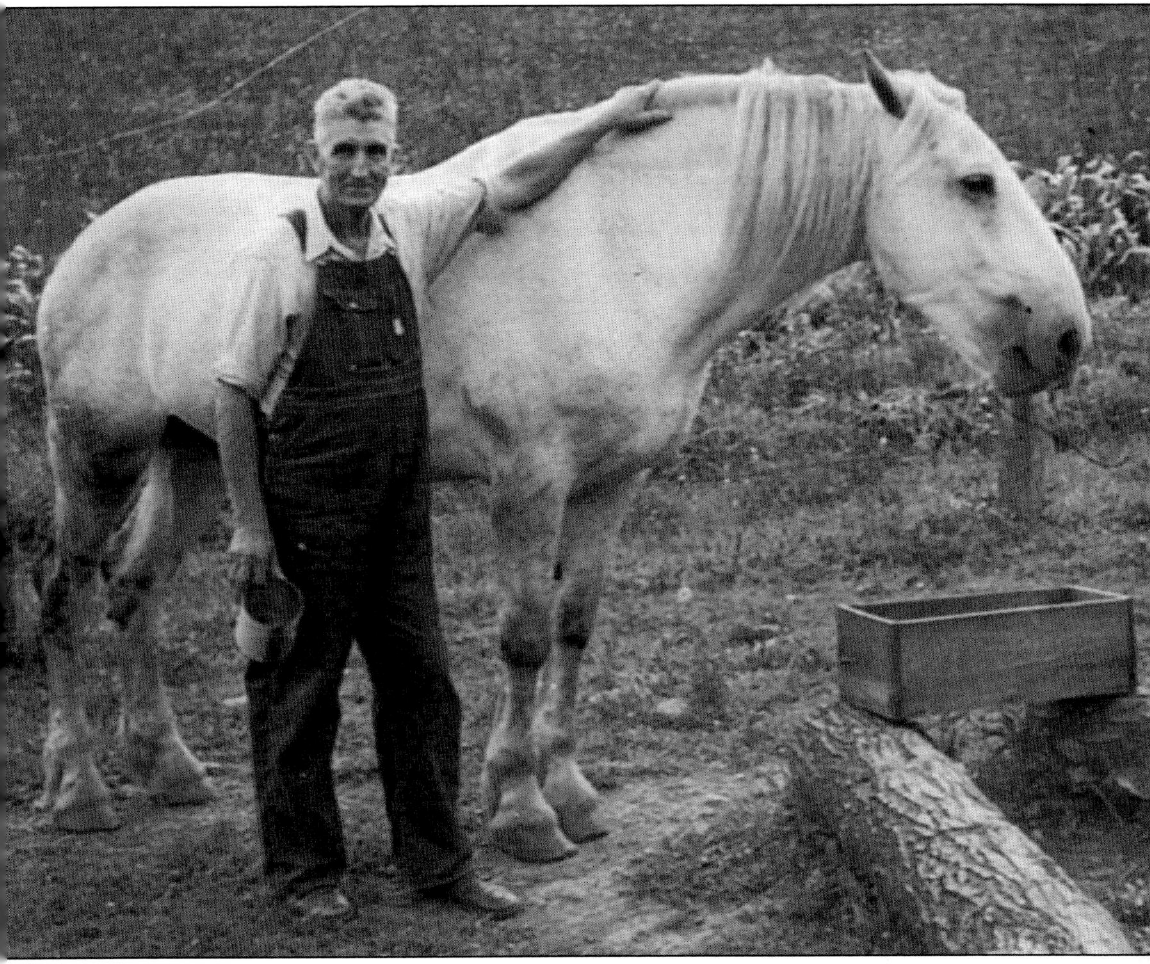

Marcus Bearden Jones stands with his horse Prince on family land. After he returned from serving in World War I, Bearden farmed his family's property and also hired himself out as a farmhand. He ran a few head of cattle and plowed the fields with Prince. He sat up all night with Prince on the night the horse died. (Courtesy of Starr Cash.)

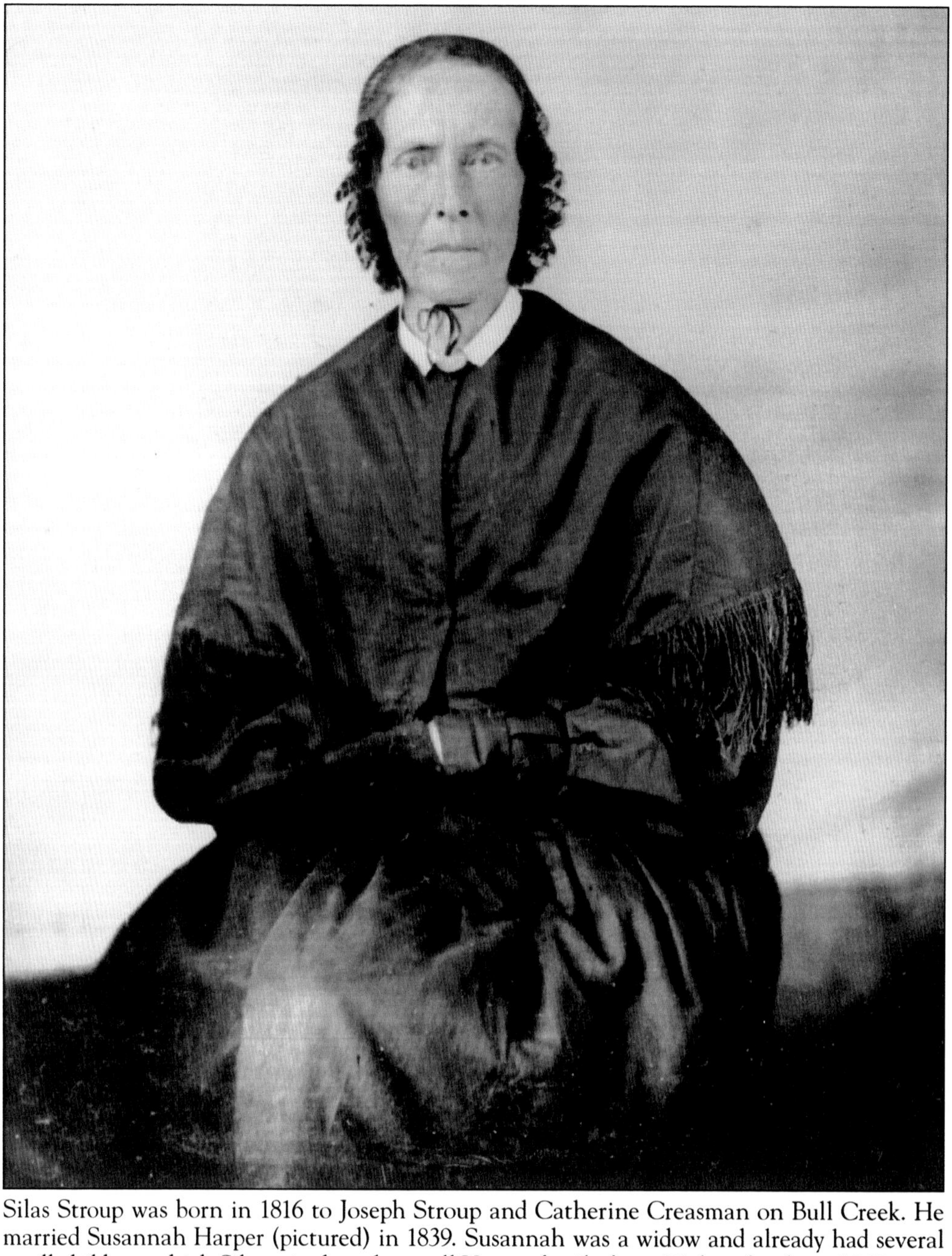

Silas Stroup was born in 1816 to Joseph Stroup and Catherine Creasman on Bull Creek. He married Susannah Harper (pictured) in 1839. Susannah was a widow and already had several small children, which Silas raised on the small Harper family farm. He bought about 1,000 acres and enlarged the old cabin. They later gave a portion of their Riceville land to the Presbyterians to build a church and school. The school was built on the site of where Silas's father, Joseph, had built Stroup's Chapel Baptist Church. The graves of Silas's parents can still be seen in the Presbyterian cemetery. Joseph Stroup dammed the Bull Creek and built a gristmill. His young daughter Lanny drowned in the mill race, and her grave was the first one in what is now the Riceville Presbyterian Church cemetery, which was part of Stroup's land at the time of Lanny's death. (Courtesy of Mike Stroupe.)

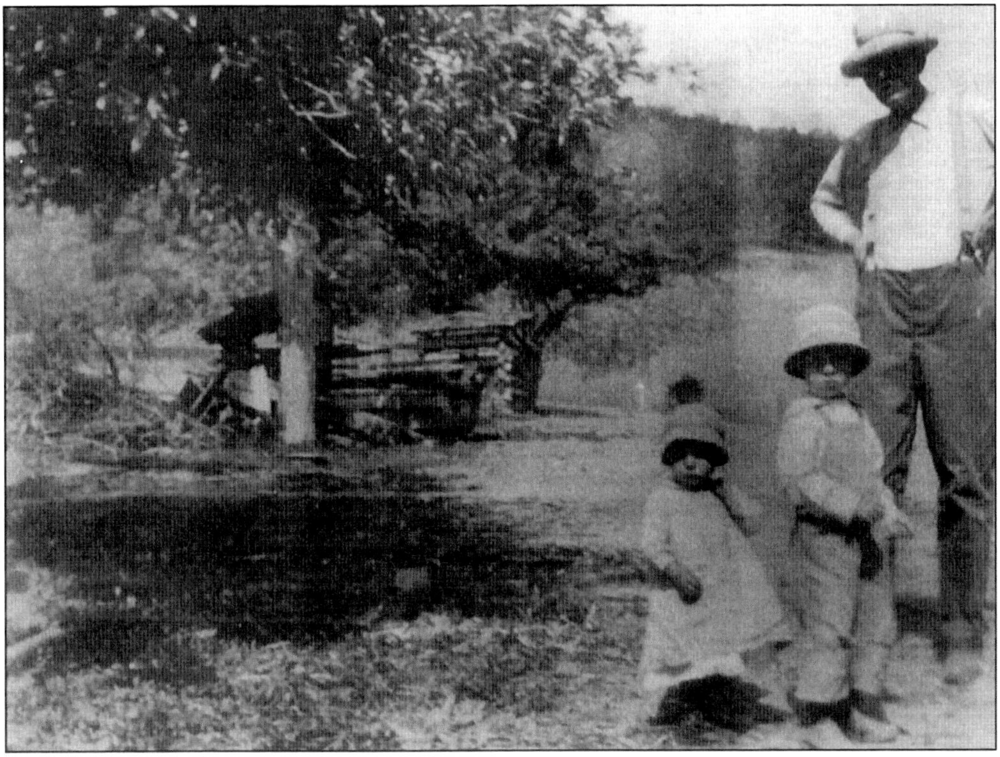

Henry Francis Ray stands with his grandsons William (right) and Ellis Ray outside their home around 1917. (Courtesy of John Weakly.)

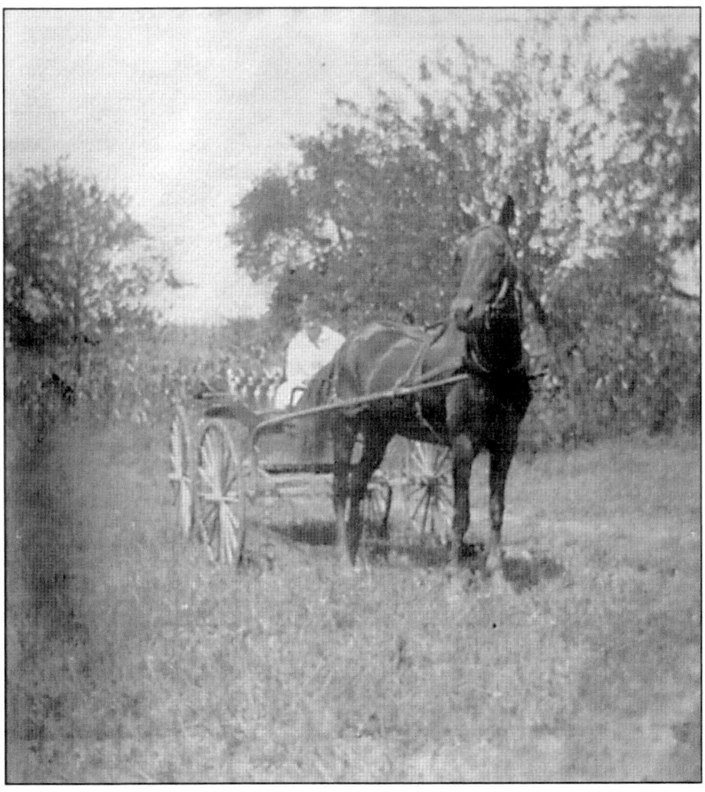

A woman drives a buggy on what was then Rice Branch Road, below the Rice home place on Old Farm School Road. Cars were uncommon in the valley until the roads were improved. In an emergency, folks would often have to call around until they found someone who could take them to the doctor in town. (Courtesy of Rafe Rice Jr.)

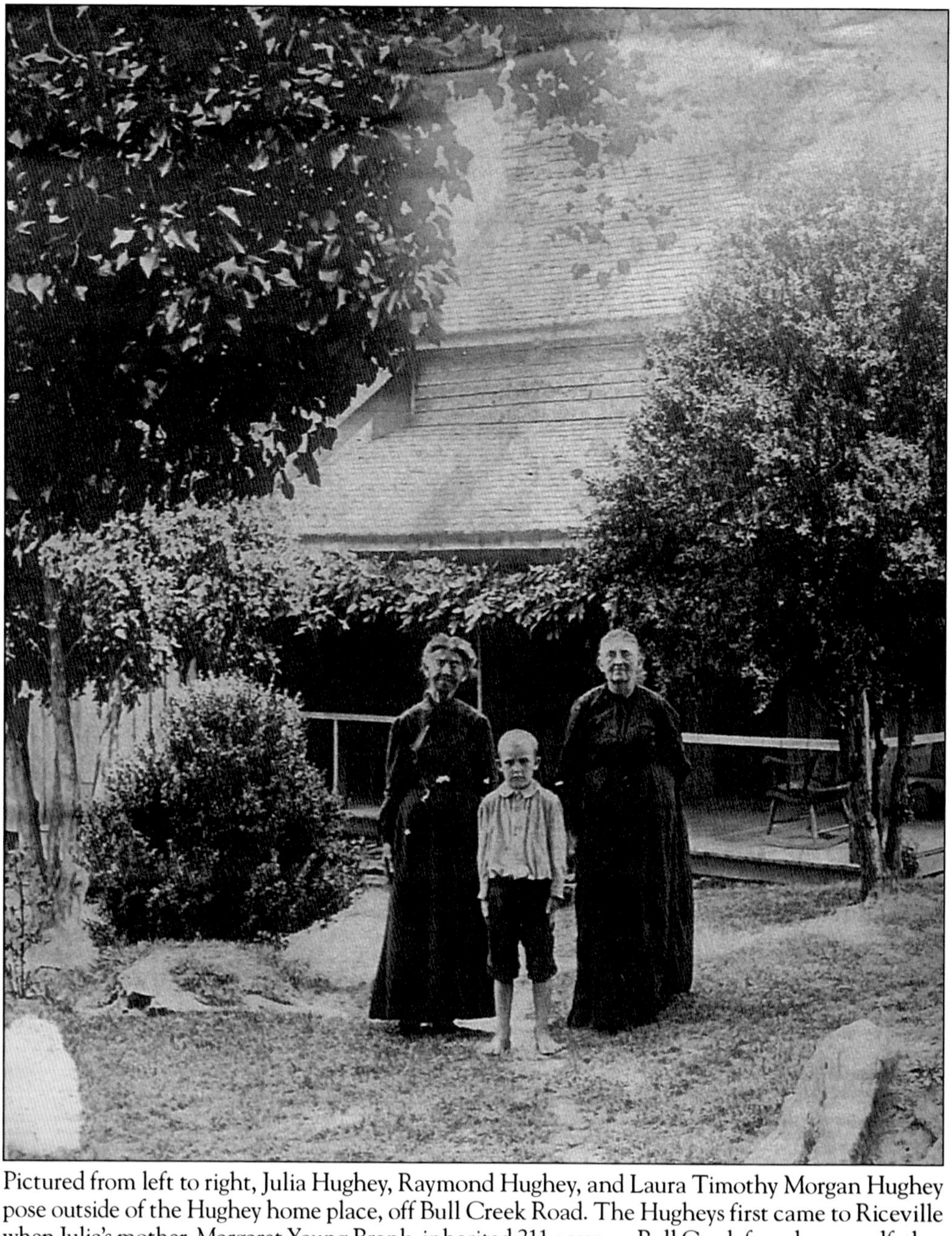

Pictured from left to right, Julia Hughey, Raymond Hughey, and Laura Timothy Morgan Hughey pose outside of the Hughey home place, off Bull Creek Road. The Hugheys first came to Riceville when Julia's mother, Margaret Young Brank, inherited 211 acres on Bull Creek from her grandfather in 1852. The Hughey's purchased another adjacent 200 acres that same year. Margaret was the daughter of Elizabeth Rice and Robert Houston Brank and the granddaughter of Joseph Marion Rice, the first settler in Riceville. Margaret married Samuel Hughey around 1825. Samuel was born in 1802 and made his living as a farmer, blacksmith, and shoemaker until his death in 1886. It was at this home that the Riceville Presbyterian Church was organized by Margaret and Samuel in 1876. (Courtesy of John Weakly.)

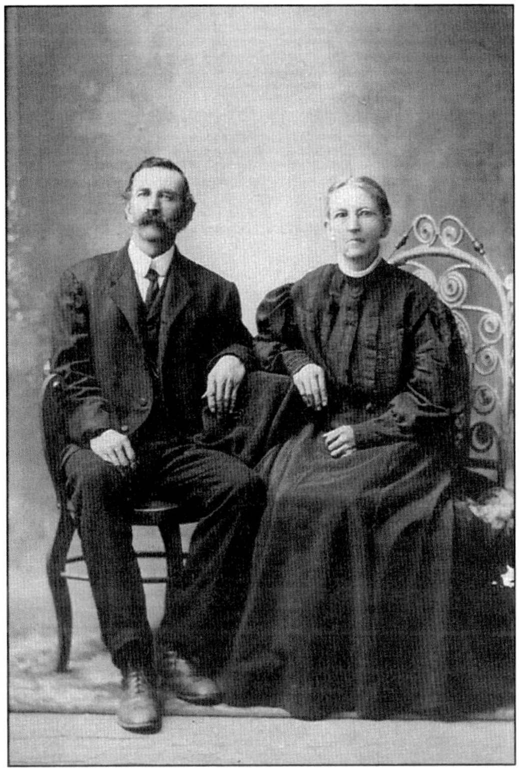

James Marion Hughey sits next to his wife, Laura Timothy Morgan, in the 1880s. James was born on November 18, 1847, to Samuel and Margaret Brank Hughey. He was a farmer and served in the Confederate army. James and Laura married on September 7, 1870, and had 12 children before Laura died in 1927. (Courtesy of John Weakly.)

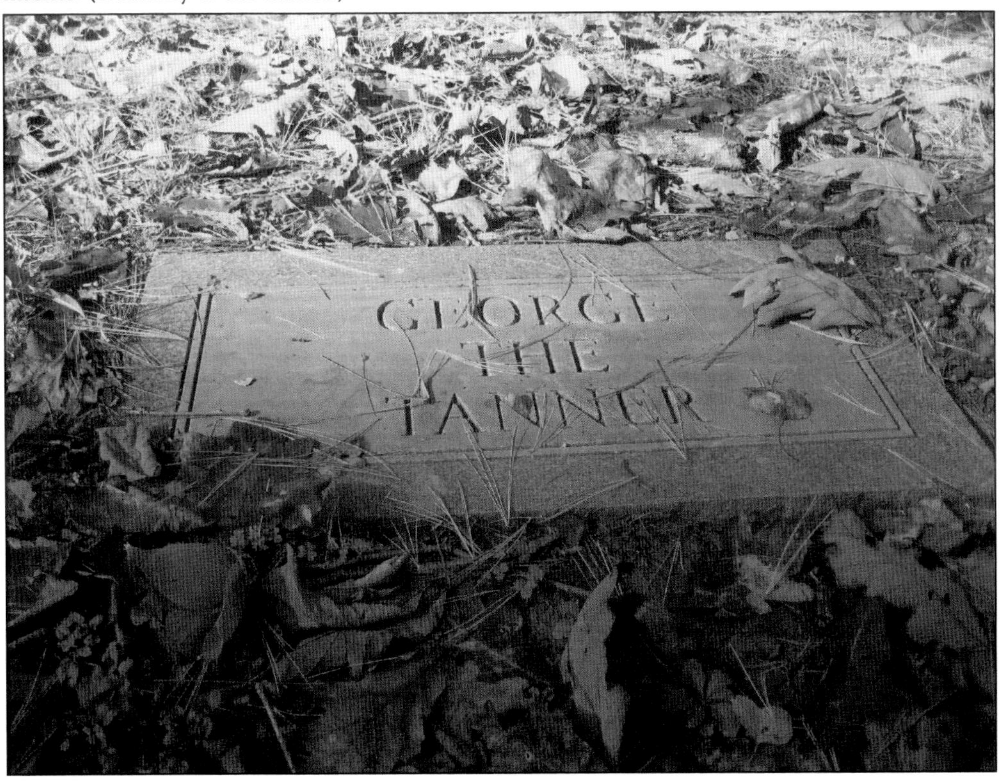

George the Tanner was willed to Margaret Young Brank and her husband, Samuel Hughey. When slavery ended, George left for Weaverville, but a few weeks later he returned to Bull Creek to live with the Hugheys and ran a local tannery, hence the nearby topographic name Tanbark Ridge. Upon his death, George was buried about 100 yards outside the Rice-Hughey cemetery. Recently, however, descendents of the Hugheys moved George's remains inside the cemetery and placed the grave marker. (Courtesy of the author.)

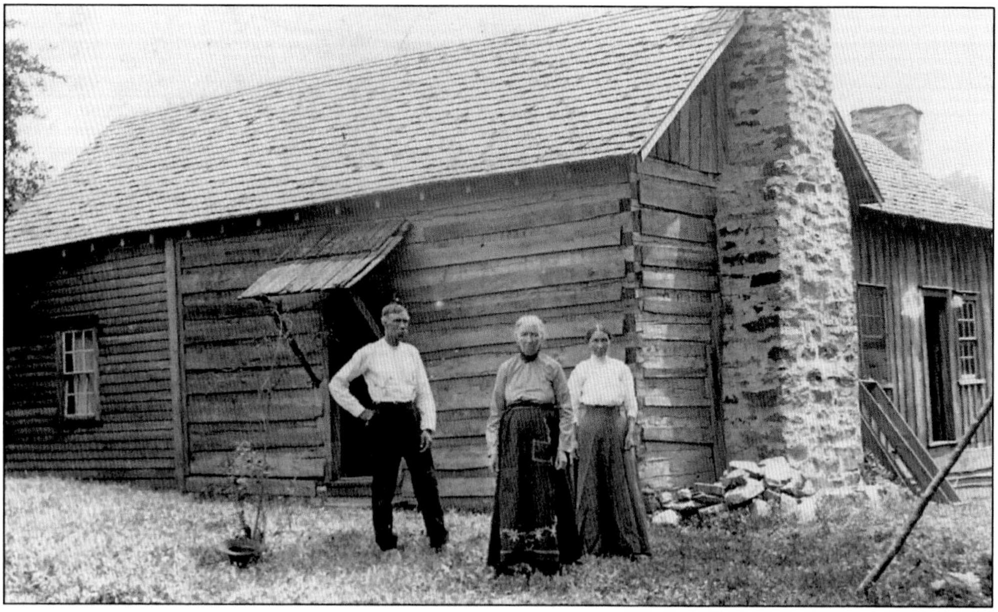

Milton Trantham stands with his mother, Charlotte, and his sister Willie Jane outside their home at the end of Jones Cove Road. Archibald Ray's son Joe Ray had lived in the house previously. Joe met Milton Trantham when Milton came up to Asheville from Tennessee in 1900 to see if he could make a living selling produce to the summer people in Montreat. At the time, Joe was an old man and was very sick. Joe asked Milton to stay and take care of him, and in return, he would bequeath Milton his home. Milton agreed and went back to Tennessee to get his mother and sister. While he was gone, Joe died. When the Tranthams returned, they moved into Joe's house, and Milton stayed there until his death in 1956. Nancy Wrenn is currently restoring the old cabin. (Courtesy of Rafe Rice Jr.)

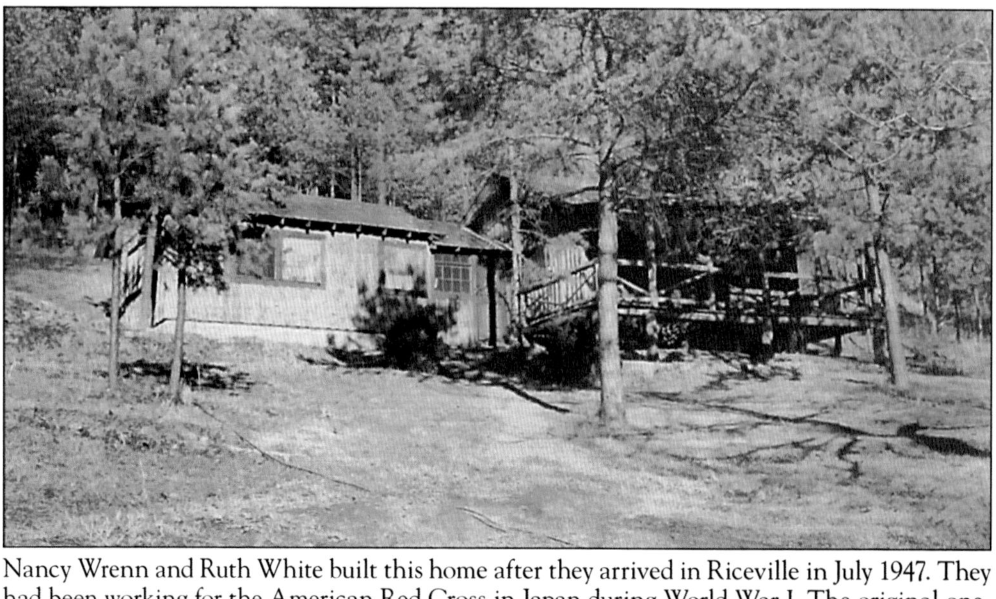

Nancy Wrenn and Ruth White built this home after they arrived in Riceville in July 1947. They had been working for the American Red Cross in Japan during World War I. The original one-room log cabin was built from trees taken down on the property and milled at Grady Maynor's sawmill, located across from the Stephenson home on Bull Creek. (Courtesy of Nancy Wrenn.)

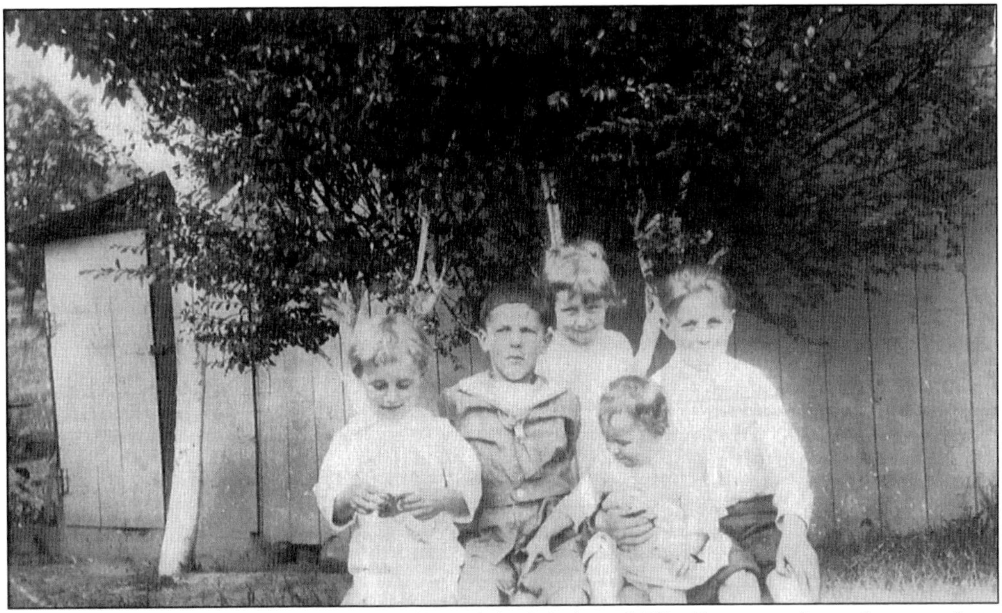

From left to right, J.M. Stroupe and Billy, Edith, Ethel, and Ellis Ray pose for a photograph in 1923. (Courtesy of John Weakly.)

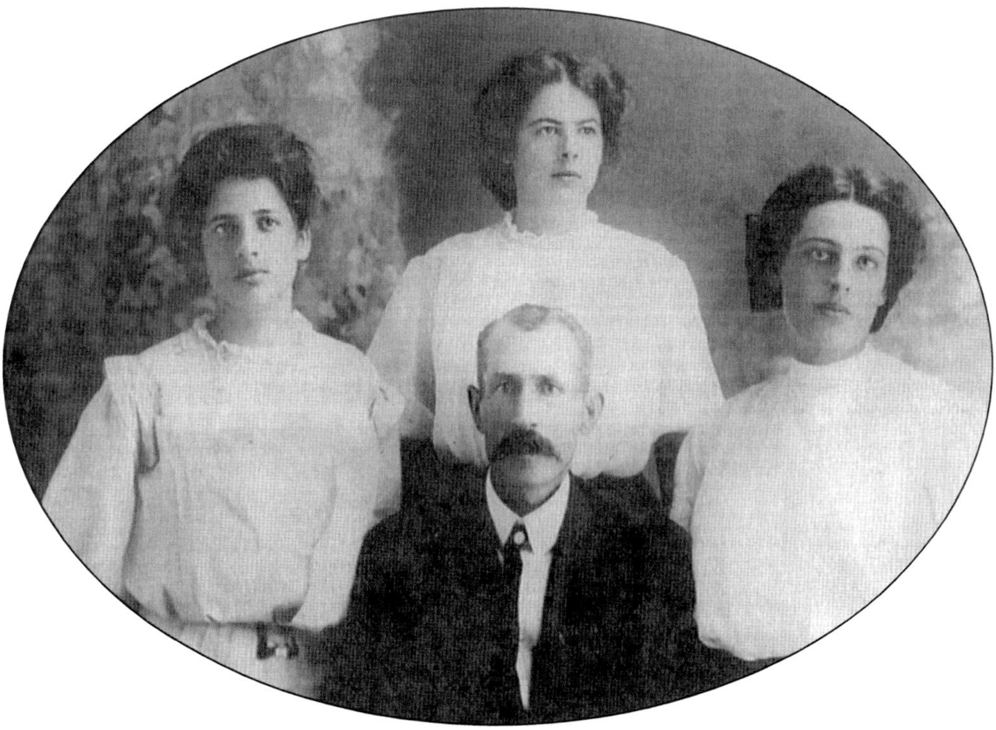

William Nelson Penland poses with his daughters (from left right) Ethel Penland Creasman, Della Penland Gregory, and May Penland Ray. (Courtesy of John Weakly.)

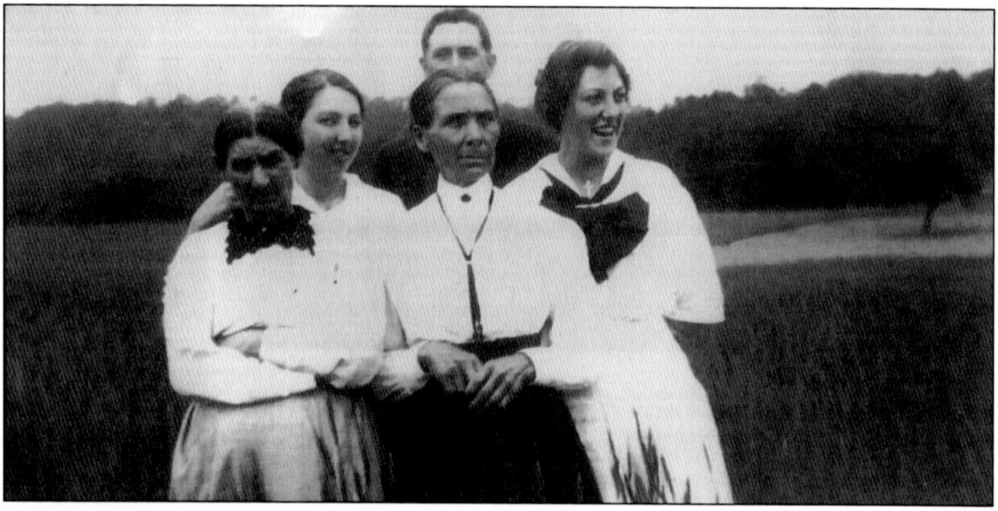

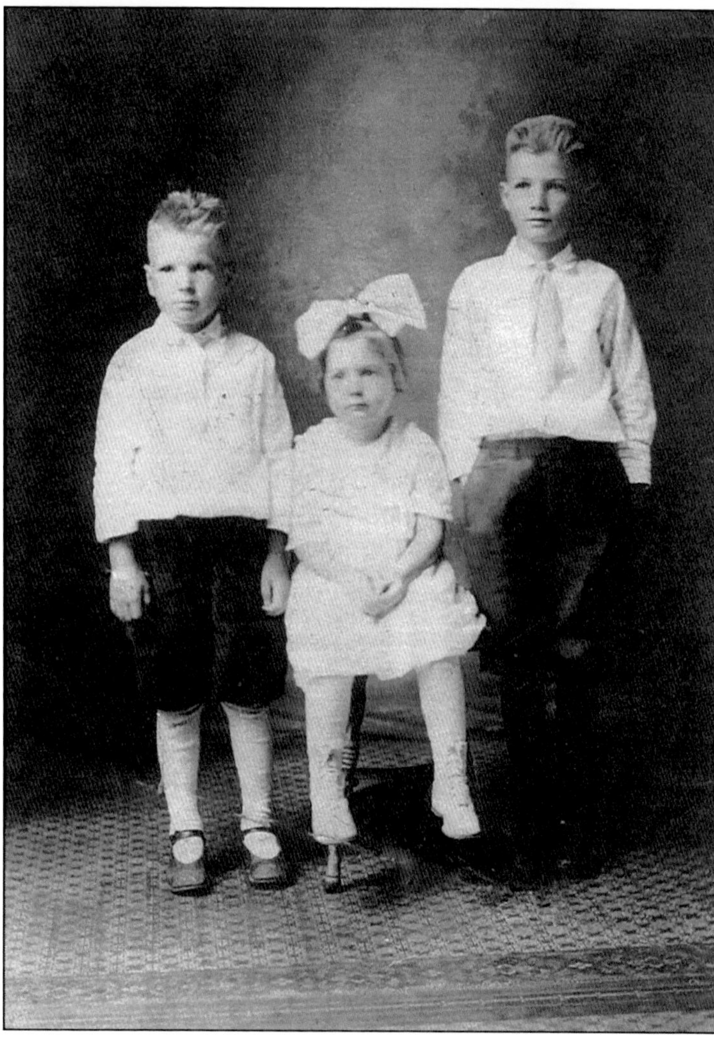

Pictured from left to right are Sophronia Ray, Neta Ray Shope, an unidentified man with an unidentified woman in front of him, and Della Ray Penley in Riceville. (Courtesy of John Weakly.)

Pictured from left to right are Bill, Beatrice, and Junis Allison. (Courtesy of John Weakly.)

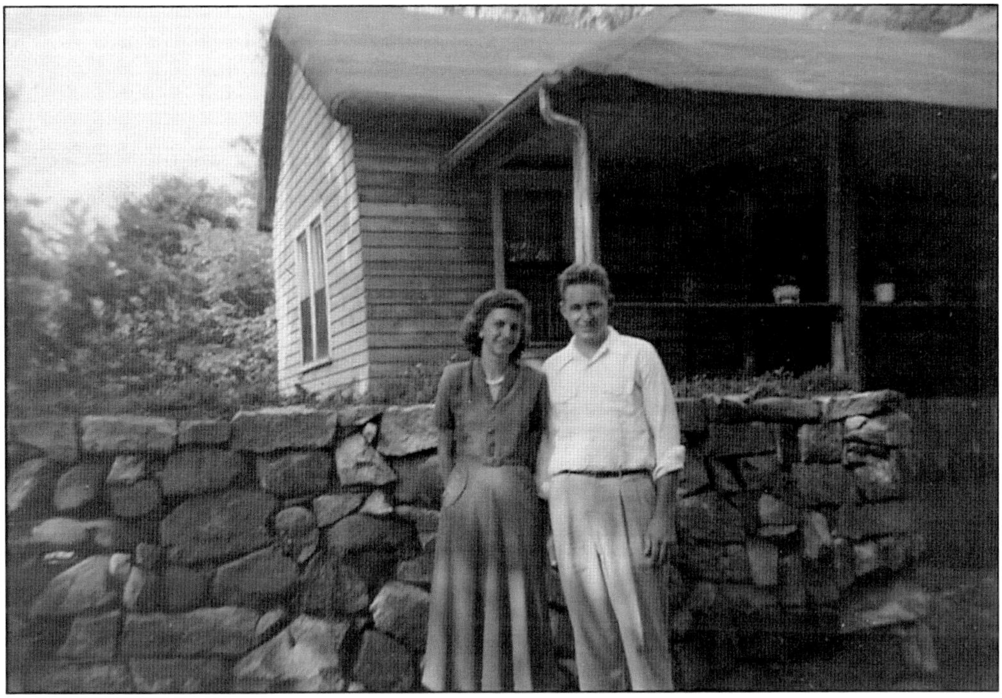

A couple stands in front of their new home in Riceville. (Courtesy of John Weakly.)

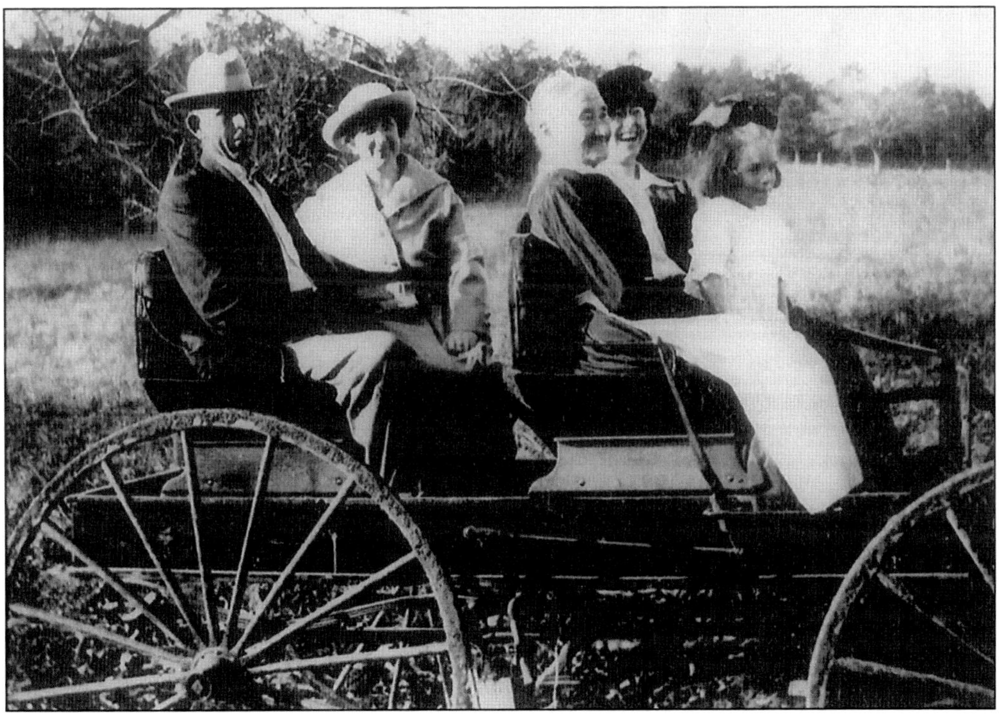

Sitting in a horse-drawn buggy are Arthur Lee Hughey and Mary Creighton Shope (woman in front, without the hat), the second wife of Leander Erwin Shope. The child is Evelyn Hughey. (Courtesy of John Weakly.)

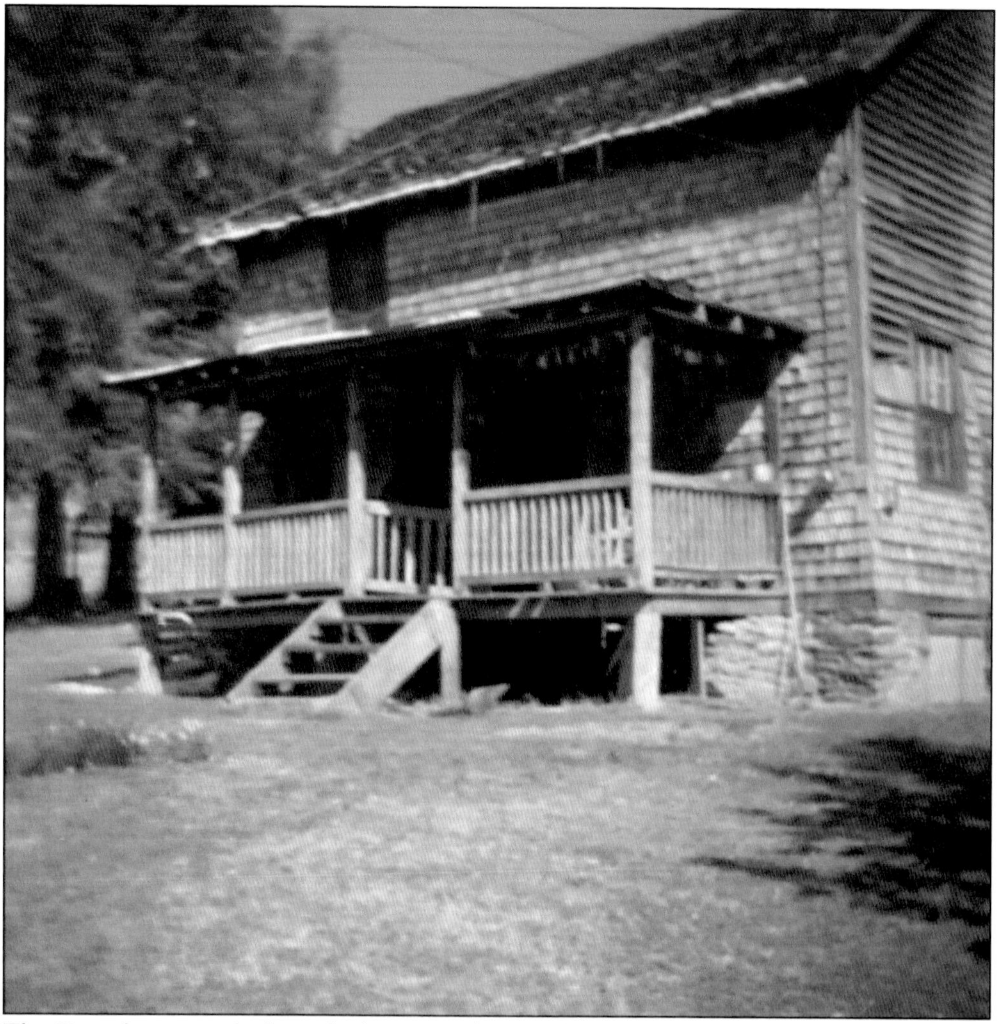

The Gregg home was built in the late 1800s by Carol Pinkney Gragg and was one of the first homes in the area during the 1800s. Most of the Gregg/Gragg family was born in or near this home. (Courtesy of Mr. and Mrs. Robin Gregg.)

Carol Pinkney Gragg was one of the first Graggs to settle in Riceville in the late 1870s. He moved to Riceville from Caldwell County and built his home place on the head of Shope Creek. He married a local girl, Eliza Caroline Shope, the daughter of Andrew Jackson Shope. Carol was born in 1846 and was referred to as "Little Granddaddy" by his relatives because of his short stature. This photograph was taken in the 1920s. (Courtesy of Mr. and Mrs. Robin Gregg.)

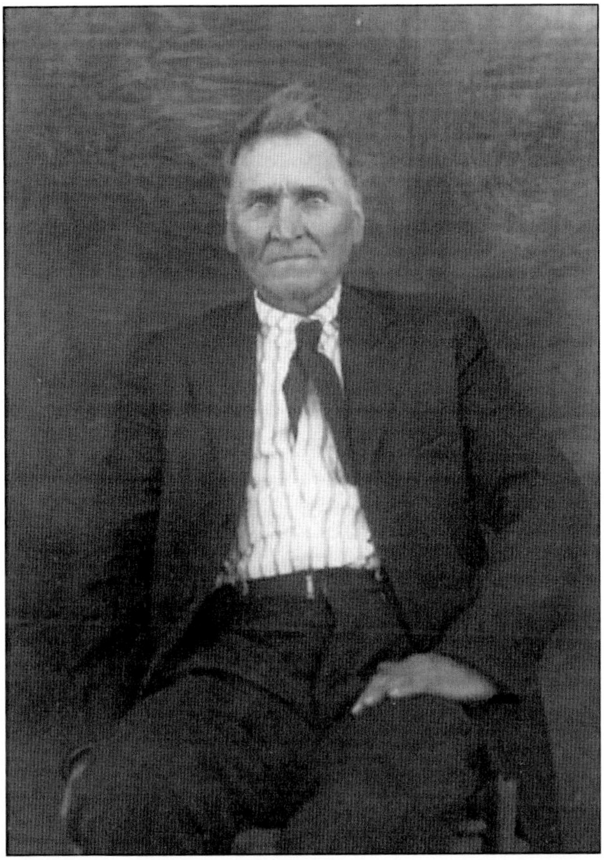

The Gregg/Gragg family poses at the head of Shope Creek. Pictured are, from left to right, unidentified, Jessie and Horace Gregg, two unidentified, Bass Gragg, a Whitsonhunt son, unidentified, Troy Gregg, and unidentified. (Courtesy of Mr. and Mrs. Robin Gregg.)

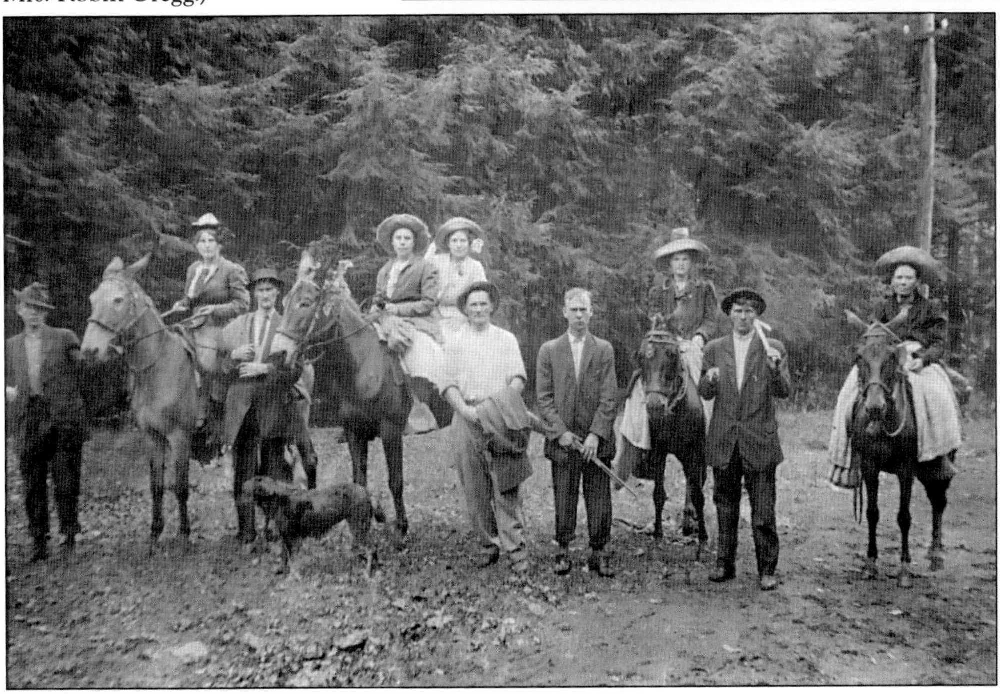

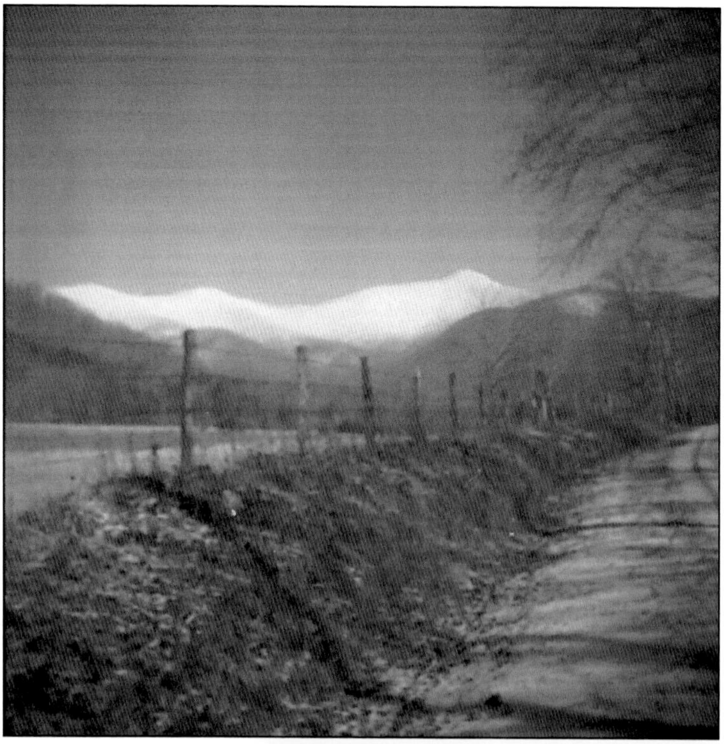

This photograph shows Shope Creek Road, near the C.P. Gragg house on the head of Shope Creek, as it looked in 1963. Snow-covered Lane's Pinnacle can be seen in the background. (Courtesy of Mr. and Mrs. Robin Gregg.)

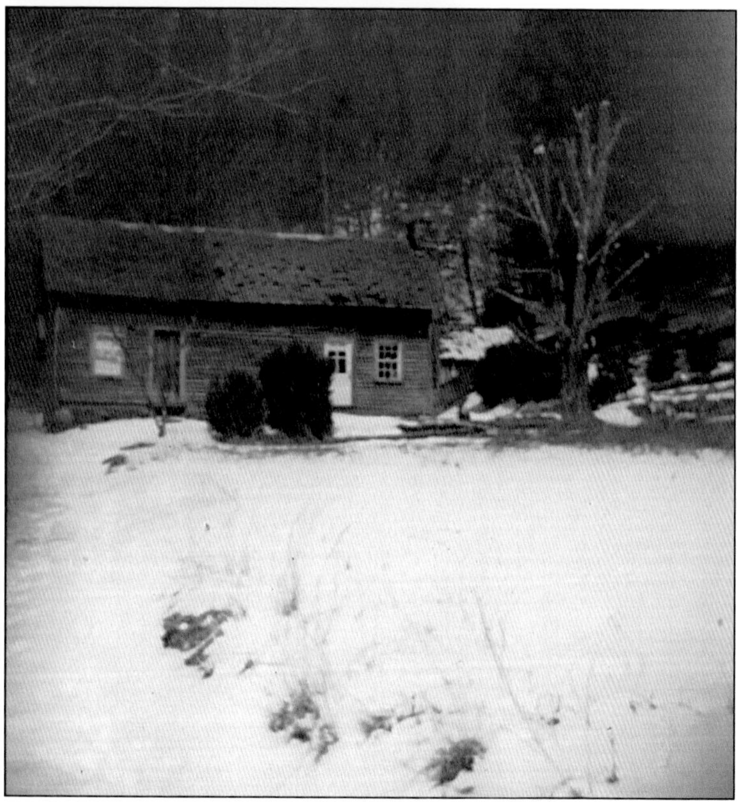

The John Burgin (J.B.) Gragg house, located at the head of Shope Creek, was originally built as a one-room cabin in 1896 by John Burgin Gragg, the son of C.P. Gragg, an early settler in the Riceville valley. Between 1916 and 1920, the left portion of the house was constructed, and the home doubled in size. This image shows the home as it looked in 1960. It has now undergone some modernizing renovations but retains the original structure. (Courtesy of Mr. and Mrs. Robin Gregg.)

Margaret Anna Clontz Gragg sits in her rocking chair in the entrance to the J.B. Gragg house in 1952. Anna sold timber from the land to H.E. Fuller, who was a logger and furniture-maker. In exchange for the wood, Fuller made several rocking chairs for the Gragg family. The seats of the rocking chairs were woven from tree bark. (Courtesy of Mr. and Mrs. Robin Gregg.)

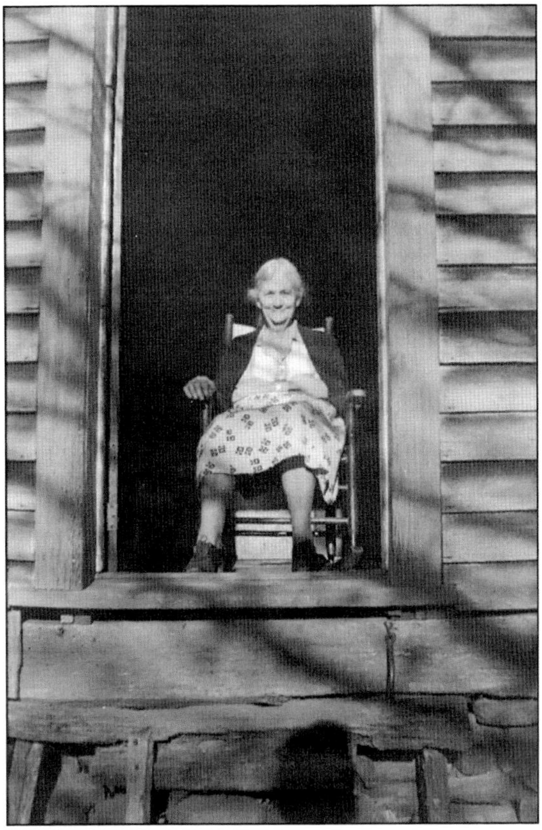

The Gregg family began holding family reunions in 1932. In the 1950s, the reunions began coinciding with the birthday of the family's matriarch, Alice Gregg Cordell. This photograph was taken on Alice's 85th birthday, May 18, 1952, at the John Cordell House. Alice stands in the front (in vest) surrounded by her family members, most from the Riceville area. (Courtesy of Mr. and Mrs. Robin Gregg.)

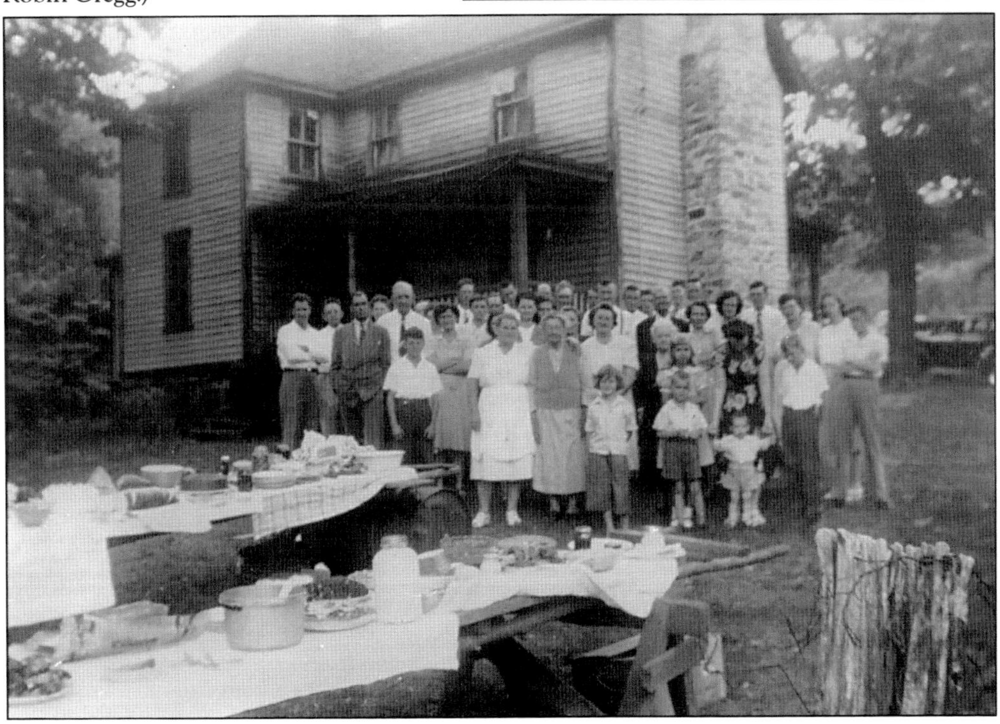

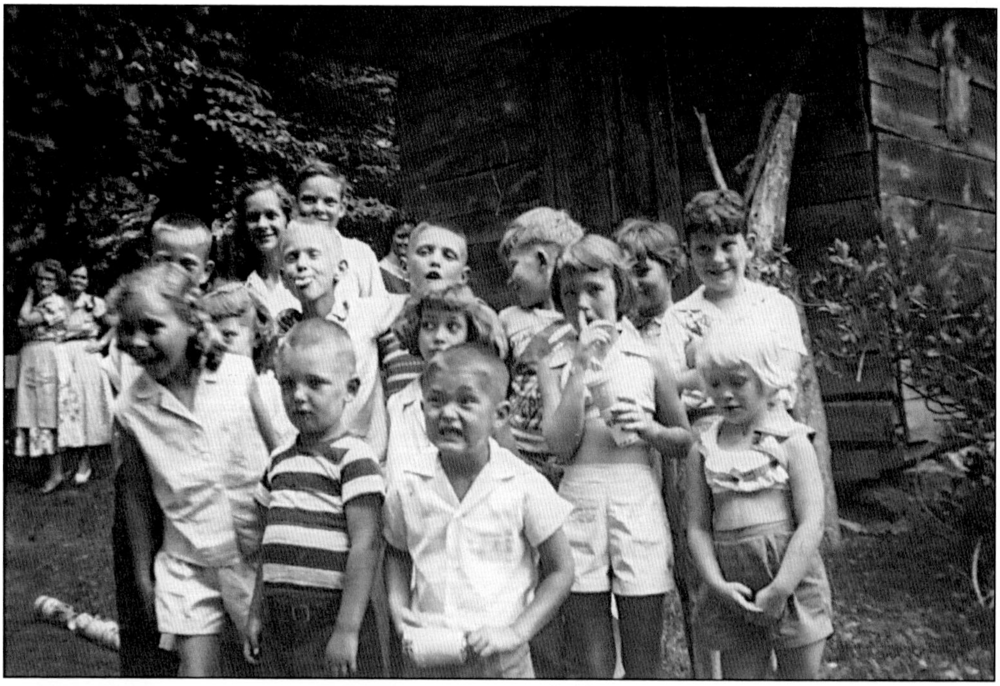

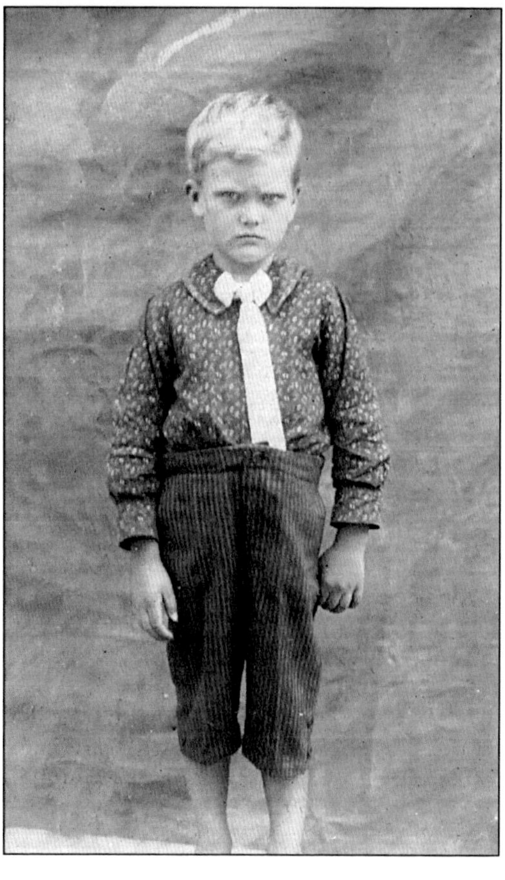

Children stand in front of the smokehouse at the J.B. Gragg house during a Clontz family reunion in the early 1950s. Pictured are Dean Robinson (boy on far left), Tommy Nichols (boy in front), and Jerry Moody (boy on far right). The smokehouse was built in the 1930s and was used to slaughter and smoke hogs raised at the residence. (Courtesy of Mr. and Mrs. Robin Gregg.)

Arthur Pinkney Gragg was the first child of John Burgin Gragg and Margaret Anna Clontz. Born just a month after the construction of the J.B. Gragg house, he was one of the first Graggs to legally change his name to Gregg. This picture was made around 1903. (Courtesy of Mr. and Mrs. Robin Gregg.)

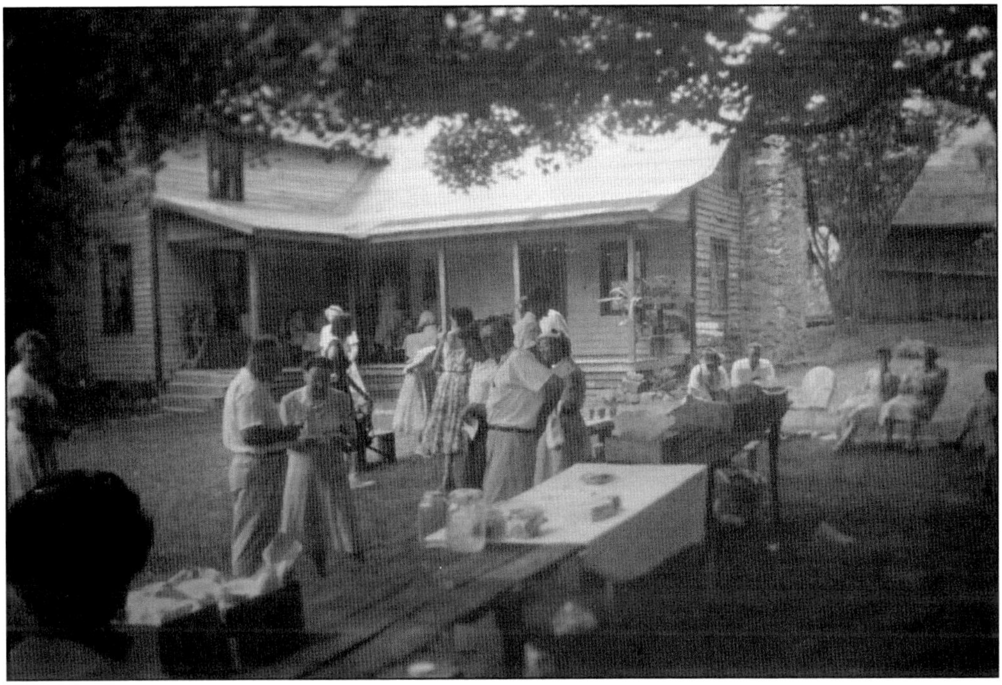

This house, known as the Creasman home, was built by William and Martha Burnette in the 1890s. The Burnettes purchased the property from Eileen Swain in 1873. In 1914, Marcus Creasman bought the property from the Burnettes and added a newer two-story wing. The older portion of the home, which is now the kitchen and dining room area, was previously a blacksmith shop, according to Ronnie King, who was raised by his grandparents in the home. (Courtesy of Nancy Wrenn.)

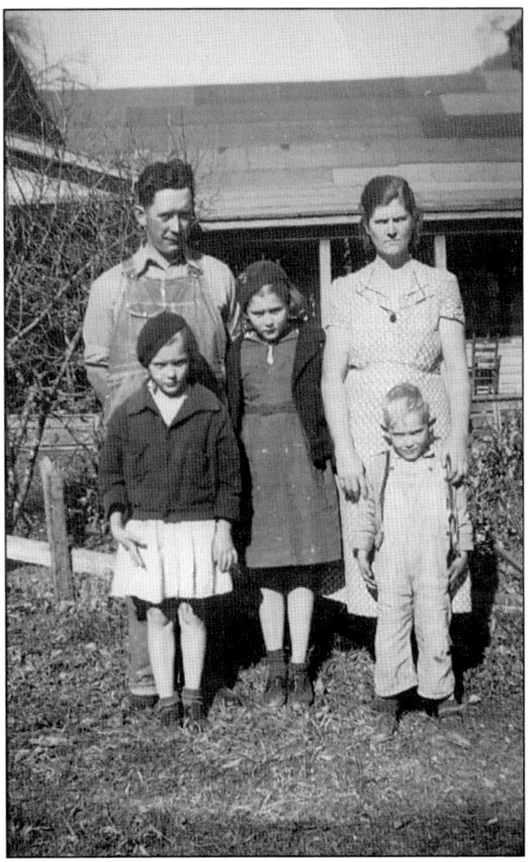

Glenn Rankin "Tom" Creasman stands with his wife, Audrey Gragg Creasman, and their children, (from left to right) Evelyn, Frances, and Wilbur "Bo" Creasman, in front of their home in 1938. (Courtesy of Mr. and Mrs. Robin Gregg.)

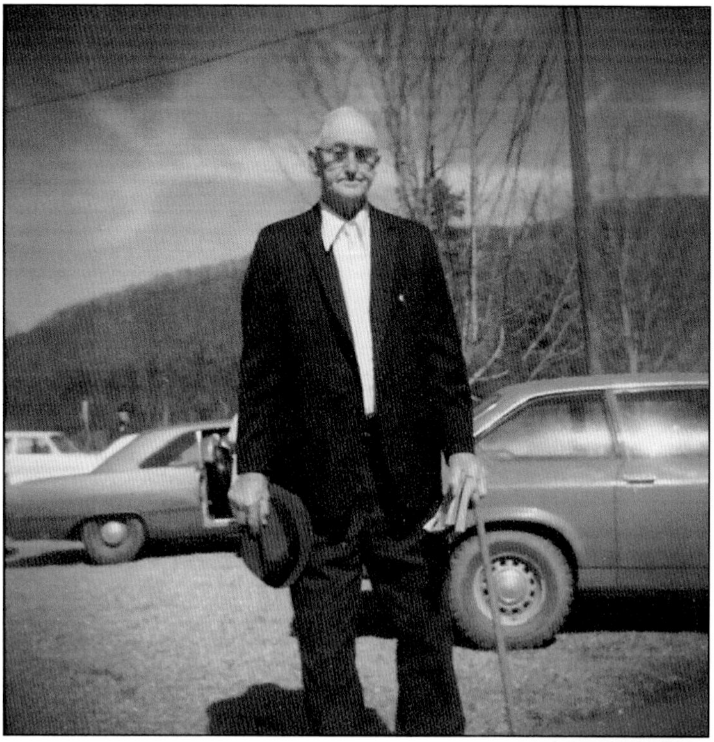

Harvey Edwin Fuller was a lumberman and had a sawmill across from his house on Fuller Lane, off Jones Cove Road. The Fullers moved to Riceville from Bryson City when their home was flooded by the creation of Fontana Lake. Harvey was born in 1895 and died in 1988. His wife, Fannie Whiteside, was born in 1893 and died in 1966. (Courtesy of Mr. and Mrs. Robin Gregg.)

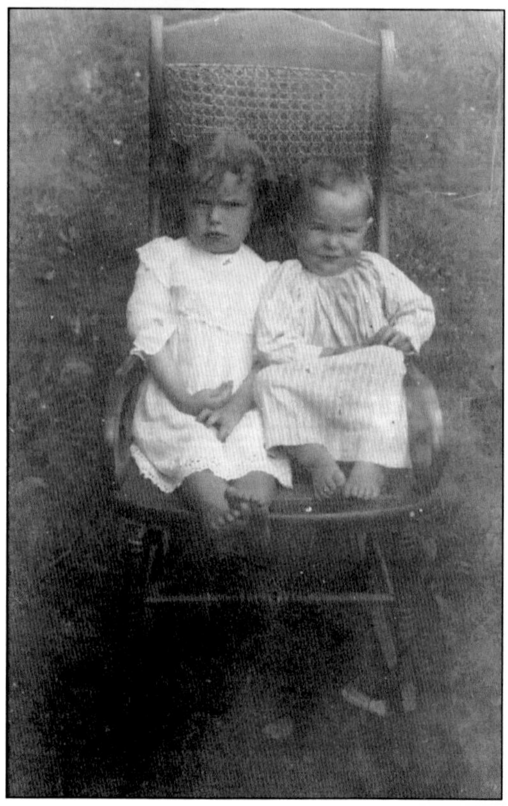

Fleta Reed and her brother Robert Carson are pictured around 1911. Fleta married Horace Reed and kept house most of her life. She was born on September 26, 1908, and died January 25, 1997. Her parents operated the power dam at Warren Wilson College. (Courtesy of Butch and Judy Reed.)

The original Reed home place was located in the hollow on Reed Mountain. Pictured around 1942 are Jim (left), George (center), and Bruce Reed. Most of the logs from the cabin, which was built around 1930, were moved from the old home place to build a new cabin on Sun Bird Lane. (Courtesy of Butch and Judy Reed.)

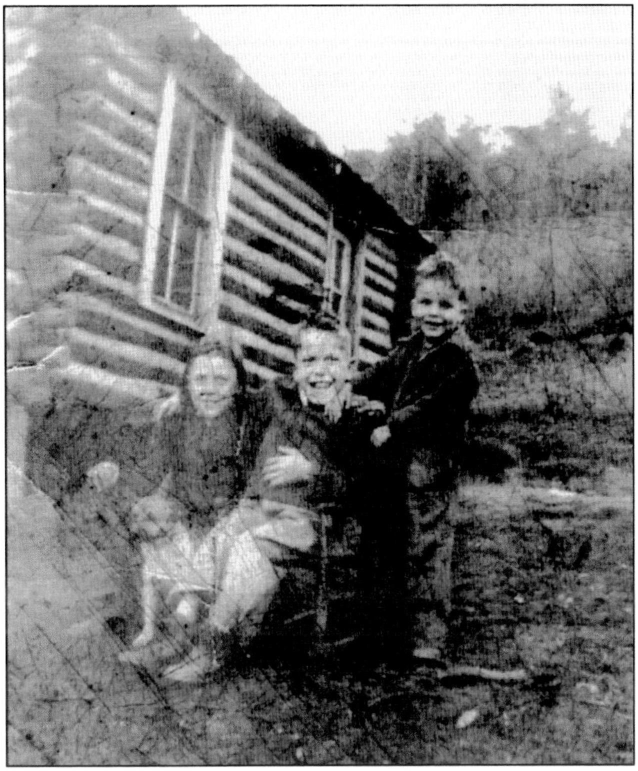

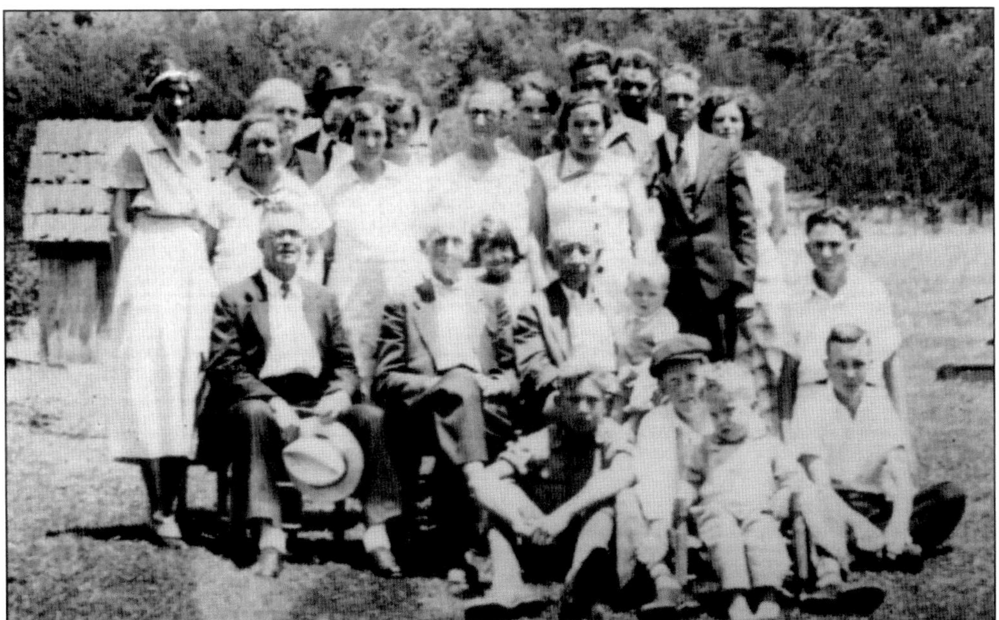

This photograph was taken at a Reed family get-together around 1935. George Reed, as a baby, sits in the front. Grandpa Reed is sitting in the middle, and Grandpa Carson is to his right, with Jim Reed on his lap. Loys Reed stands on far left, and Elmer Reed stands in the far back. (Courtesy of Butch and Judy Reed.)

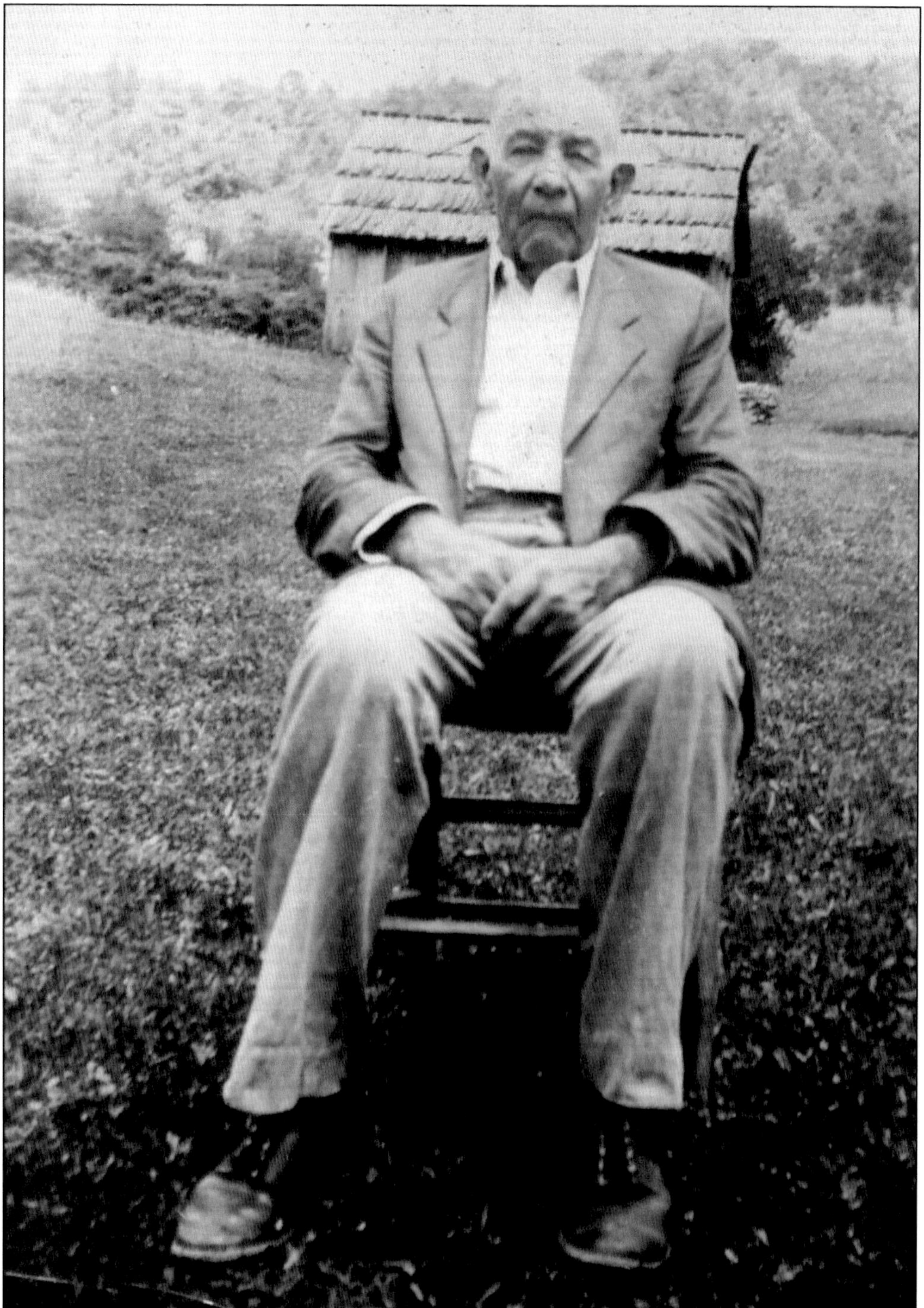

The Reed family came to Riceville in the mid-1800s. George Weldon Reed was one of the first Reeds to settle in Riceville. His barn can be seen behind him. He made his living as a farmer and a minister. (Courtesy of Butch and Judy Reed.)

In this view of the valley, taken from the porch of the Reed home place, Upper Grassy Branch Road can be seen on the on left, and Bethel Methodist Church is just past the frame of the photograph on the far right. The Reed family found arrowheads and Indian artifacts in this area when they plowed the fields. (Courtesy of Butch and Judy Reed.)

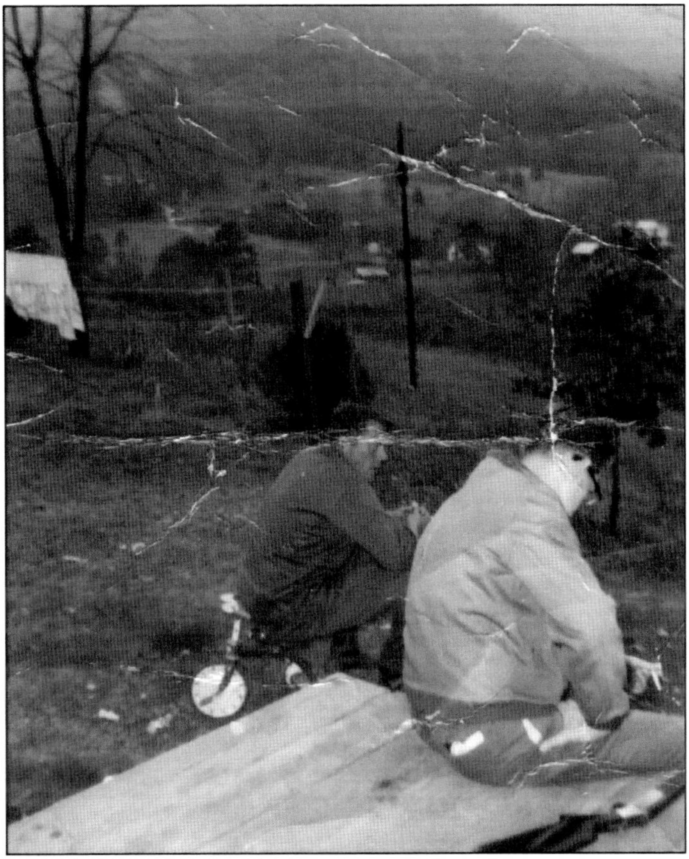

The Reed home is pictured in 1957. A young Dean Reed stands in the foreground while his relatives Horace, Edna, and Fleta (wearing glasses) Reed visit. (Courtesy of Butch and Judy Reed.)

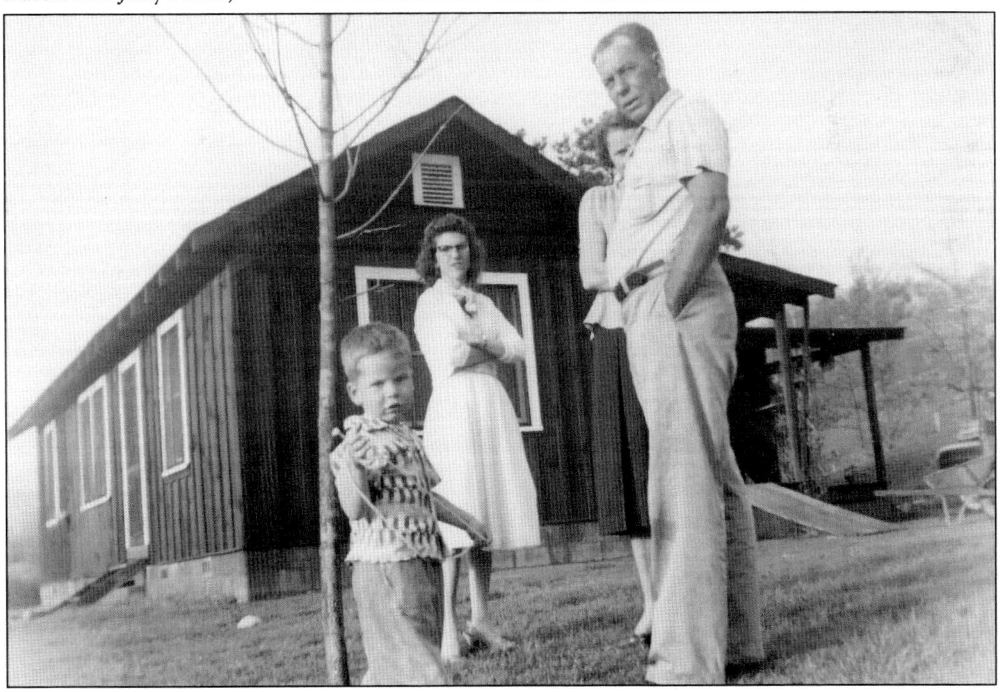

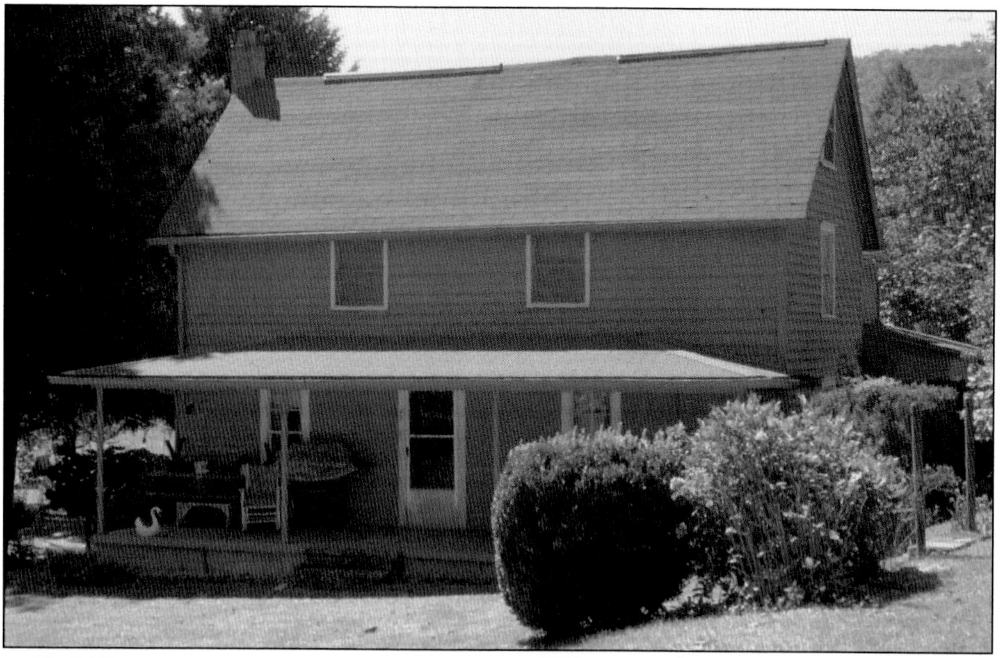

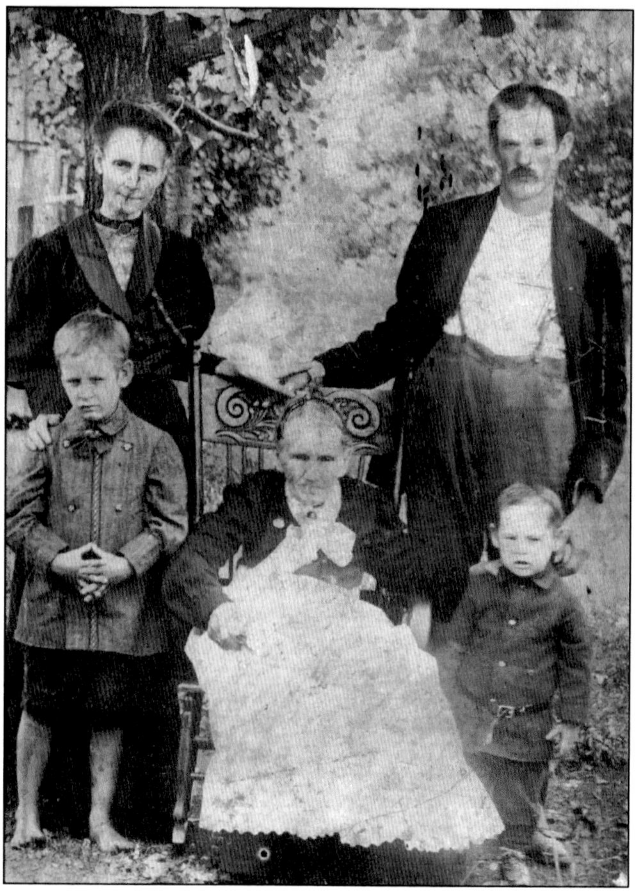

The Stephenson home, located off Bull Creek Road, once served as the post office when Democrats were in office in the county. Lilly Stephenson was a school principal in Biltmore. There used to be a big oak tree in the yard that was a favorite of Lilly's. When the state came to pave the road, they wanted to cut down the tree. Lilly got out her shotgun and told them to leave the tree, and now Bull Creek Road curves around the spot where the tree once stood. (Courtesy of Nancy Wrenn.)

The Bradley's lived near Berea Baptist Church. Paul Bradley (standing in back) was a weaver. (Courtesy of Butch and Judy Reed.)

Two

EDUCATION AND RELIGIOUS LIFE

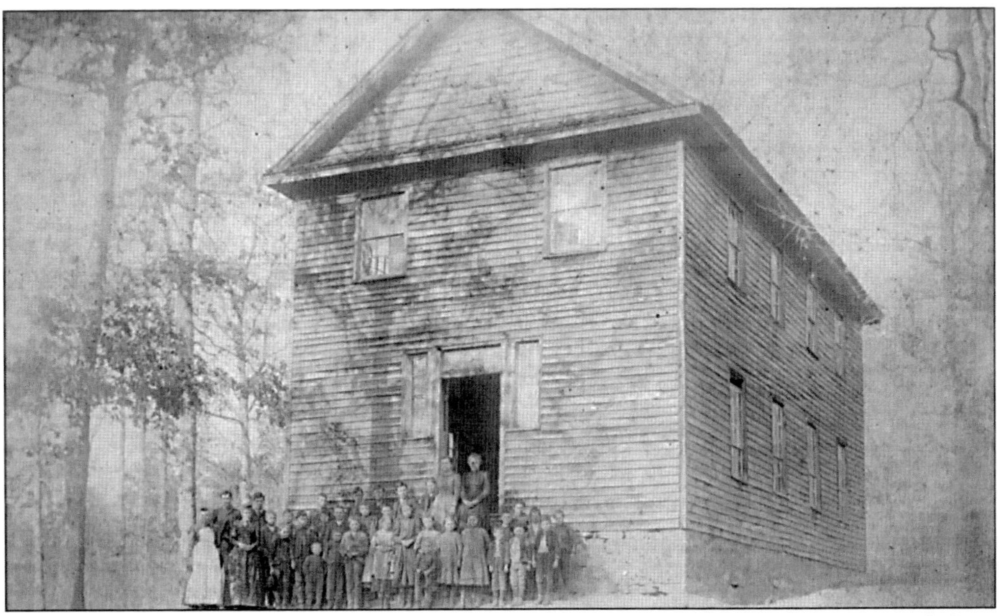

The Presbyterian church sent missionaries to the Blue Ridge Mountains. This photograph from 1892 is featured in the album kept by Frances Louisa Goodrich (1856–1944), the founder of Allanstand Craft Industries. She first came to western North Carolina as a teacher with the Presbyterian Board of Home Missions and was posted in one of Riceville's early schools, the Montanic Institute. The figures in the doorway are identified as Eva Gorbold and Frances Louisa Goodrich. (Courtesy of Mr. and Mrs. Robin Gregg.)

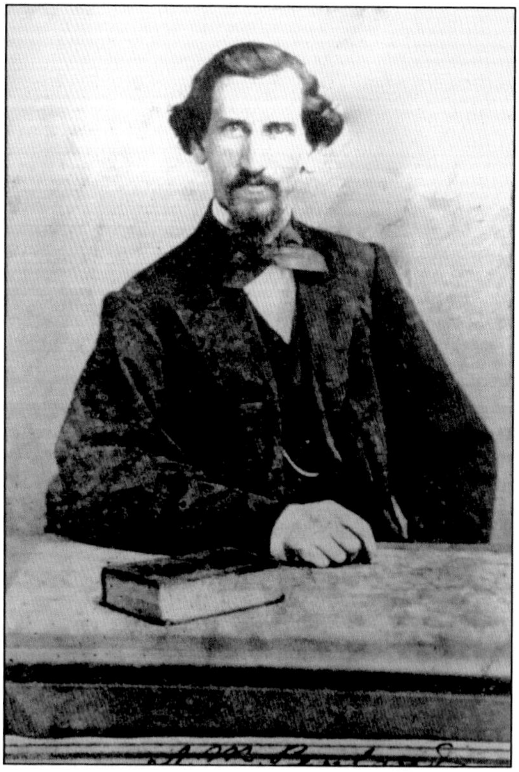

A.M. Penland founded schools across the Asheville area. On September 15, 1873, he founded and became the first principal of the Montanic Institute, which was located on the hill adjacent to Riceville Presbyterian Church. The school closed in 1885, and Penland moved back to Reems Creek. The schoolhouse was sold to the trustees of the College Hill Church for a dollar. (Courtesy Warren Wilson College Archives.)

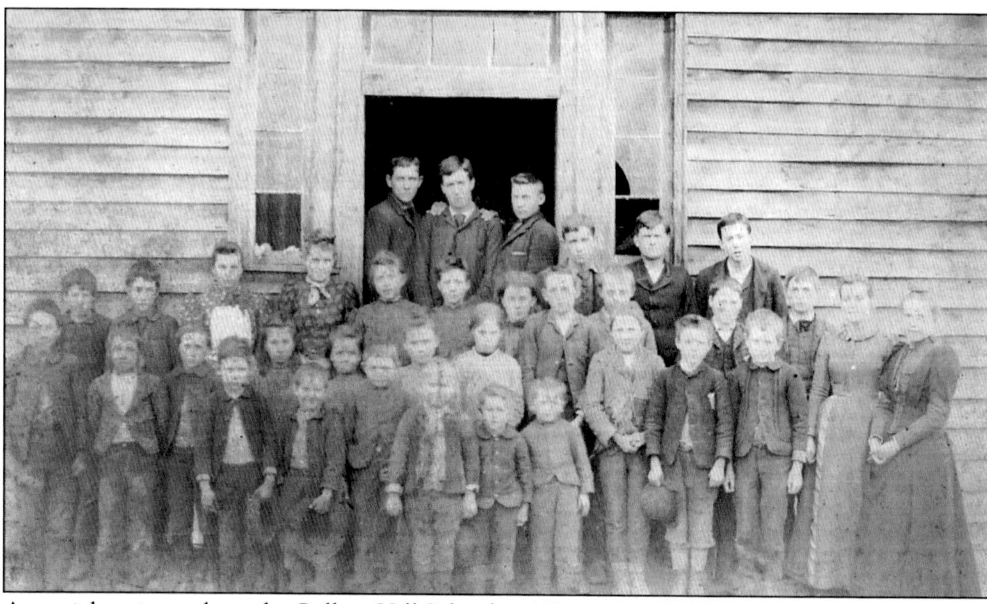

An article written about the College Hill School in 1891 reported, "If needy boys and girls wished to attend school, Penland made no charges for admittance and instruction; school expenses of older youths he was accustomed to lighten by allowing them to cut wood and do odd jobs in part payment." Penland's original diary from his days in Riceville indicates that students paid tuition in cash as well as in farm goods. In 1874, the school had 151 students and required two teachers. (Courtesy of Mr. and Mrs. Robin Gregg.)

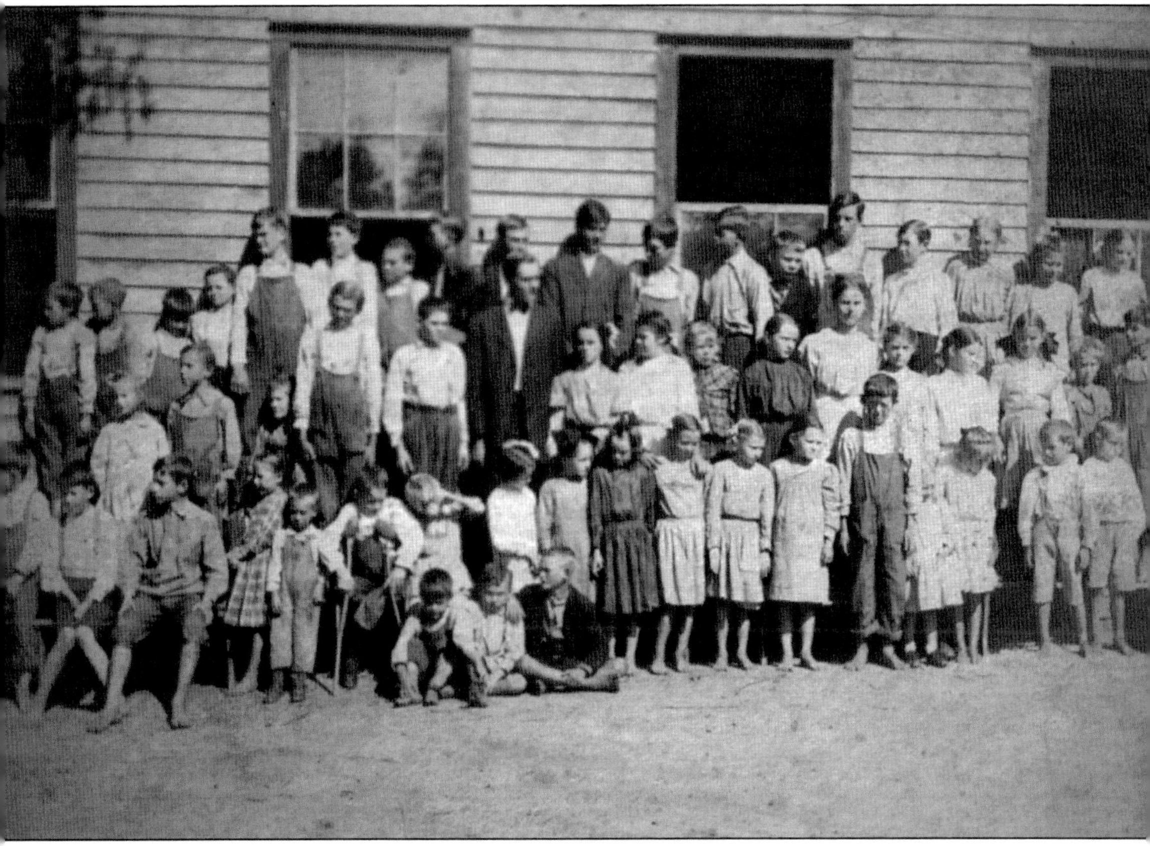

Three schools operated in this location after the Montanic Institute: Vaughn Academy, Peabody School, and College Hill School. For the little ones, there was "Read'n, Rite'n, and 'Rithmetic," and for the older ones, Greek and Latin. During the day, the schoolhouse was a hive of activity. The older children studied downstairs with the younger children in the two rooms upstairs. The rooms were called the big room and the small room, even though they were the same size. The names "big" and "small" referred to the size of the children. (Courtesy of John Weakly.)

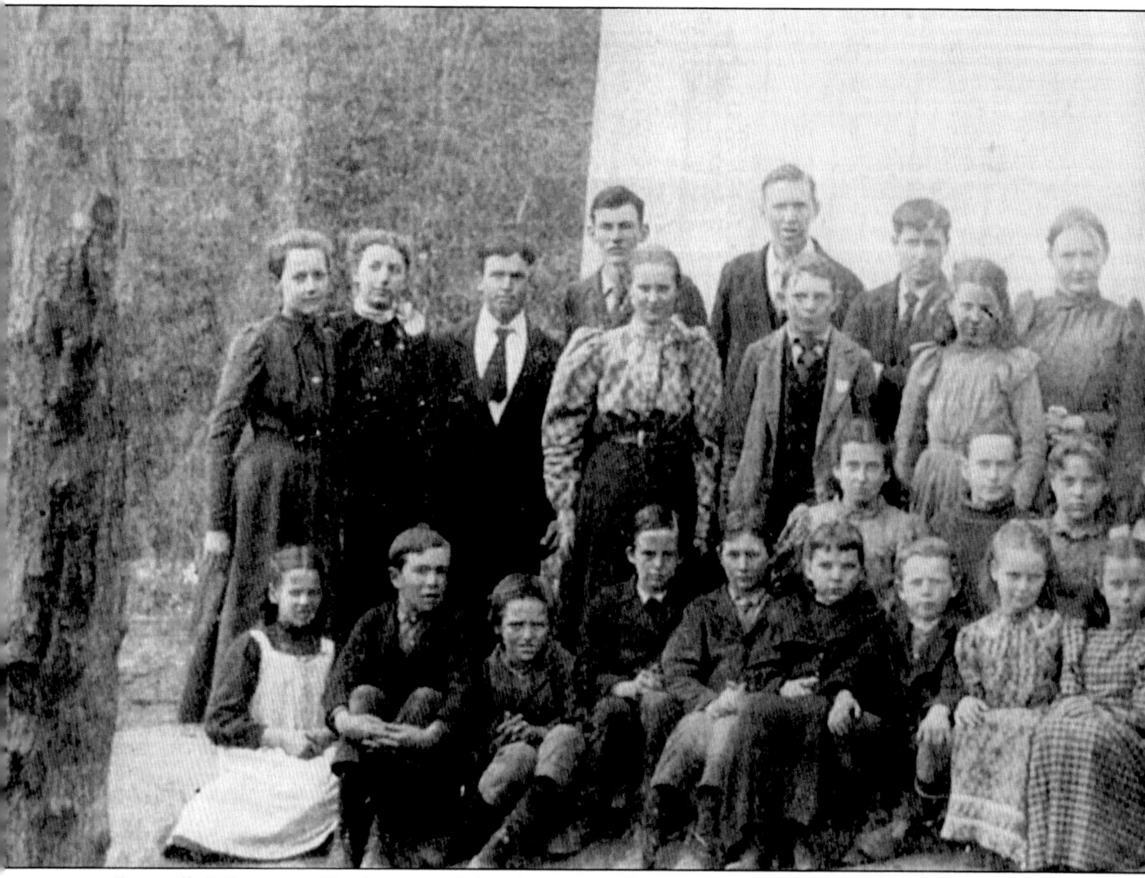

Riceville Missionary Presbyterian School is pictured around 1900. The teacher was Ollie Hendricks (standing far right), from Indiana. Her sister "Miss Flo" came with her and kept house. Pictured from left to right are (first row) May Penland, Jack Rice, Will Jones, Jim Burnett, Estes Rector (adopted son of D.L. Stevenson), Bessie Clark, Walter Hughey, Sue Swann, Heslop Creasman, Dawton Gallimore, John Hughey, Horace Stevenson, Newman Clark, Raphael Rice, Luther Creasman, and Frank Stevenson; (second row) Isabell Hall, Wayne Shope, Althea Reed, Della

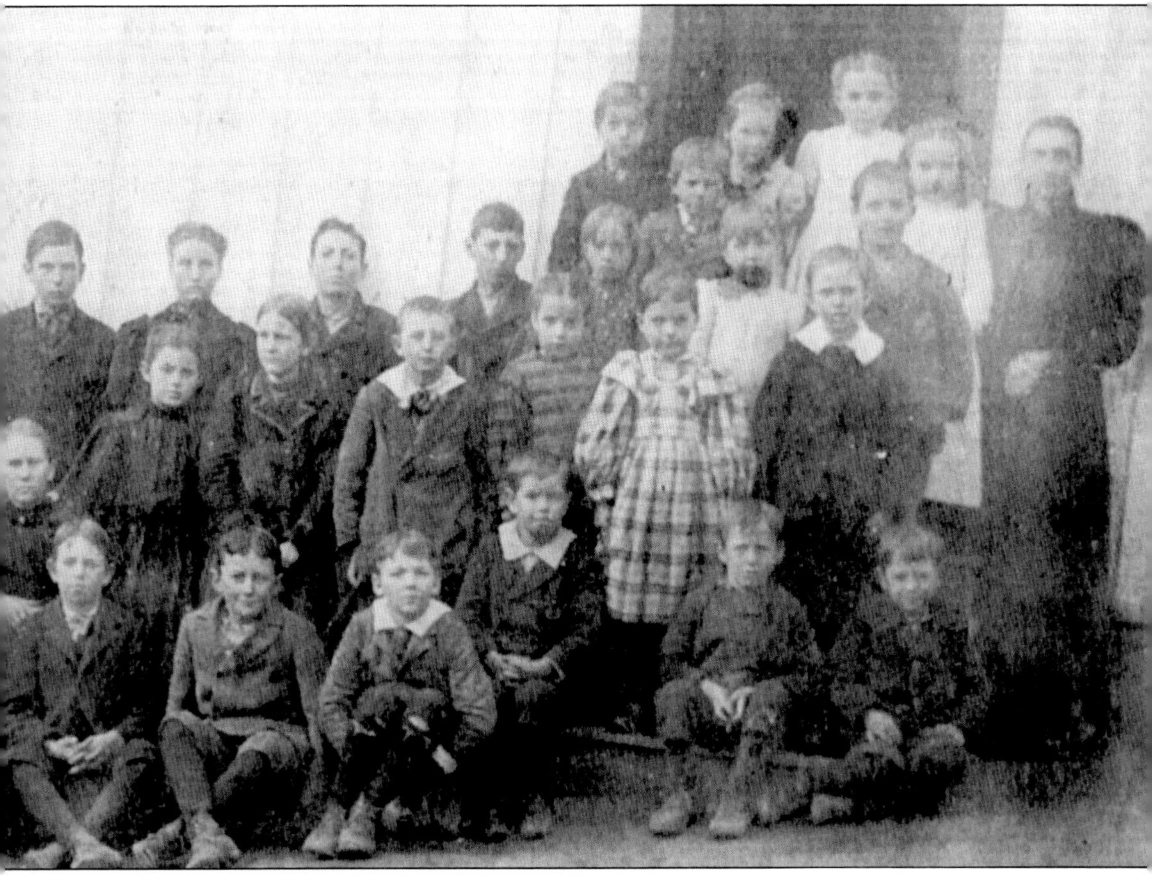

Penland, and Cora Stokes; (third row) Ethel McDaris, Ernest Hughey, Mamie Keesler, Ethel Roberts, Ella Stringfellow, Therron McDaris, Retta Reed, Edith Clark, and Lafayette "Fate" Burnett; (forth row) Cleo Bartlett, Sigourney Hughey, Charlie Hall, Frank Clark, Chester Head, Carroll Hall, Mary Jones, Herman Clark, Charlie Burnett, Ida Swann, John Ray, Will Ray, Ollie Fox, Florence Stringfellow, and Brannon Jones; (fifth row, on steps) Wilton Bartlett, Ivan Hughey, Sallie Burnett, Elsie Reed, and Hettie Reed. (Courtesy of John Weakly.)

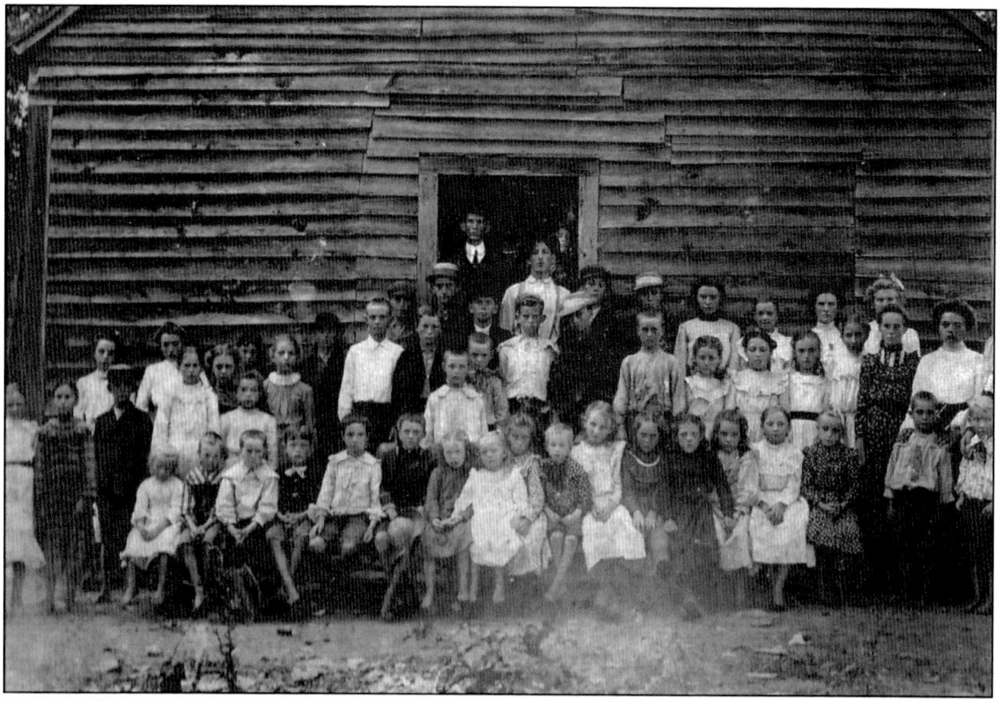

The Brush Hill School was the other school for local children. It was on Old Farm School Road, across from the old Rice home place. The schoolchildren would walk on the road to the school, located right off Riceville Road. Brush Hill was torn down about 1935, and the lumber was taken by Rafe Rice's uncle Jack, who used it to build a cabin in the woods near the Grassy Branch Church. (Courtesy of Rafe Rice Jr.)

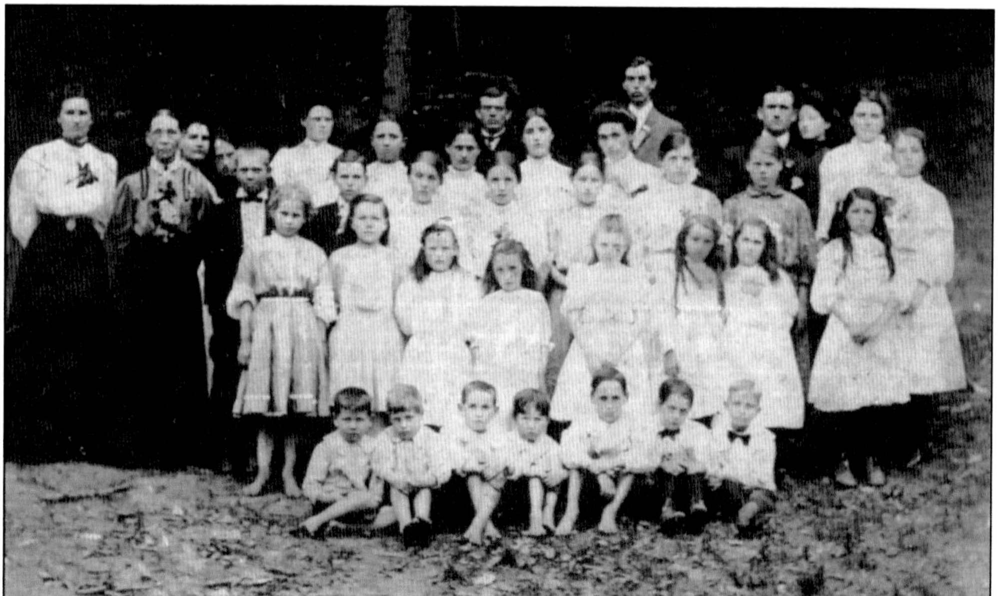

The students and teachers at Brush Hill School, also called "the Little Red Schoolhouse," are pictured around 1912. The boy with the bow tie standing beside the teacher is Elmer Reed. His brother Horace Reed is in the front row, second from the left. (Courtesy of Butch and Judy Reed.)

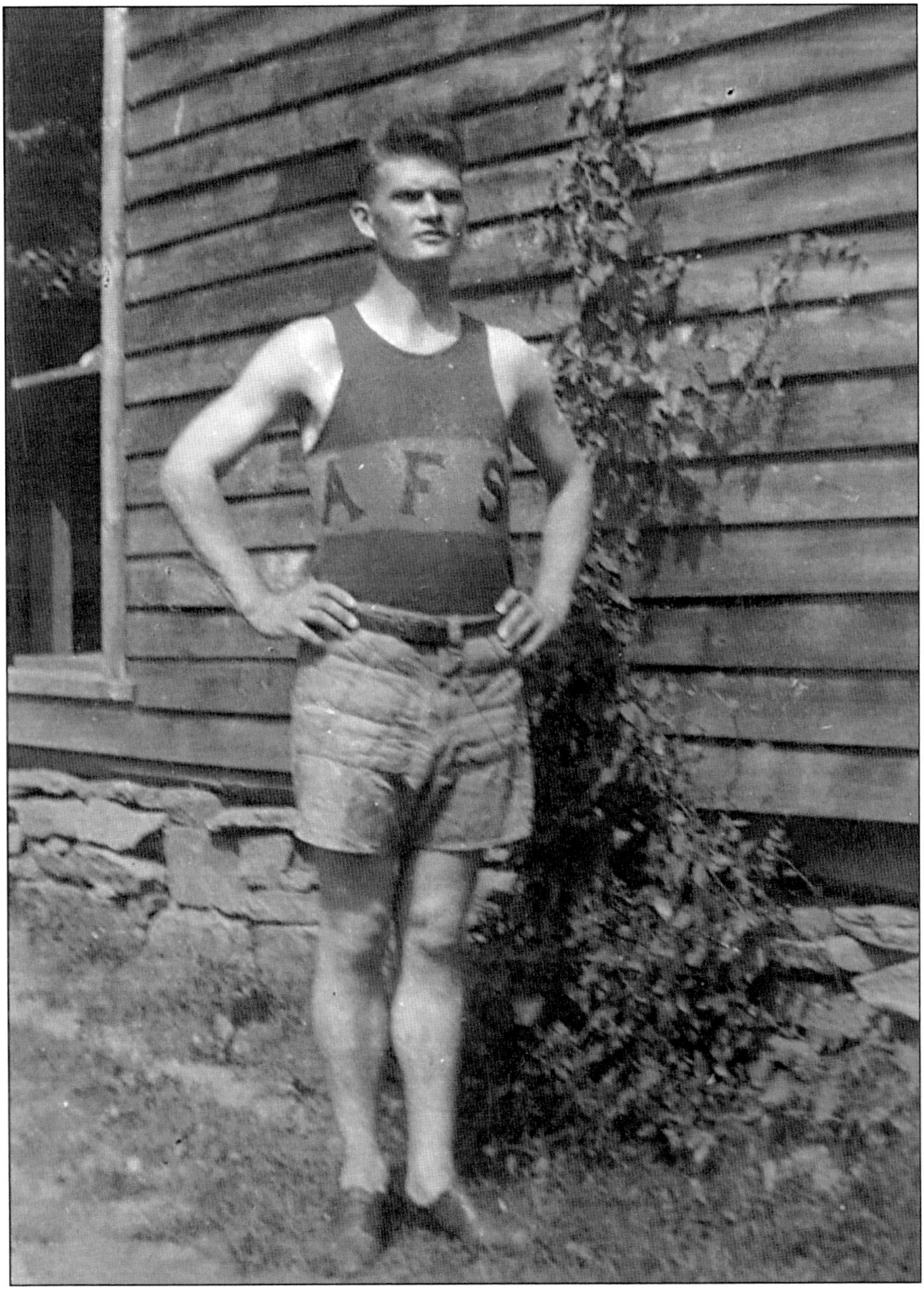

Arthur Pinkney Gragg, pictured in his basketball uniform, was the first child of John Burgin Gragg and Margaret Anna Clontz. From 1914 to 1918, he attended the Asheville Farm School (now known as Warren Wilson College), which, in the early 20th century, was such a journey from the head of Shope Creek that Arthur was unable to regularly visit, so he corresponded with his family through the US mail. (Courtesy of Mr. and Mrs. Robin Gregg.)

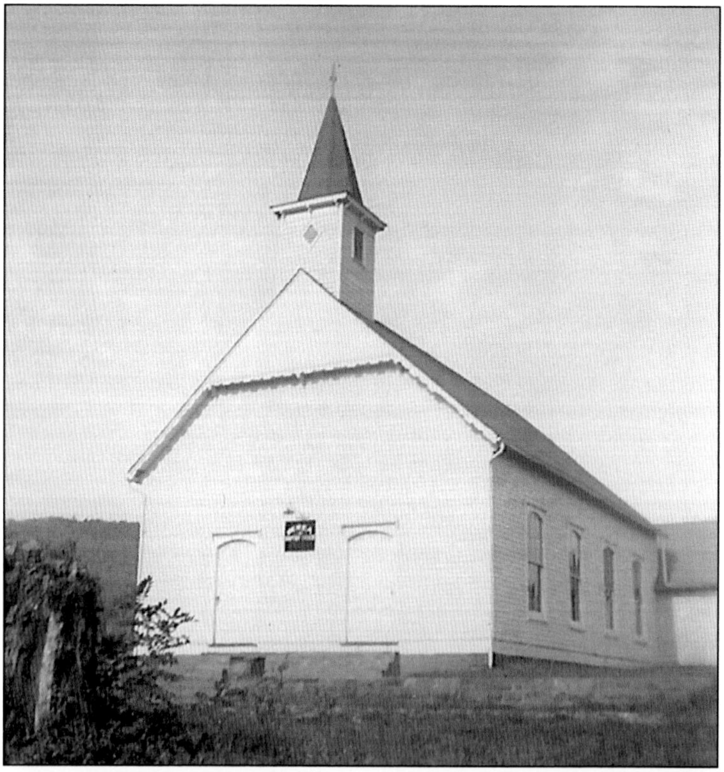

Berea Baptist Church is Riceville's oldest church. In 1853, Berea Baptist Church, located on Riceville Road south of Bull Creek, was organized. The first pastor of the church was Thomas Stradley, from the First Baptist Church of Asheville. (Courtesy of Riceville Community Center.)

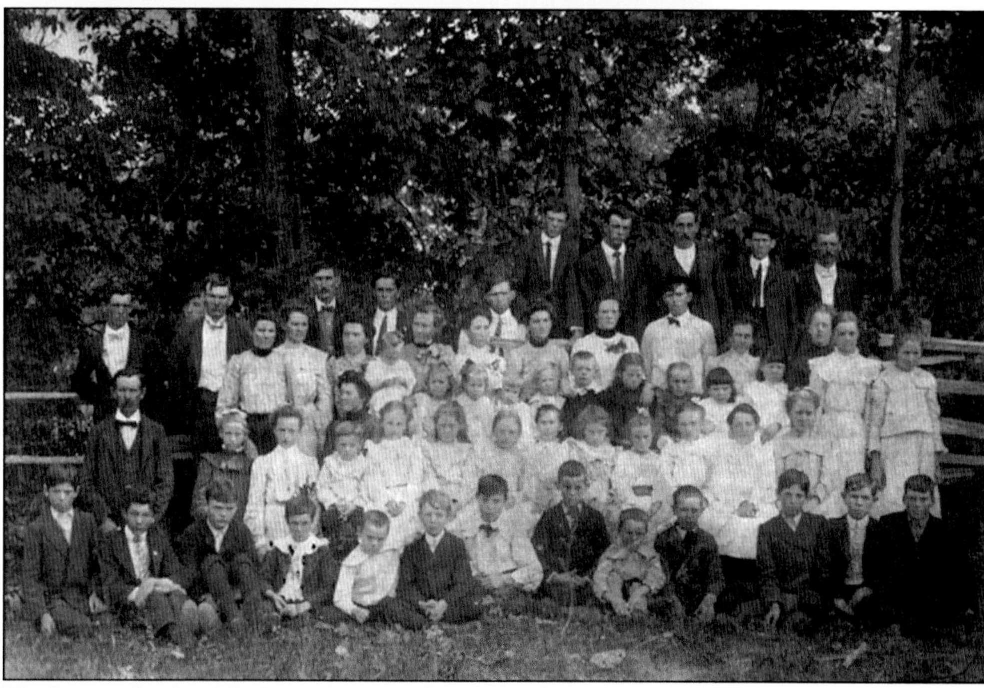

The boys and girls of the Berea Baptist Church Sunday School pose with their teachers in front of a split-rail fence in 1903. At the time Berea was organized, there were only threes houses in the area surrounding the church: the Bartletts, Reeds, and Alexanders. (Courtesy of John Weakly.)

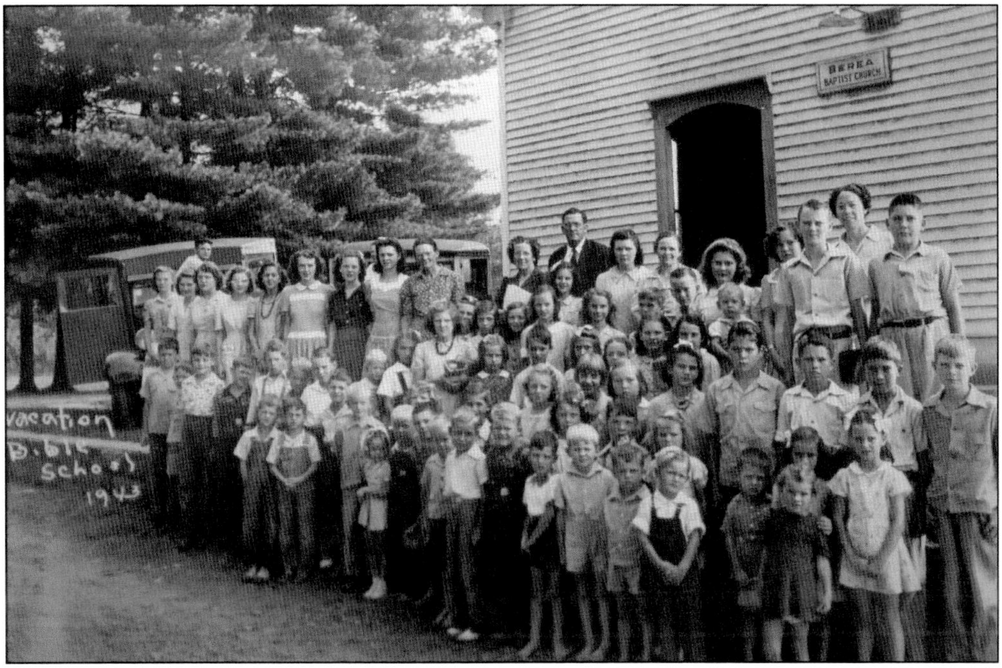

Berea Baptist Church's Vacation Bible School is shown in 1943. On May 17, 1953, the church celebrated its centennial with special services in the morning and afternoon. A picnic lunch was served, finishing with a birthday cake topped with 100 candles. Special music was furnished by the First Baptist Church of Asheville. (Courtesy of John Weakly.)

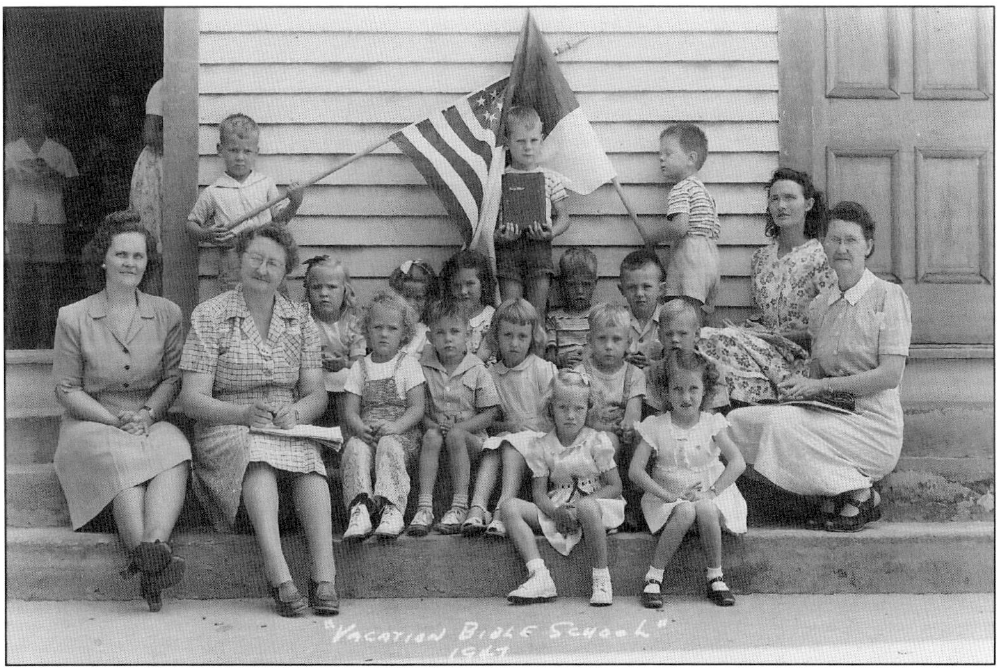

Berea Baptist Church's Vacation Bible School is shown in 1947. Bible school teacher Pauline Gregg Ingle sits far left beside Gus Cordell Creasman. Thelma Gregg Buckner sits far right. (Courtesy of Mr. and Mrs. Robin Gregg.)

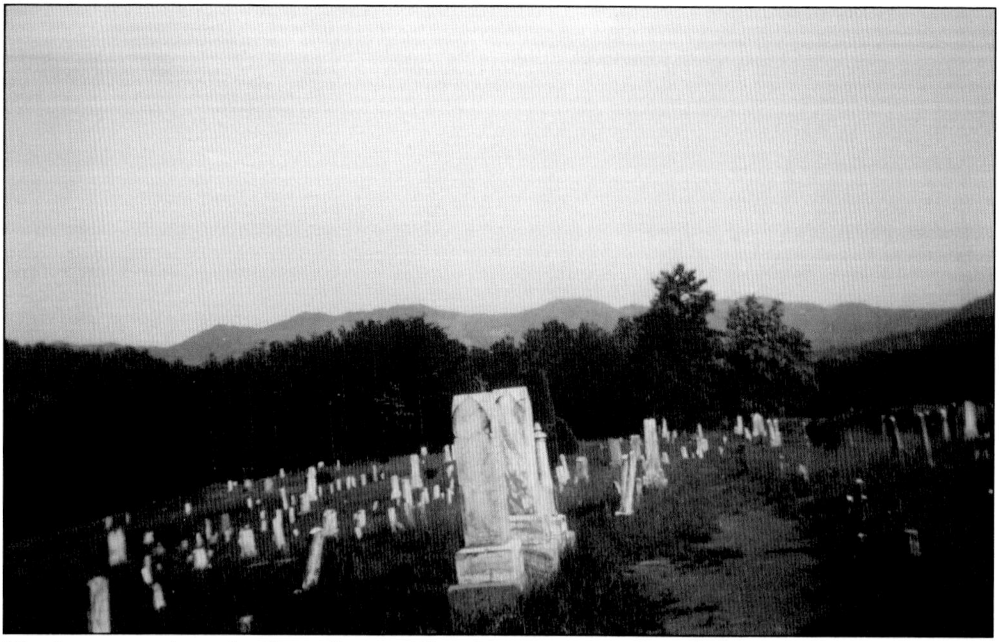

The first person buried at Berea Baptist Church cemetery was Joseph Stroupe, a charter member. He was buried in 1856. These photographs are from the 1950s. (Courtesy of the Riceville Community Center.)

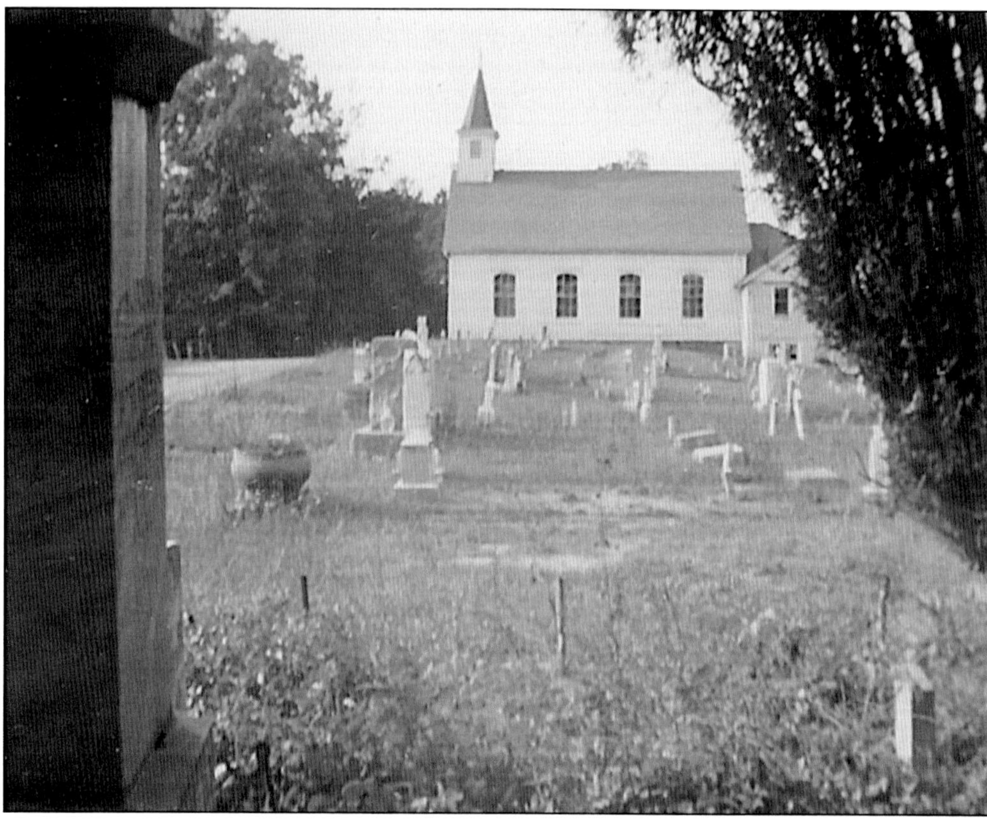

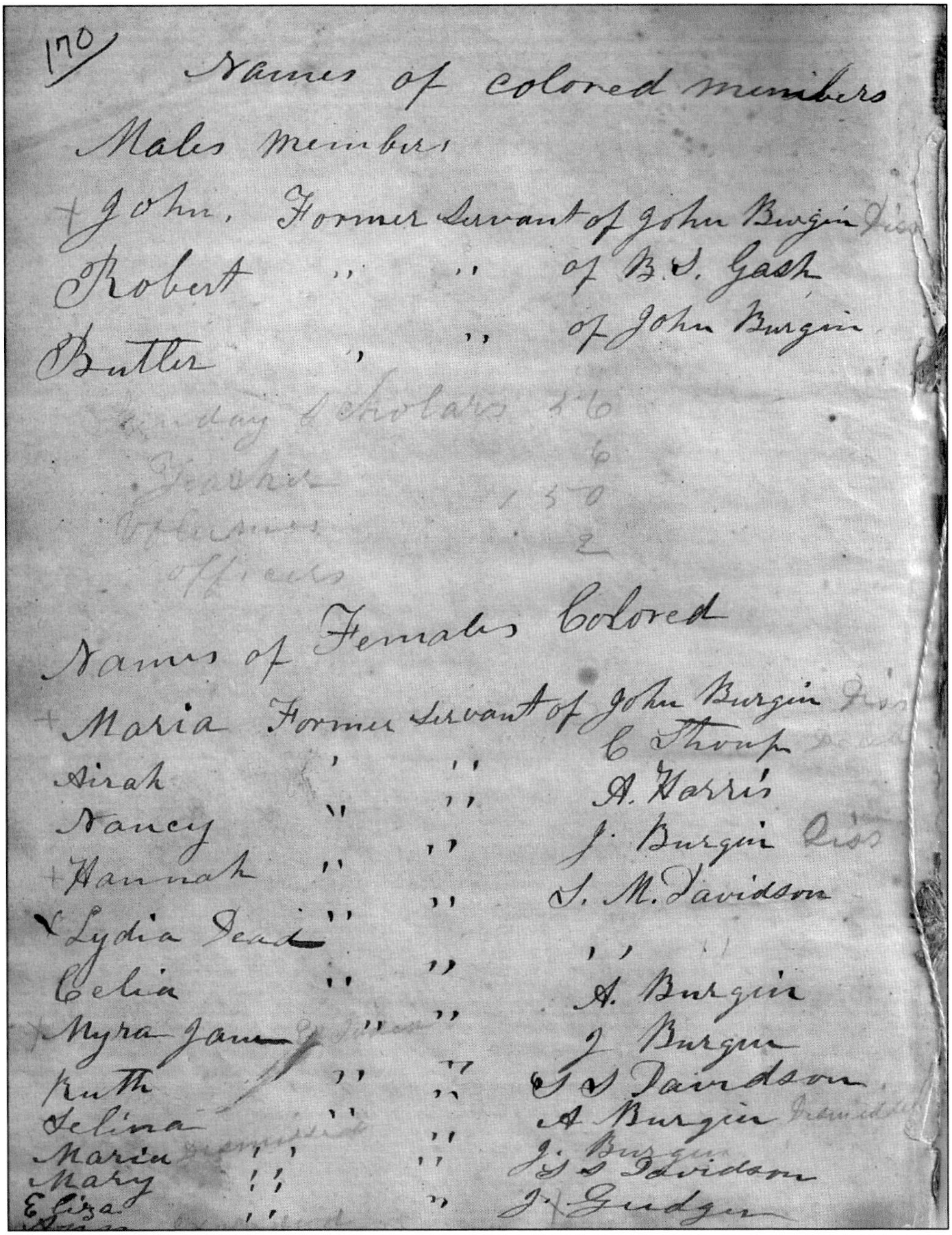
170

Names of colored members

Males members

+John, Former servant of John Burgin Dis

Robert " " of B.S. Gash

Butler " " of John Burgin

Names of Females Colored

+Maria Former servant of John Burgin Dis

C Thorp

Airah " " A. Harris

Nancy " " J. Burgin Dis

+Hannah " " S. M. Davidson

Lydia Dead " " "

Celia " " A. Burgin

Myra Jane " " J Burgin

Ruth " " T S Davidson

Selina " " A Burgin

Maria " " J. Burgin

Mary " " T S Davidson

Eliza " " J. Gudger

Berea Baptist Church's records are very thorough and perhaps the only written documentation of early African American members of the Riceville community. The records indicate that two of the first five founding members, Seneca and his wife, Maria, were African American servants of T.T. Patton. Later entries record births, deaths, and honors, as well as several occasions when women—of both races—were dismissed from the congregation for immoral conduct, such as dancing. In another entry, member Joshua Bartlett and his wife, Jane Rymer, were excluded from the church because she convinced him to desert the Confederate army, and he hid in the woods. (Courtesy of Mr. and Mrs. Robin Gregg.)

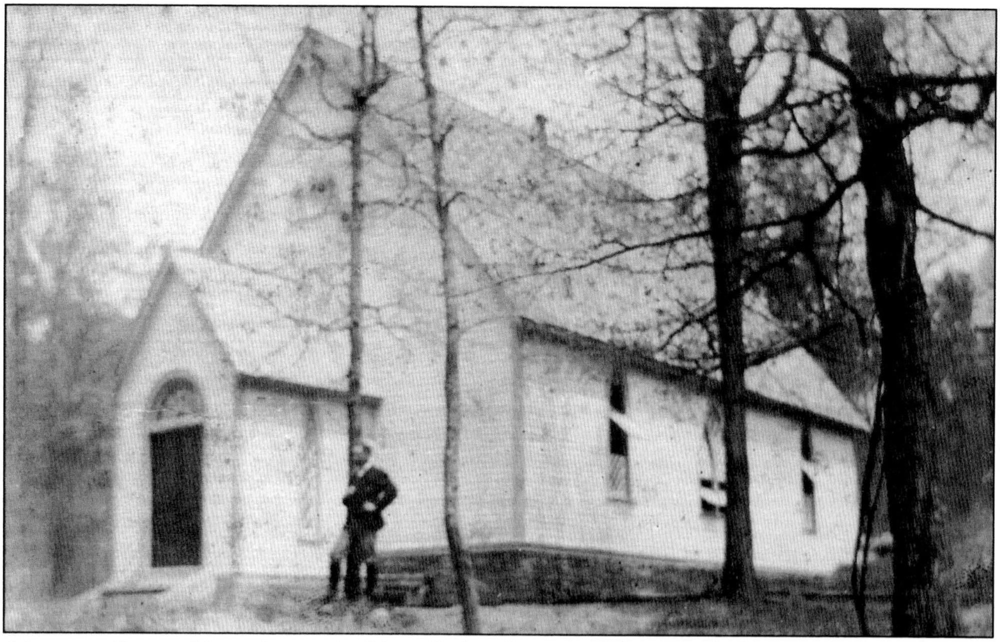

About a mile past Berea Baptist is Riceville Presbyterian Church, which was established in the spring of 1876 and met at the Bull Creek home of Samuel and Margaret Hughey. Jim Craig sold the land to the church, and the building was constructed around 1895. There were 19 charter members of the College Hill Presbyterian Church (as it was originally called): Samuel and Margaret Hughey, Matilda Roberts, Walton Roberts, Marion Roberts, Cornelius and Nanny Clark, Harriet Hughey, Laura Hughey, Julie Hughey, Addie Hughey, Newton Hughey, Chris Hughey, Doc and Sarah Stephenson, Daniel Stephenson, Silas and Clarissa Stroupe, and George and Brasaka Reed. (Courtesy of Sara Sawyer.)

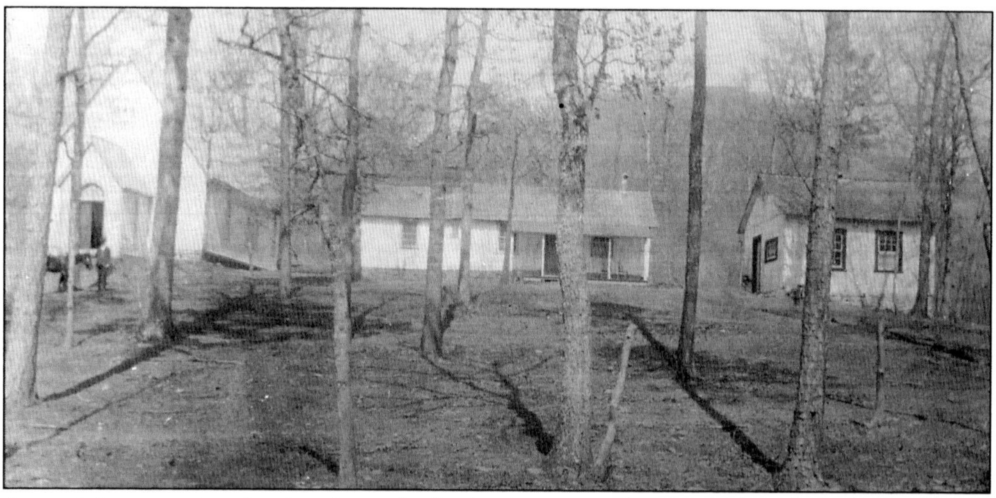

Around the same time the church was built, the first manse (middle building) was built on what is now part of the parking lot. A few preachers lived in the manse, but more often, they lived in Reems Creek, coming by horseback over Bull Creek Gap for Sunday preaching. One young preacher—evidently not raised on a farm—rode over with his saddle backwards on the horse. One of the men kindly changed it for him when he wasn't looking. The manse came to be used as a residence by the women who taught in the Riceville School. (Courtesy of Sara Sawyer.)

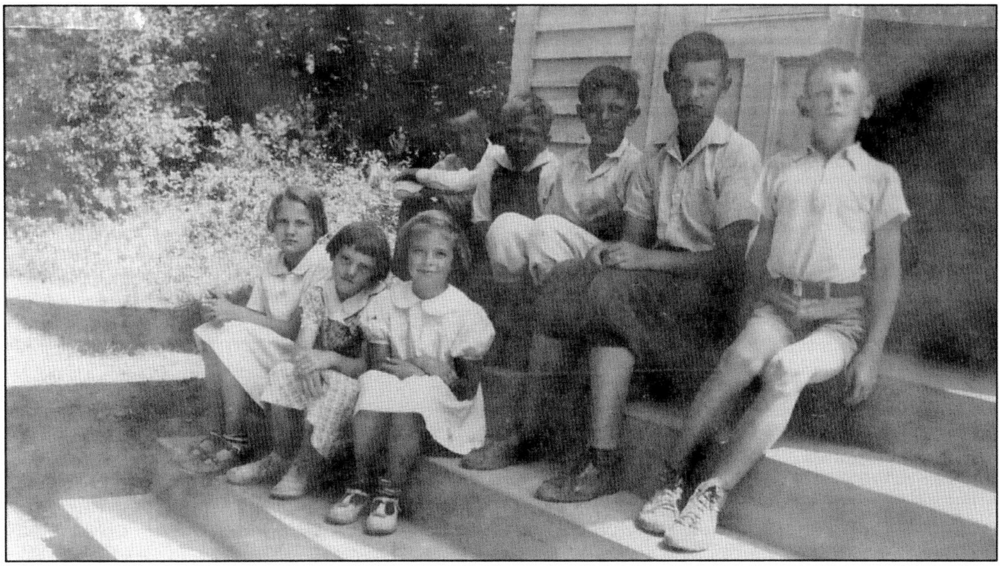

The Rice family children sit on the steps of the Riceville Presbyterian Church in the 1930s. (Courtesy of Sara Sawyer.)

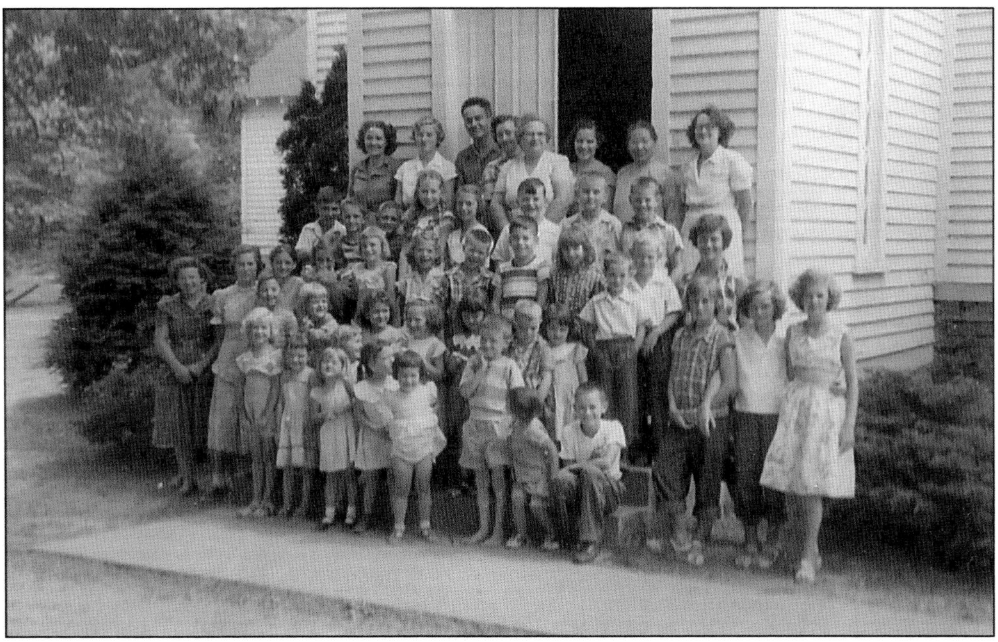

Riceville Presbyterian Church held its first Vacation Bible School in July 1953. Approximately 50 children enrolled in the school. (Courtesy of the Riceville Community Center.)

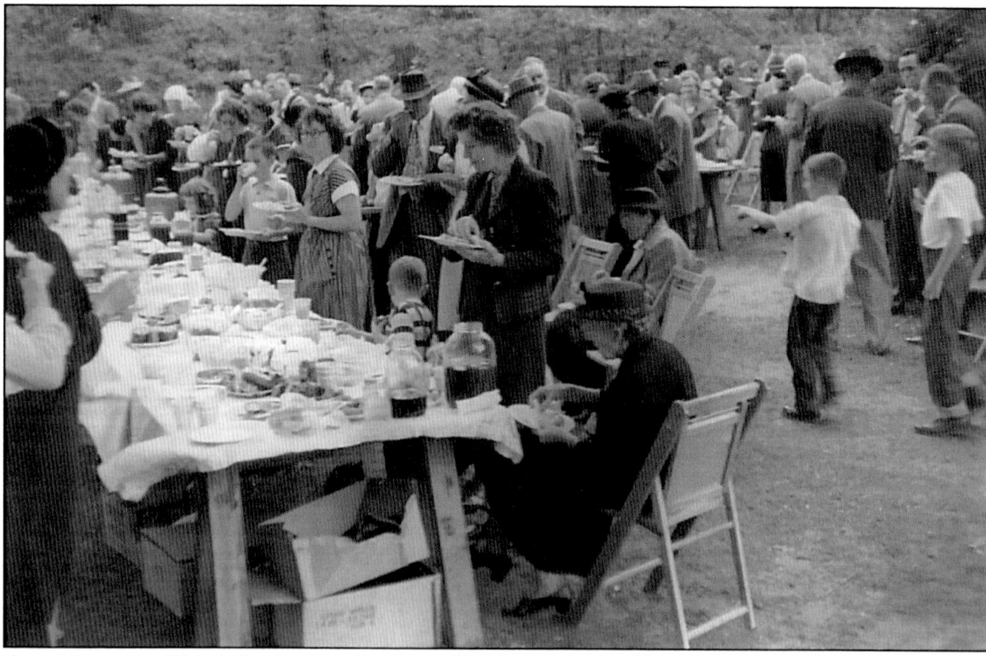

A yearly event, Old Folks Day at the Riceville Presbyterian Church is pictured in 1953. During the event, the congregation—old and new—gathers for a picnic lunch after the service and shares the history and fellowship of the church. The tradition continues today. (Courtesy of the Riceville Community Center.)

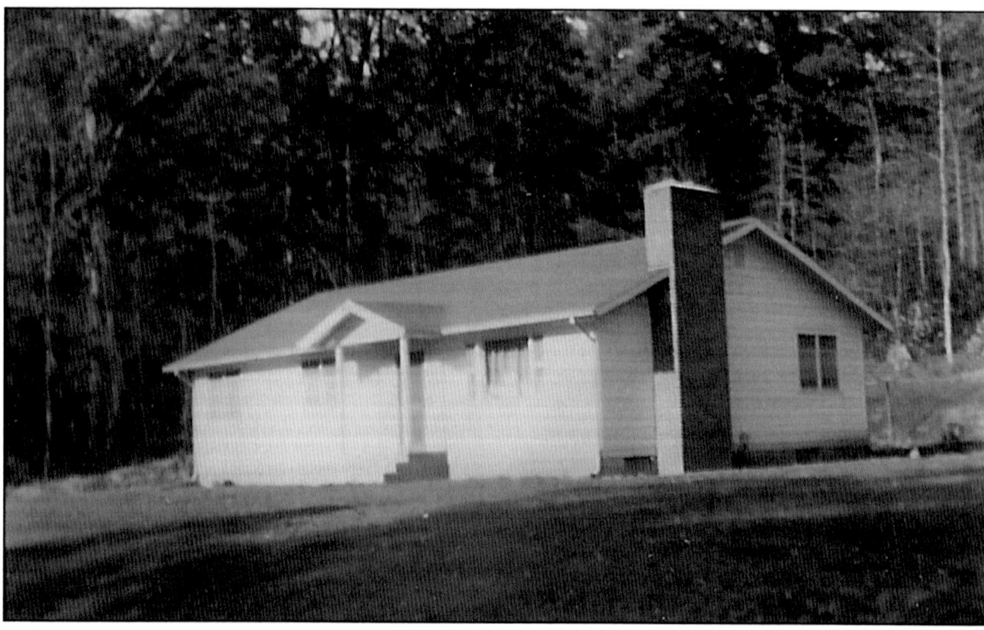

In December 1952, the new Riceville Presbyterian manse was completed. Remarkably, it was built entirely through volunteer labor. Members of the church and community gave up vacations, weekends, and many evenings. Within the congregation were carpenters, electricians, plumbers, and plasterers. The manse stands as testimony to the spirit of the church—and the community. (Courtesy of the Riceville Community Center.)

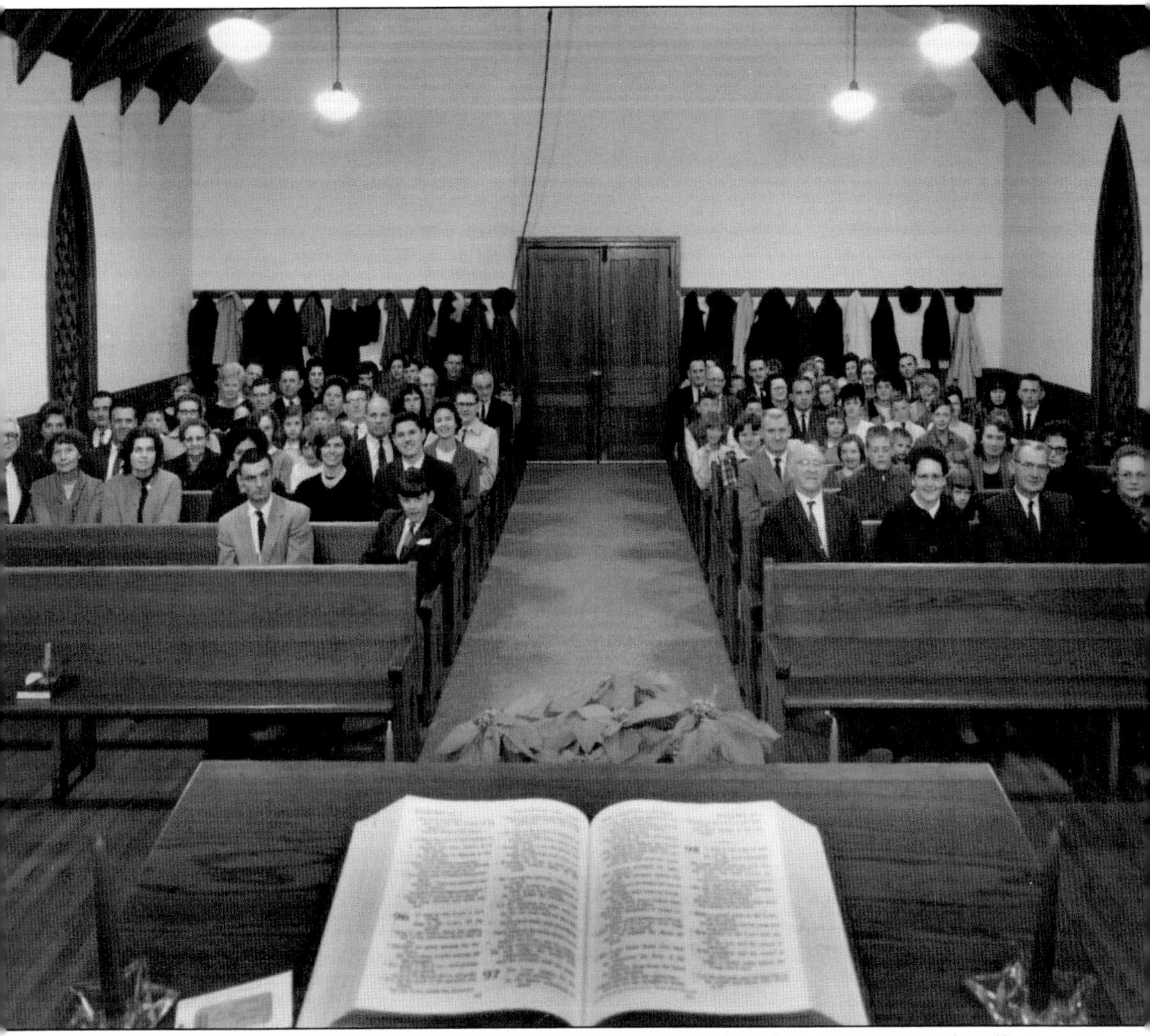

In 1952, Rev. Keith Mitchell was ordained and installed as the first full-time pastor of College Hill Church. In 1953, the College Hill Church officially became the Riceville Presbyterian Church. The church still holds weekly services in the original sanctuary, as seen in this early 1960s photograph. (Courtesy of Sara Sawyer.)

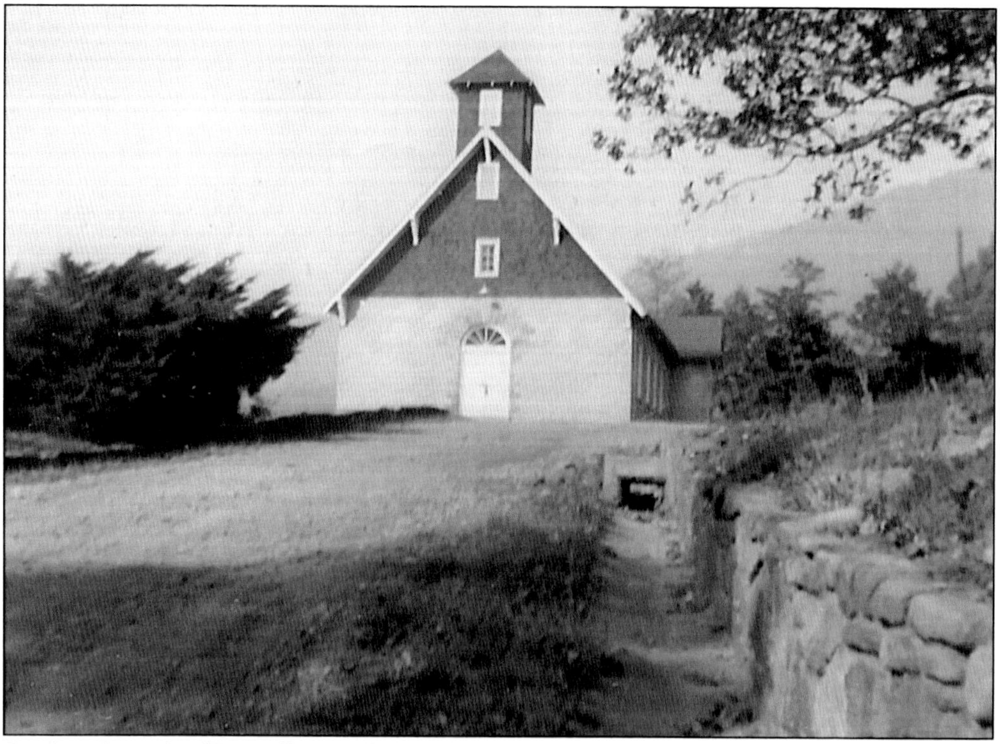

On the other side of Riceville is Bethel Methodist Church. In 1886 and early 1887, the Reverend E.H. Reynolds encouraged Methodists to build a church on a section of what is now Riceville Road. The church building was constructed in 1888 on land donated by Joseph and Hannah Glass, by mostly volunteer labor. The building was dedicated in 1890 and services were held by circuit riders once a month. In 1923, the first church building burned but was reconstructed by 1925. (Courtesy of the Riceville Community Center.)

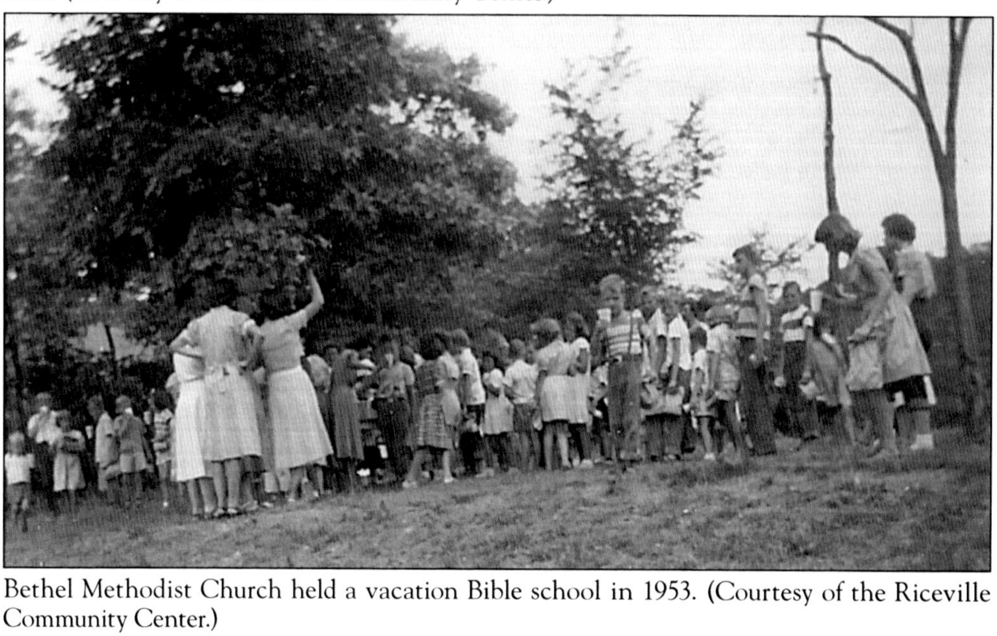

Bethel Methodist Church held a vacation Bible school in 1953. (Courtesy of the Riceville Community Center.)

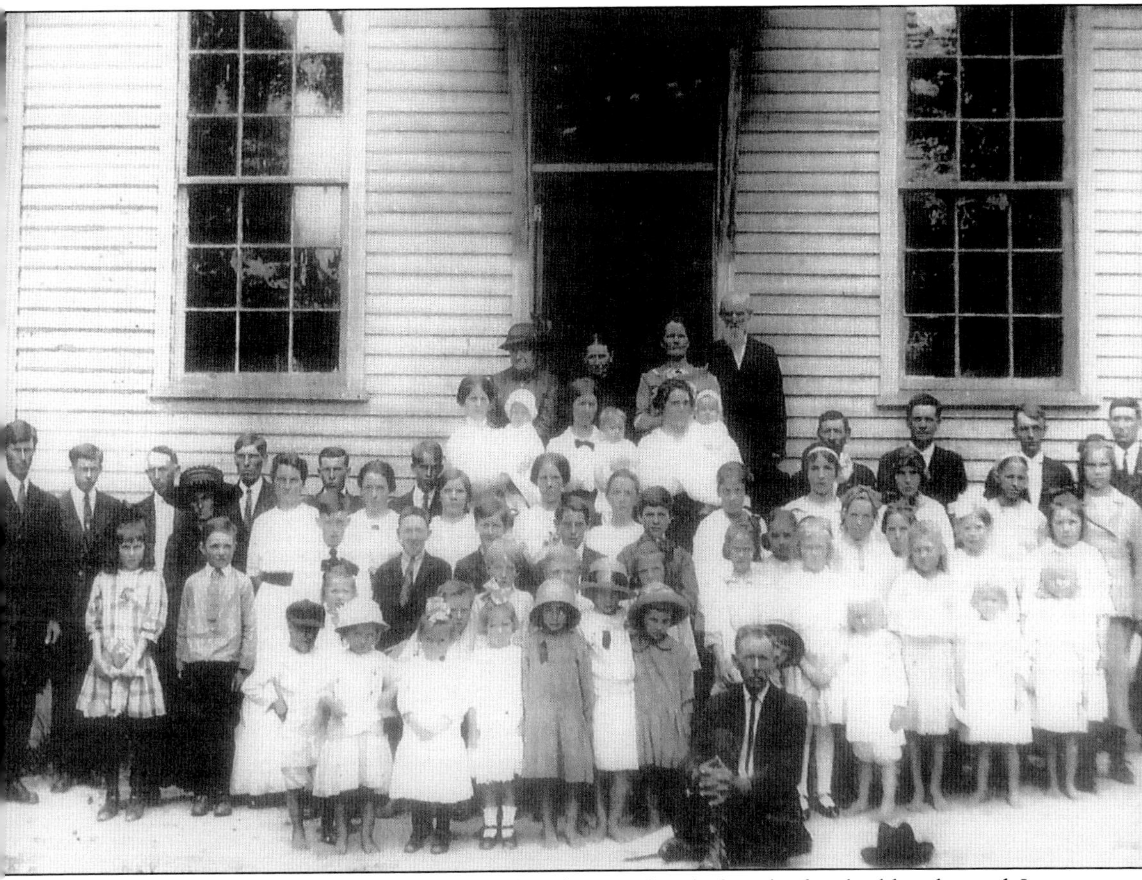

This early photograph of Bethel Methodist Church was taken before the first building burned. In the back row are, standing in doorway from left to right, Rhoda Shope Rice, unidentified, Harriet Shope Sales (Rhoda's sister), and W. Cornelius Sales (Harriet's husband). The tallest man near the right window is Arthur Rice, the son of Joseph Rice, and the man at the far right end of the same row is Sandy Sales, the son of Harriet and Cornelius Sales. (Courtesy of John Weakly.)

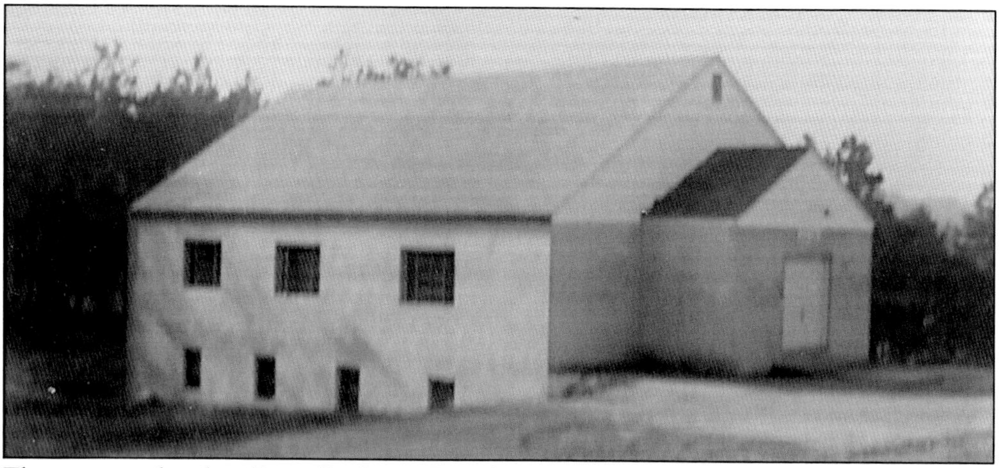

The youngest church in Riceville, Grassy Branch Baptist, was organized in the fall of 1949. It has outgrown its original building twice and currently meets in the new sanctuary, which was built in 1986. (Courtesy of the Riceville Community Center.)

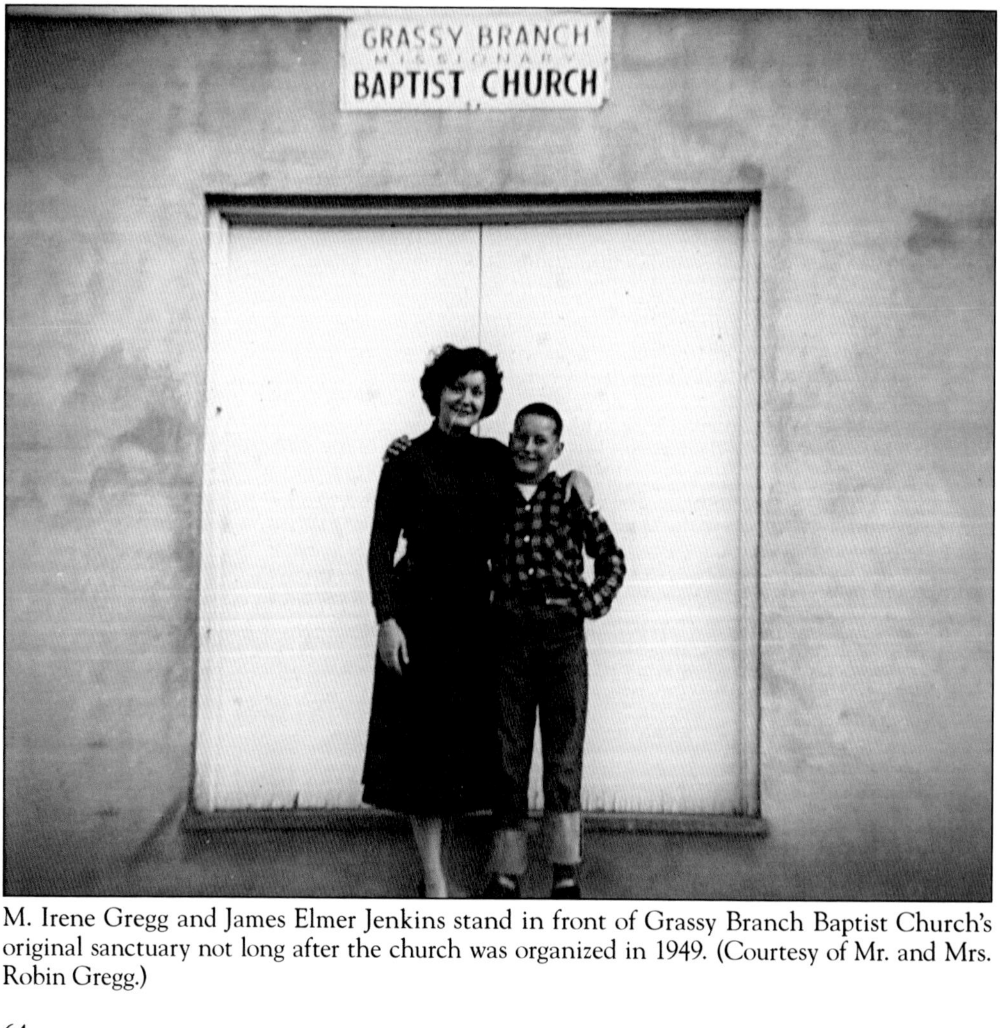

M. Irene Gregg and James Elmer Jenkins stand in front of Grassy Branch Baptist Church's original sanctuary not long after the church was organized in 1949. (Courtesy of Mr. and Mrs. Robin Gregg.)

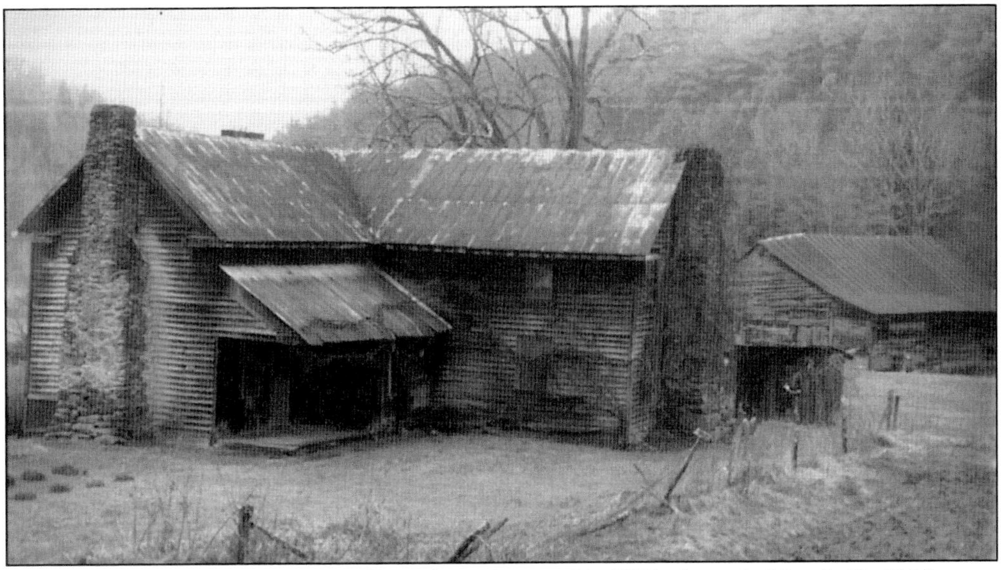

Riceville was home to two post offices from August 28, 1876, through March 31, 1906—one that served the community while the Democrats were in office and the other while Republicans governed. The Clark house is located on Parker Road and was the first post office in the Riceville area. It was built by Marion Carter in the 19th century. According to Clark family stories, the Clark house served as the post office when the Republican Party was in charge of the county. E.F. Clark was the first postmaster. Mail was delivered semi-weekly by horseback. (Courtesy of Cobb Hughey.)

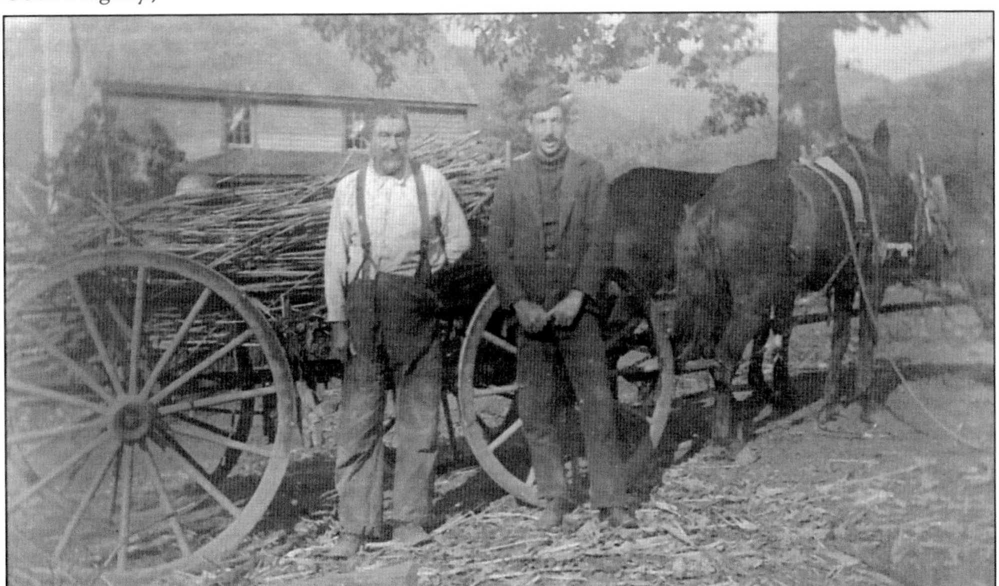

During the early 1900s, a cane mill operated on Bull Creek. In the background of this photograph is the Stephenson home, which served as the Riceville post office for many years. The Stephenson home was built around 1900. It is now known as the Glenn Ray house. When the Democratic party was in office, a rider from Reems Creek, via Bull Gap from Swannanoa, is said to have picked up the mail at this house. A.L. Stevenson was the first postmaster at this home. (Courtesy John Weakly.)

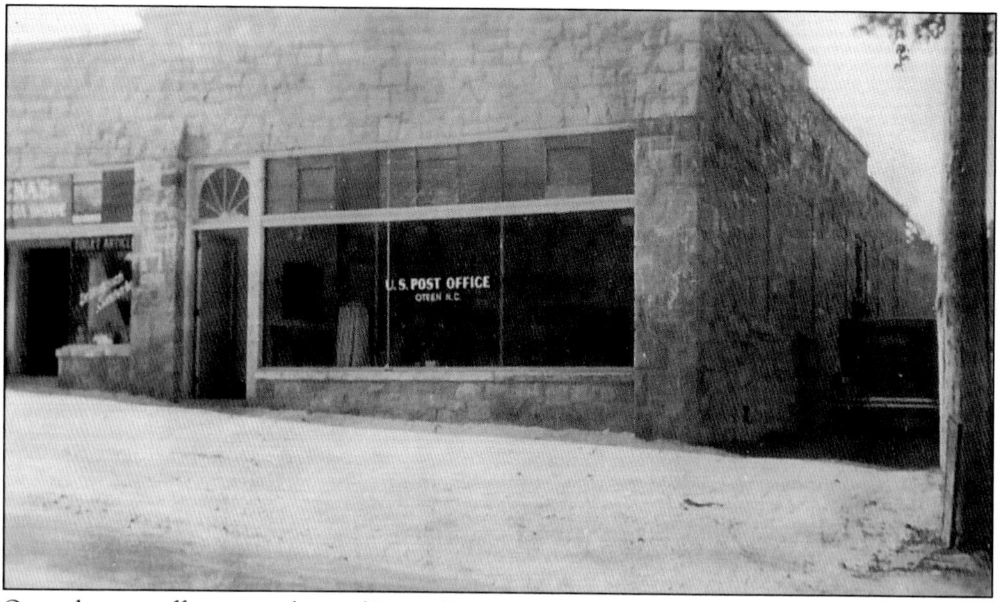

Once the post offices moved out of Riceville, residents' mail came through the office at Oteen. This post office was located across Tunnel Road from the Veterans Affairs (VA) Hospital and was abandoned around 1945. The office of postmaster was still a political job during this time. Rafe Rice's father, Raphael, was the postmaster for about 10 years after World War I but lost his job when the administration changed. (Courtesy of Rafe Rice Jr.)

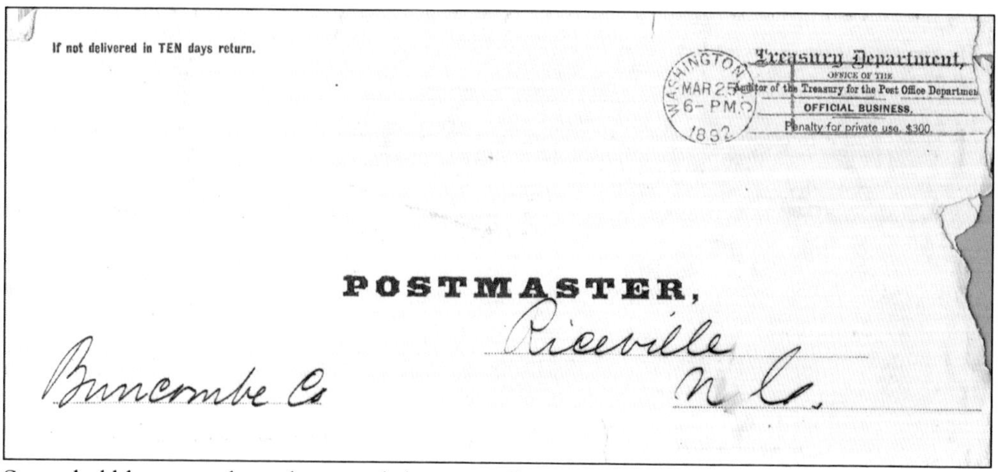

Several old letters and envelopes and the post office account book are kept in the Stephenson home by its current owners. Shown is an early letter addressed to the postmaster at the Stephenson home in Riceville. (Courtesy of John Weakly.)

Three

LIVELIHOODS

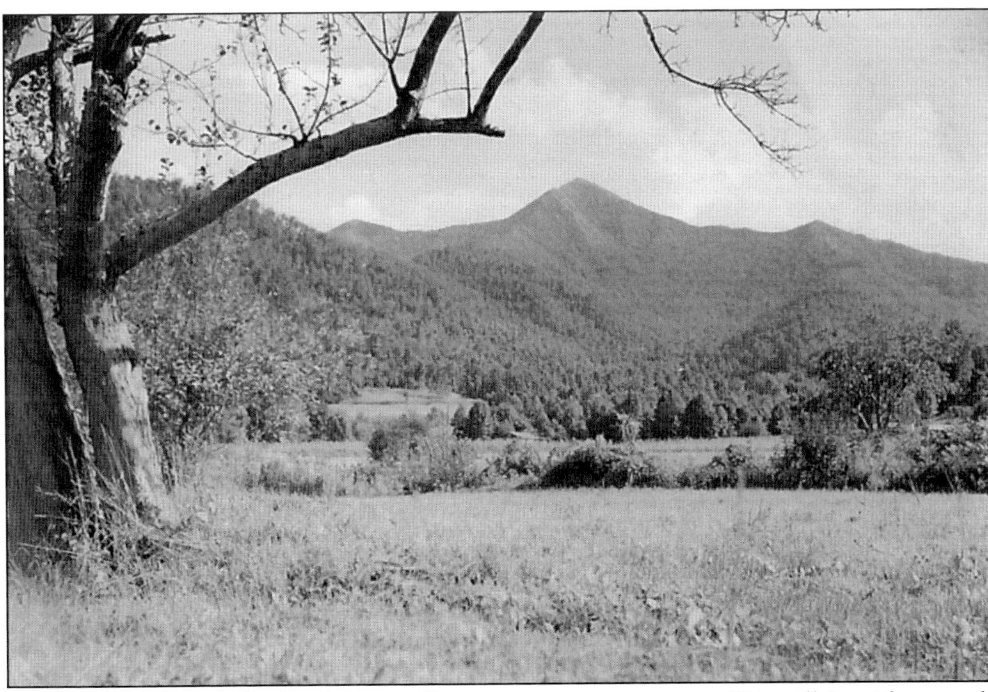

Infrastructure, like a school and a post office, was necessary, as most of Riceville's residents made their living farming within the community, and transportation out of the valley was difficult and time-consuming. (Courtesy of Rafe Rice Jr.)

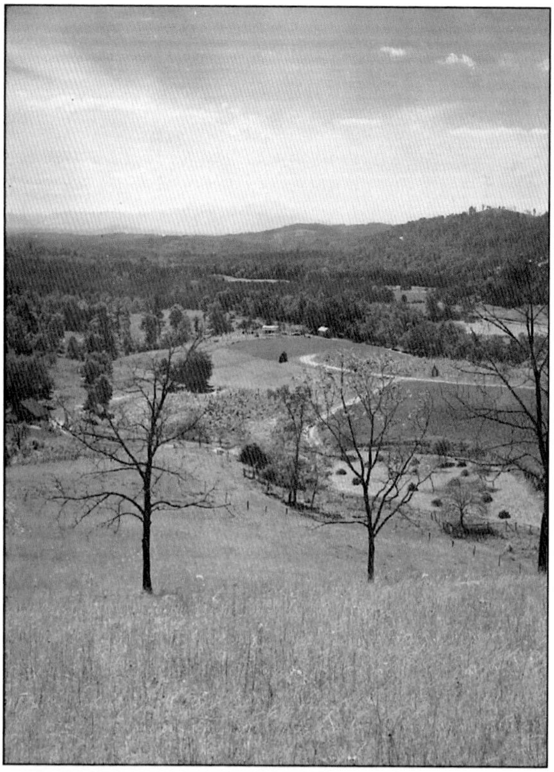

Baxter Shope's property was only one of the many farmsteads in the valley. The 1883 *Buncombe Gazetteer* listed Riceville's prominent residents, their occupations, acreage, and the distance of their property from the post office: G.W. Burnett sold general merchandise at a local store, J.C. Clark operated a sawmill and gristmill, and J.A. Reed was a gunsmith. Other listed residents—S.W. Glass, C.P. Gragg, Samuel Hughey, A.J. Rice, W.R. Shope, B.G. Shope, J.M. Shope, S.A. Stroup, S.F. Stroup, and D.C. Stephenson—all owned around 100 acres in the area and made their livings farming. Also, a blacksmith shop operated at the end of Jones Cove. (Courtesy of Rafe Rice Jr.)

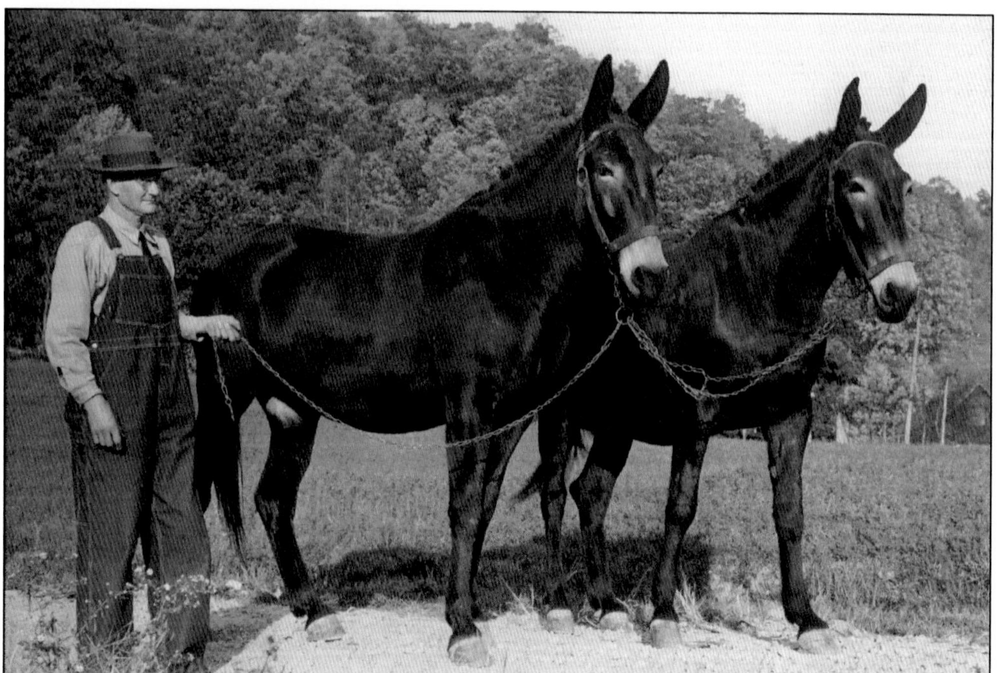

Baxter Perry Shope poses with his two mules. Most plowing was done with horsepower, as large machines were expensive and hard to come by in the valley. (Courtesy of Butch and Judy Reed.)

Harry W. Plumber drives his horse Dandy on Riceville Road in 1912. Riceville Road was one of the only routes into and out of the valley during this time and remained unpaved until the 1950s. (Courtesy of Rafe Rice Jr.)

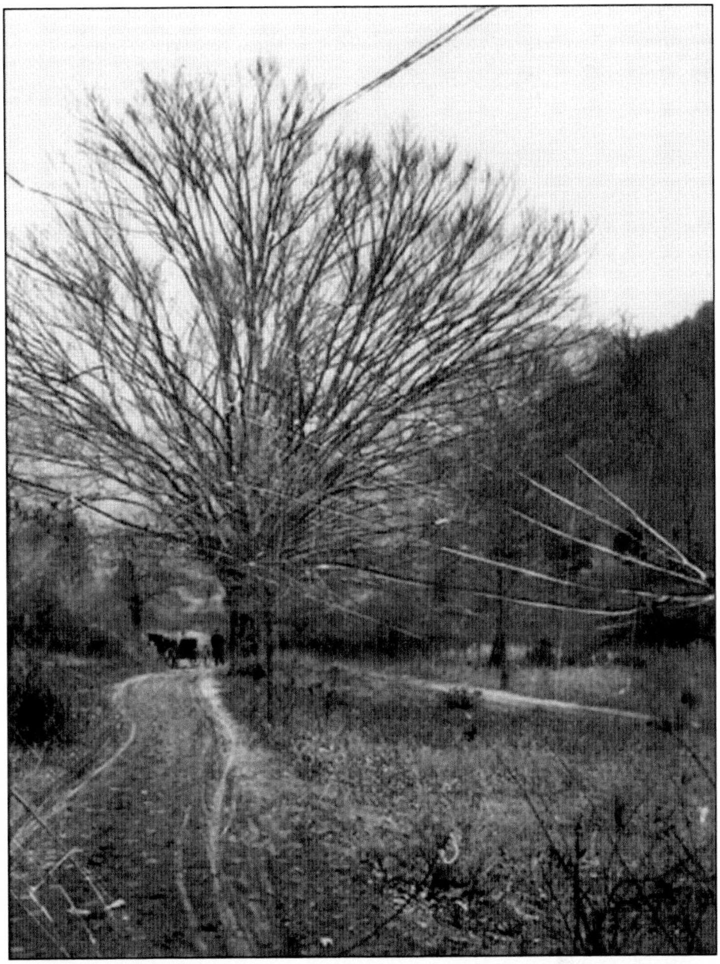

The Rice family used this sled to haul wood and do chores from the old log barn on the Rice home place. Arthur Rice stands on the left and Jack Rice is on the right. Edwin, Arthur's son, is driving the horse, Nell, around 1925. (Courtesy of Rafe Rice Jr.)

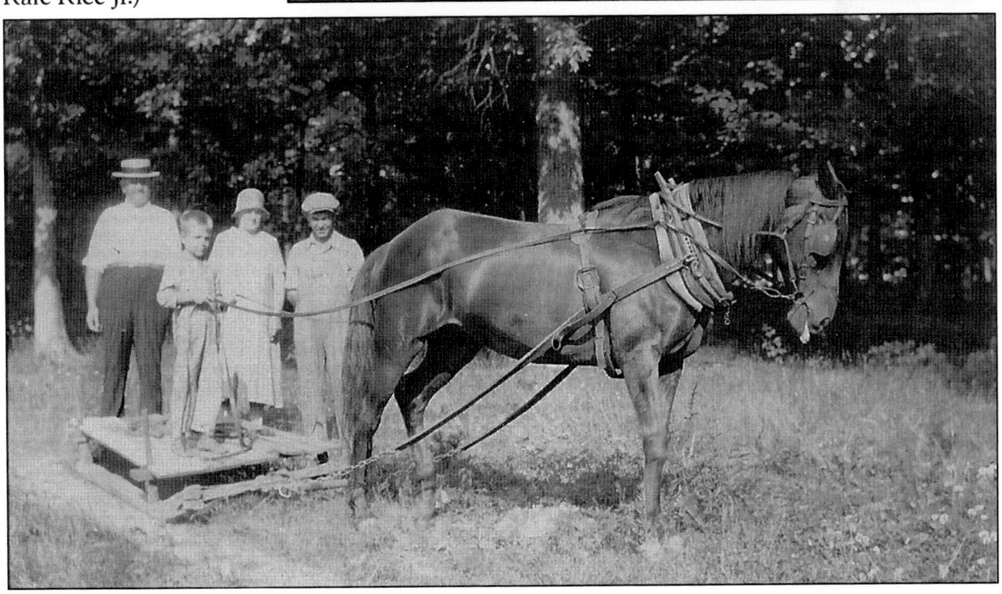

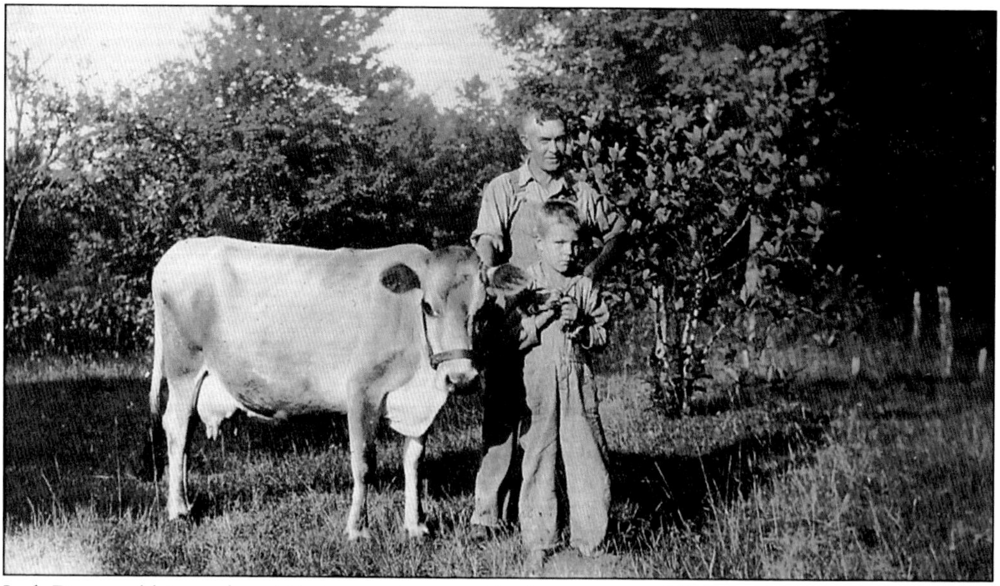

Jack Rice and his nephew Edwin are shown with their cow on Old Farm School Road, in front of the old Rice home place. (Courtesy of Rafe Rice Jr.)

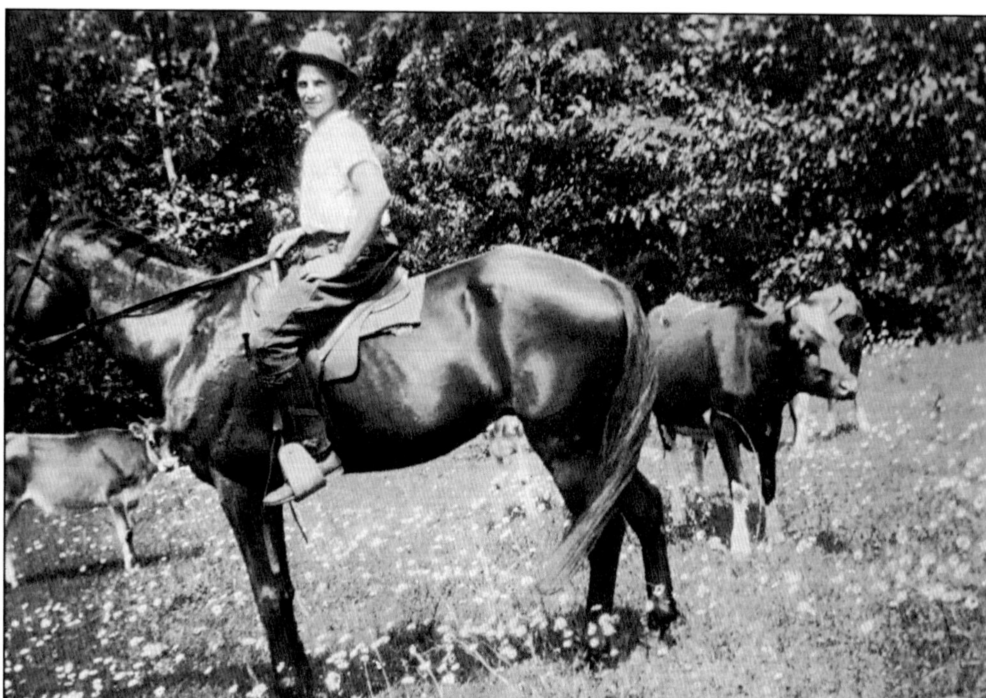

Up until the 1930s, cattle grazed freely throughout Riceville without fencing. Here, Burgin Clinton Gregg rides his horse Britt around the head of Shope Creek to herd cattle. (Courtesy of Mr. and Mrs. Robin Gregg.)

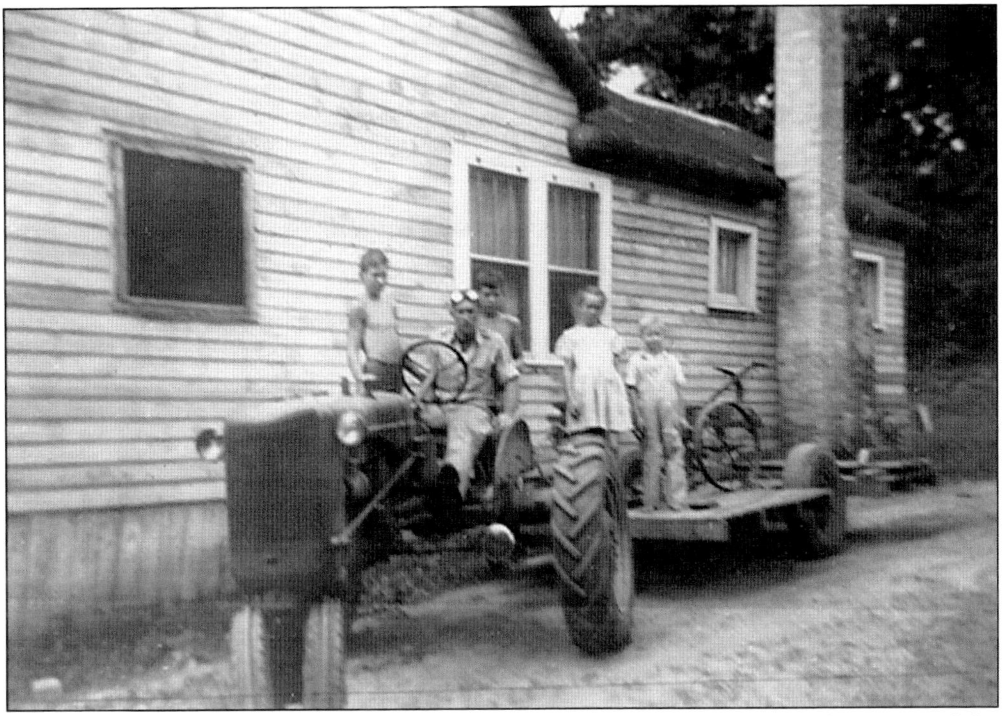

Eventually, residents were able to invest in some heavy machines to help reduce some of the drudgery of farm work. Children were often expected to help bring in the harvest. (Courtesy of John Weakly.)

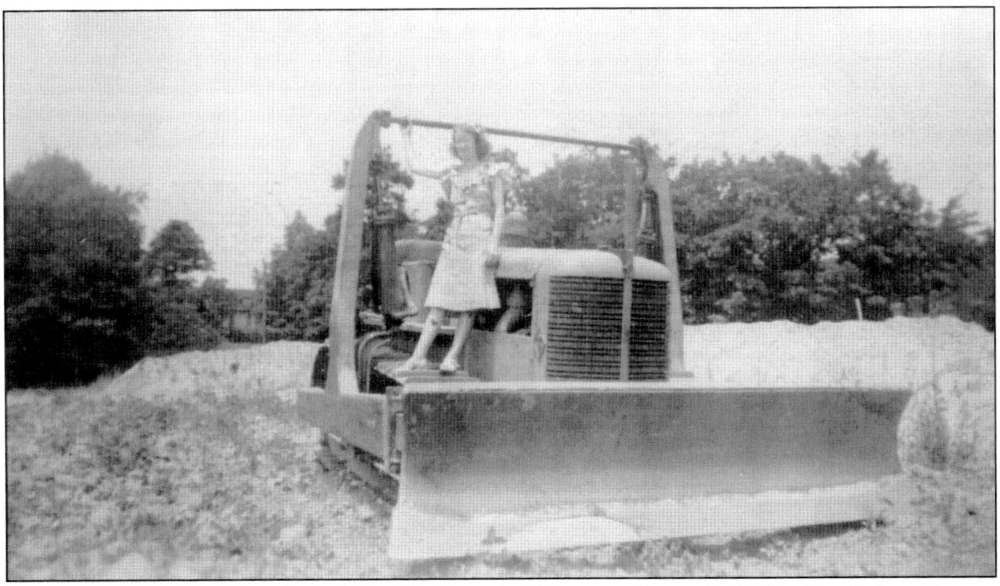

Fleta Reed stands on top of an Allis-Chalmers bulldozer in the early 1940s. Her father, Horace Reed, owned several bulldozers and worked on many of the roads in the Riceville area through the 1960s. He helped create the Riceville Forest subdivision and many of the homesites. At one time, the bulldozer turned over on him. It was lying on top of him and had to be jacked up so he could crawl out. (Courtesy of Butch and Judy Reed.)

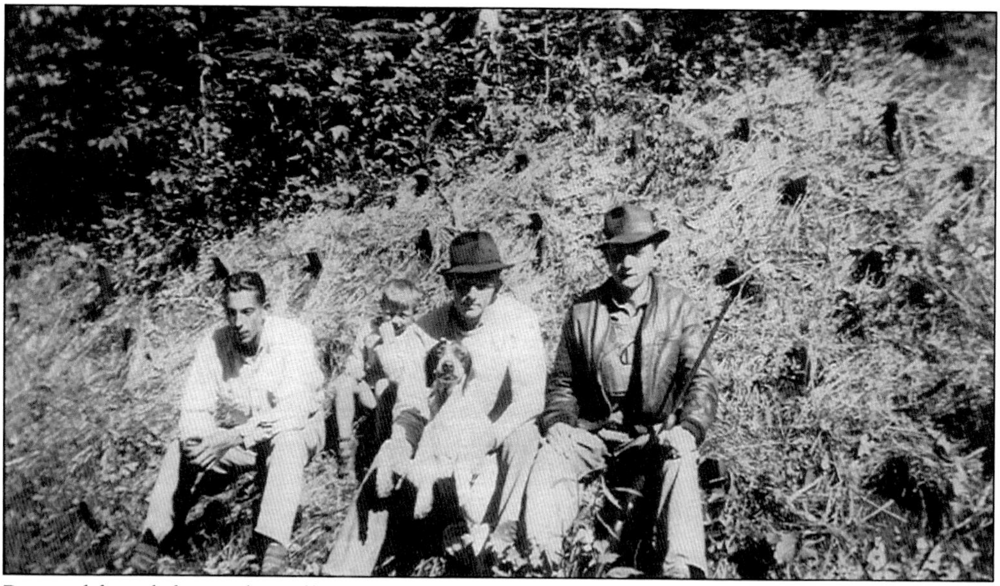

Pictured from left to right, Billy Ray, Bobby Reed, Ray Penley, and Marvin Creasman pose with their hunting dog. Hunting was a very important livelihood and leisure activity for people in the Riceville valley. (Courtesy of John Weakly.)

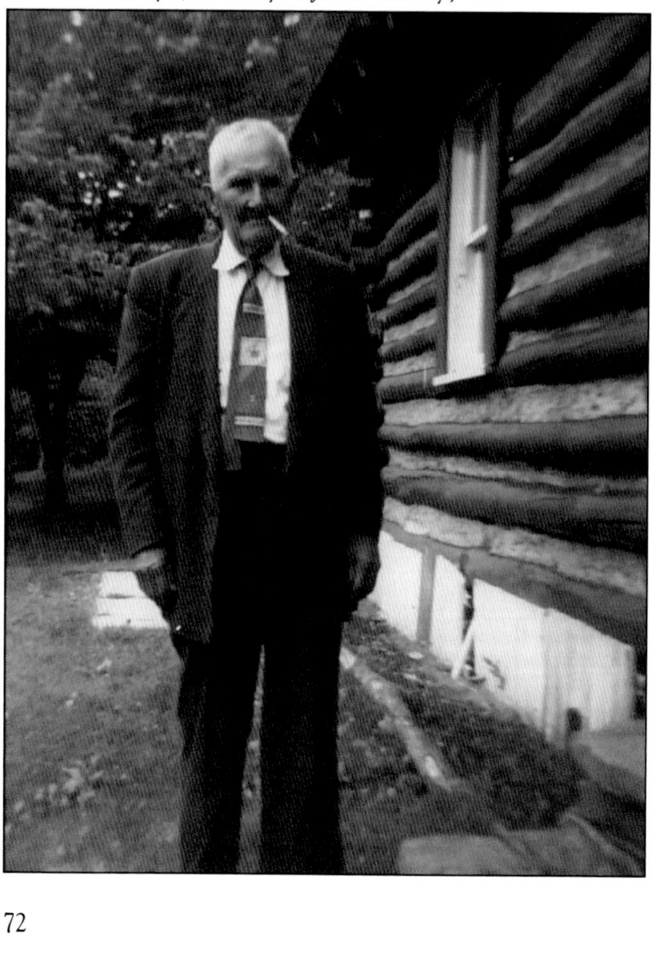

Though farming was the main livelihood of Riceville's residents, moonshining was another way to earn money during this time. Finley Bascom "Bass" Gragg made his living as a moonshiner (and herb gatherer) in the 1920s and 1930s, until he was apprehended by police and spent a year in prison for selling his brew. In the summer of 1962, Bass poses in front of Burgin Clinton Gragg's log cabin on Shope Creek. Bass was a son of C.P. Gragg and Eliza Carolina Shope Gragg. He continued to dig ginseng later in life and always carried a pistol with him. There were several other known stills in the Riceville area. For certain customers, one store owner would not only fill up their car tank with gasoline, but would also fill other containers with moonshine. (Courtesy of Mr. and Mrs. Robin Gregg.)

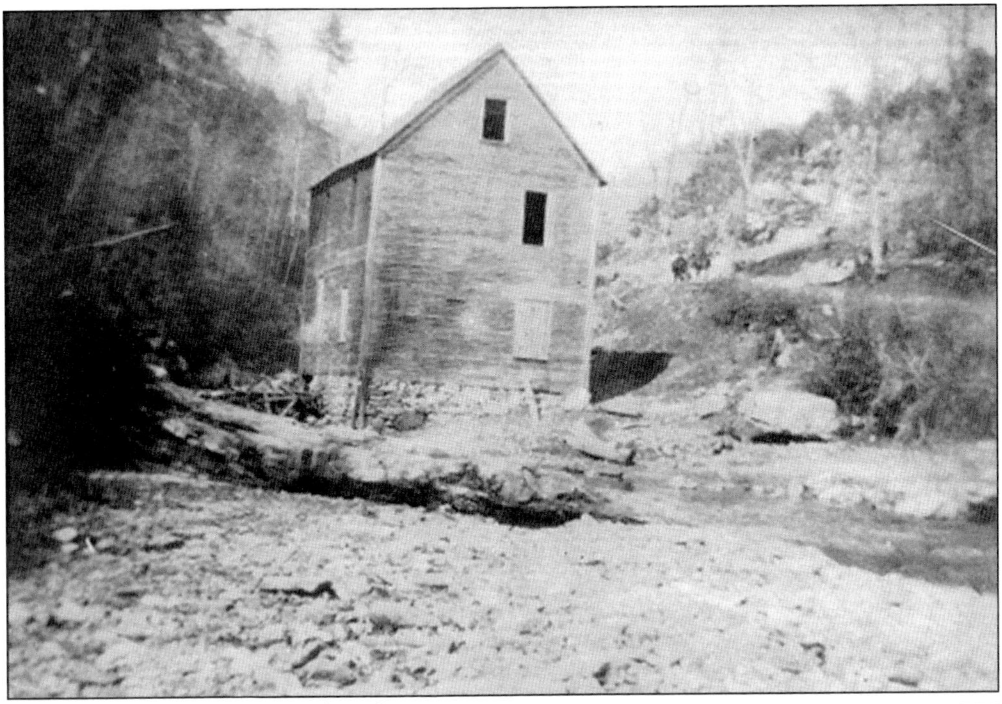

There were many mills located on the rivers around Riceville. The water was used to power the mills. In the 1940s, Grady Maynor operated a sawmill on Bull Creek Road. Much of the lumber used to build homes in Riceville came from this mill. Located across the street from the current community center and fire station was another a gristmill, which used the power of the creek to grind corn. (Courtesy of John Weakly.)

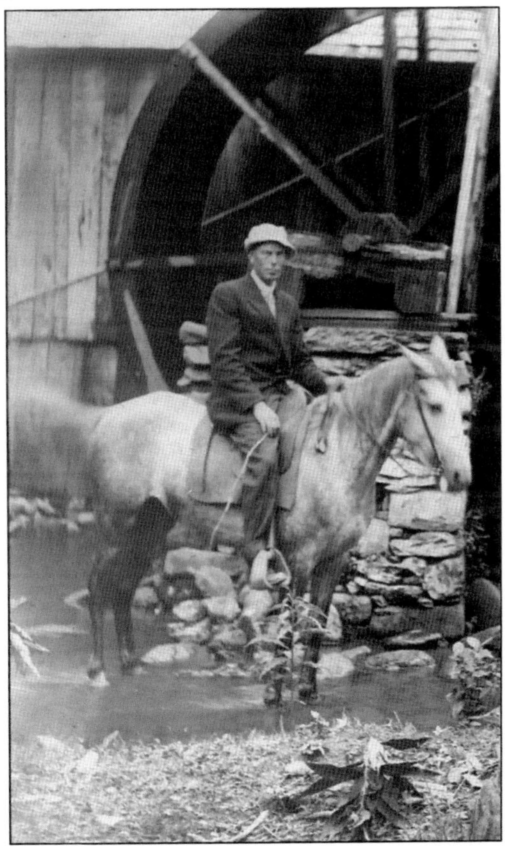

James B. Carson and his wife, Althea, operated the power dam at Warren Wilson College. Althea Carson was Fleta Reed's mother. Walter Williams, Althea's brother, is shown on his horse in front of the Warren Wilson College waterwheel. (Courtesy of Butch and Judy Reed.)

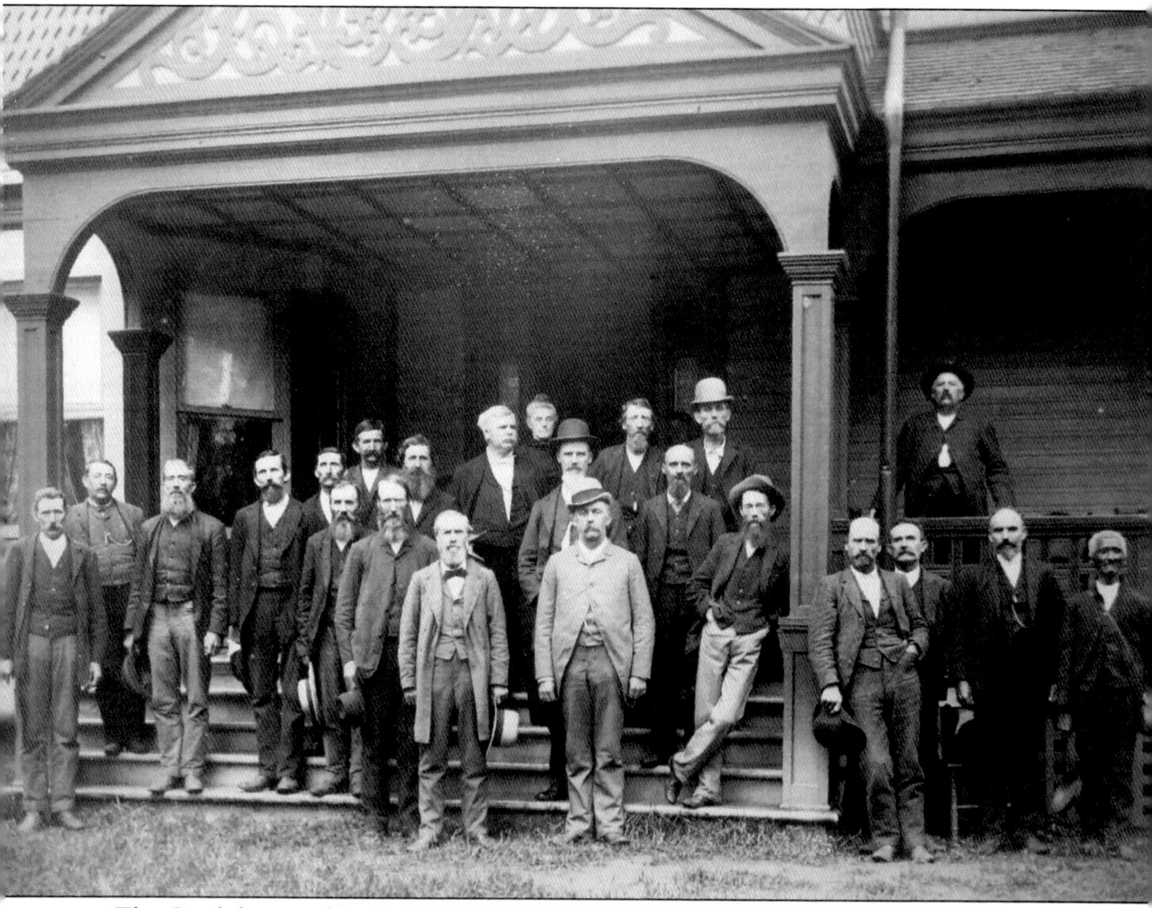

The Confederate soldiers of Company F, 14th North Carolina Regiment, also known as the "Rough and Ready Guard," were run by Zebulon Vance. Jim Hughey, of Bull Creek (seventh from left), was a part of this company, which often drilled in Riceville on the muster field. According to George B. Coggins, "The muster field was part of the Craig Farm and is located about where Henry West owned land on the Old Farm School Road. On the north flank of the Swannanoa River there was a field, the only flat place in these mountains, and it was hidden from view of the valley and passerbys, although the first wagon road came right by, so everybody could get there. That's where the soldiers met and were mustered into the Civil War. They came from all over the place. And they would parade there and drill and learn how to carry their rifles properly. It was also a shooting ground for the Civil War soldiers." (Courtesy of Rafe Rice Jr.)

Arthur Pinkney Gragg served in the US Navy during World War I. He lived much of his life in Topeka, Kansas, but moved back to the Gregg home place in Riceville in 1965, living there for the remainder of his life. He passed away in 1989. (Courtesy of Mr. and Mrs. Robin Gregg.)

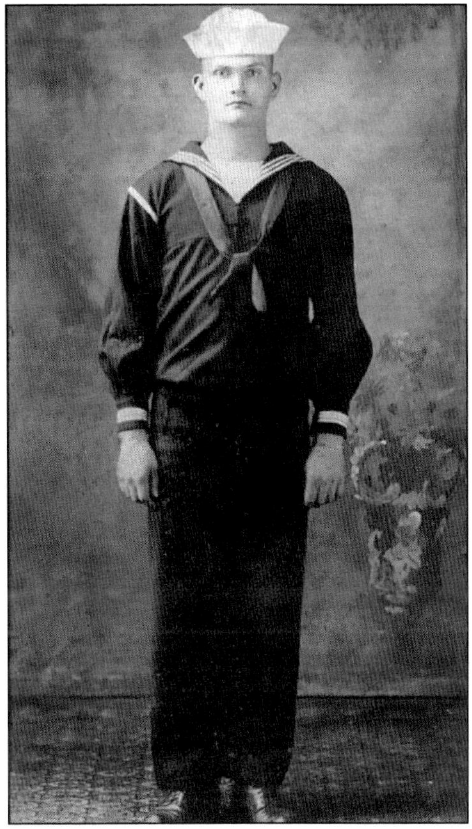

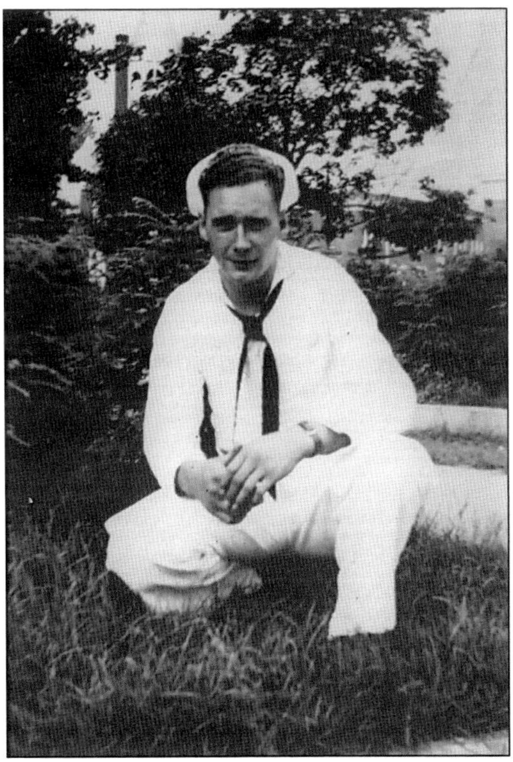

Herbert Gregg served in the US Navy as a pilot during World War II. When he returned home on the train, he went to the Black Mountain airport, rented a plane, and flew over the Riceville valley to let his family know he was home and needed to be picked up at the airport. (Courtesy of Mr. and Mrs. Robin Gregg.)

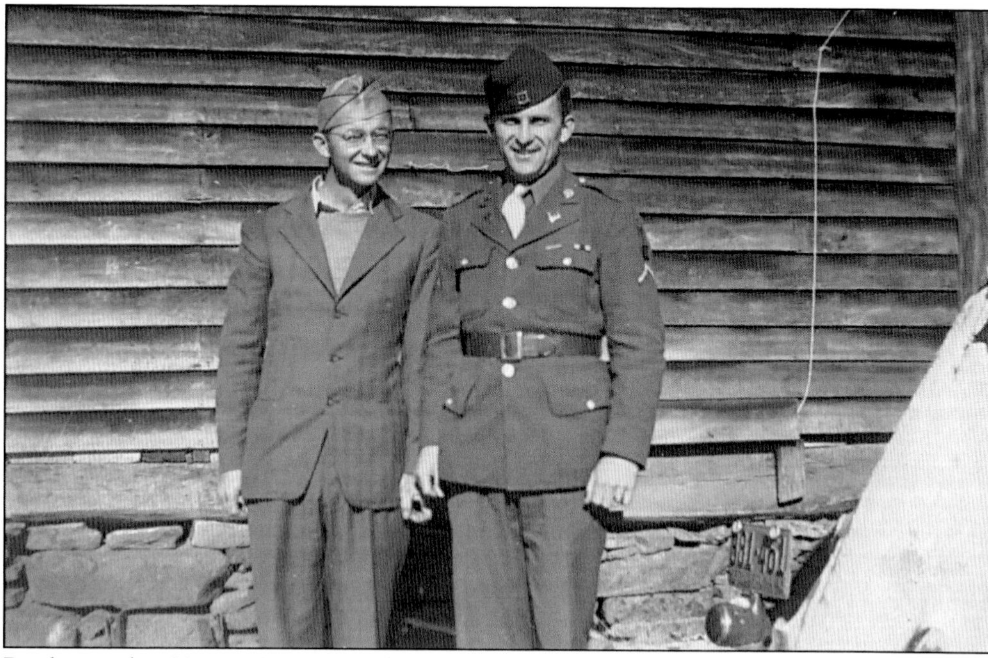

Brothers-in-law Henry Harrison Ingle (left) and Burgin Clinton Gregg, both from Riceville, served in the European theatre during World War II. This photograph was taken in front of the J.B. Gregg home place on Shope Creek, on December 13, 1942, before the two men departed. (Courtesy of Mr. and Mrs. Robin Gregg.)

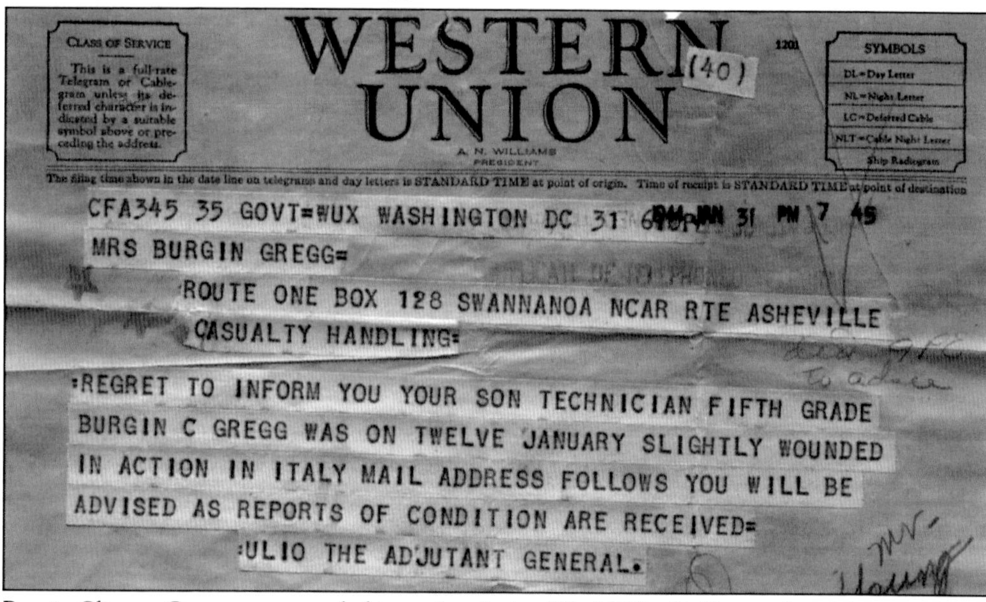

CLASS OF SERVICE
This is a full-rate Telegram or Cablegram unless its deferred character is indicated by a suitable symbol above or preceding the address.

WESTERN UNION (40)

A. N. WILLIAMS
PRESIDENT

1201

SYMBOLS
DL=Day Letter
NL=Night Letter
LC=Deferred Cable
NLT=Cable Night Letter
Ship Radiogram

The filing time shown in the date line on telegrams and day letters is STANDARD TIME at point of origin. Time of receipt is STANDARD TIME at point of destination

CFA345 35 GOVT=WUX WASHINGTON DC 31 6 1944 JAN 31 PM 7 45
MRS BURGIN GREGG=
ROUTE ONE BOX 128 SWANNANOA NCAR RTE ASHEVILLE
CASUALTY HANDLING=
=REGRET TO INFORM YOU YOUR SON TECHNICIAN FIFTH GRADE BURGIN C GREGG WAS ON TWELVE JANUARY SLIGHTLY WOUNDED IN ACTION IN ITALY MAIL ADDRESS FOLLOWS YOU WILL BE ADVISED AS REPORTS OF CONDITION ARE RECEIVED=
=ULIO THE ADJUTANT GENERAL.

Burgin Clinton Gregg was wounded in action during World War II. His mother, Margaret Anna Gregg, received a telegram, but no other details of where he was or how he was doing. For months, Anna heard nothing, but would make the long trek down to the mailbox each afternoon, hoping for word of her son. Months later, she finally received a letter from her son, who had taken shrapnel through the left side of his body and was soon returning home. (Courtesy of Mr. and Mrs. Robin Gregg.)

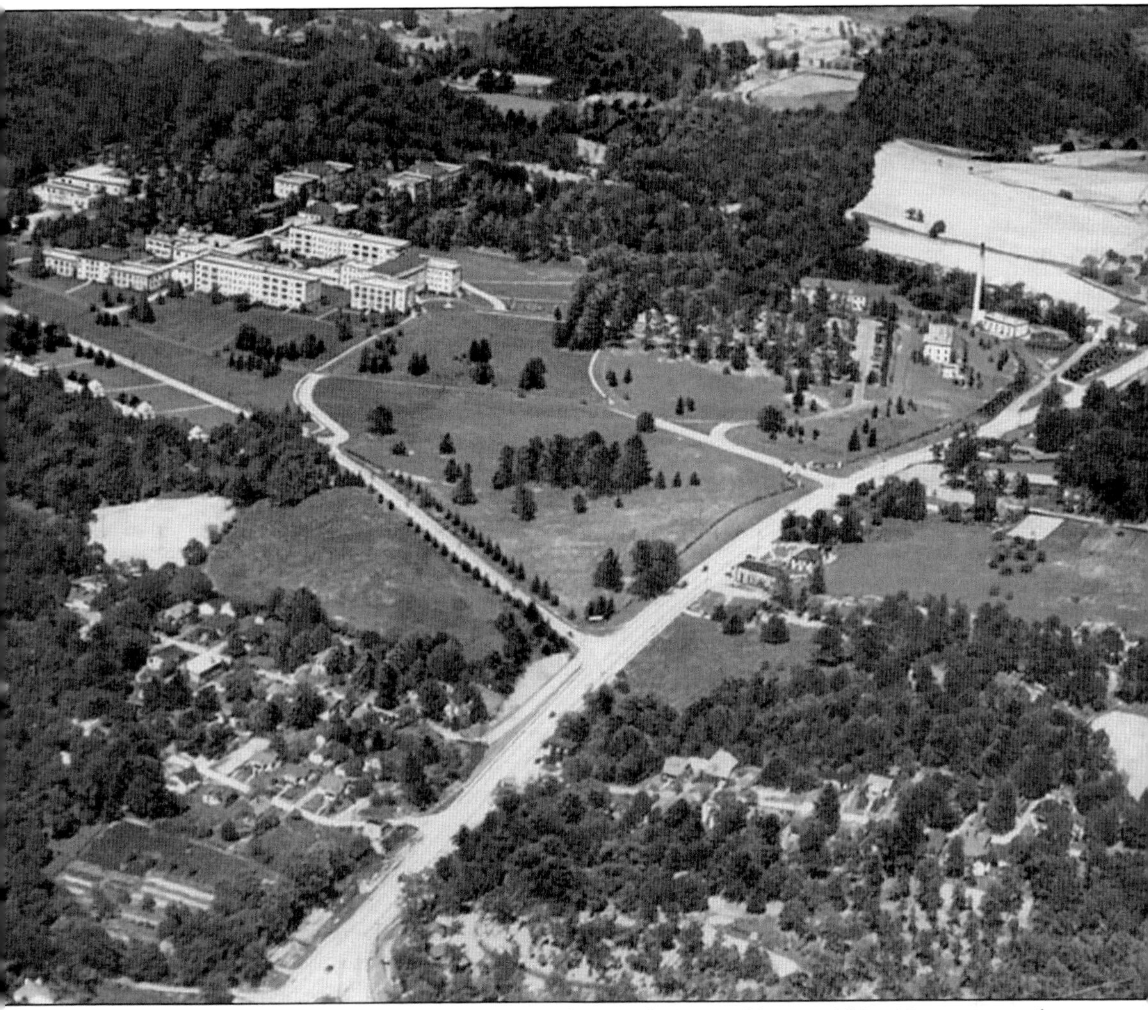

An aerial view shows the VA Hospital off Riceville Road. General hospital No. 19 was opened in 1918, in Oteen, North Carolina, to treat soldiers who had been inflicted with the respiratory disease tuberculosis. During World War I and World War II, soldiers were at increased risk of getting tuberculosis because of weather conditions, close quarters, and other wartime factors that likely had negative effects on their immune systems. General Hospital No. 19 was one of two major tuberculosis hospitals during this time, and it had some of the best equipment in the country. It was highly esteemed, and hundreds were cured there. (Courtesy of Rafe Rice Jr.)

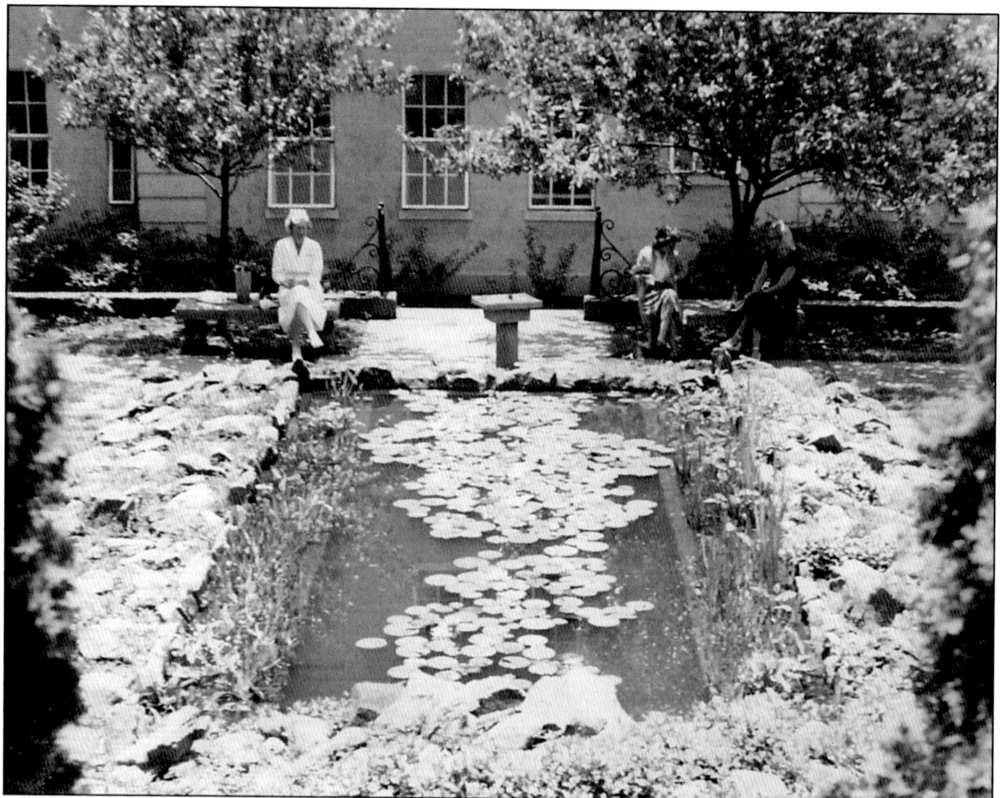

The VA Hospital was known for was its unique treatment of tuberculosis. Injections and vaccines were not used, but there was a recuperation program that involved rest, fresh air, and mental stimulation. The patients had a close relationship with one another and with their nurses, who were said to be very cheerful and friendly. Hospitals around the country considered the pure positive form of treatment to be very innovative and effective. (Courtesy of Rafe Rice Jr.)

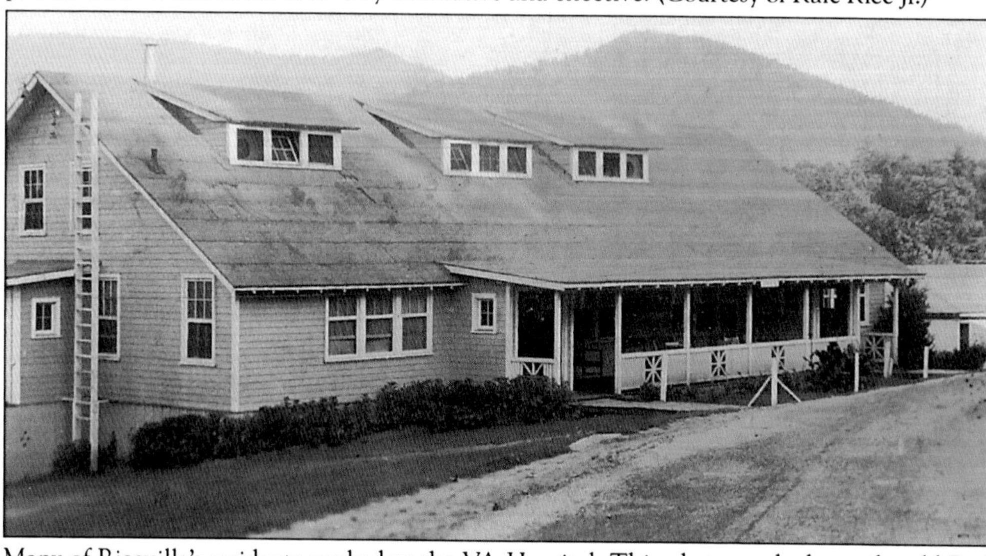

Many of Riceville's residents worked at the VA Hospital. This photograph shows the old Red Cross Building in 1920. (Courtesy of Rafe Rice Jr.)

Helen Rice, the wife of Raphael Rice, was a nurse at the VA Hospital. (Courtesy of Rafe Rice Jr.)

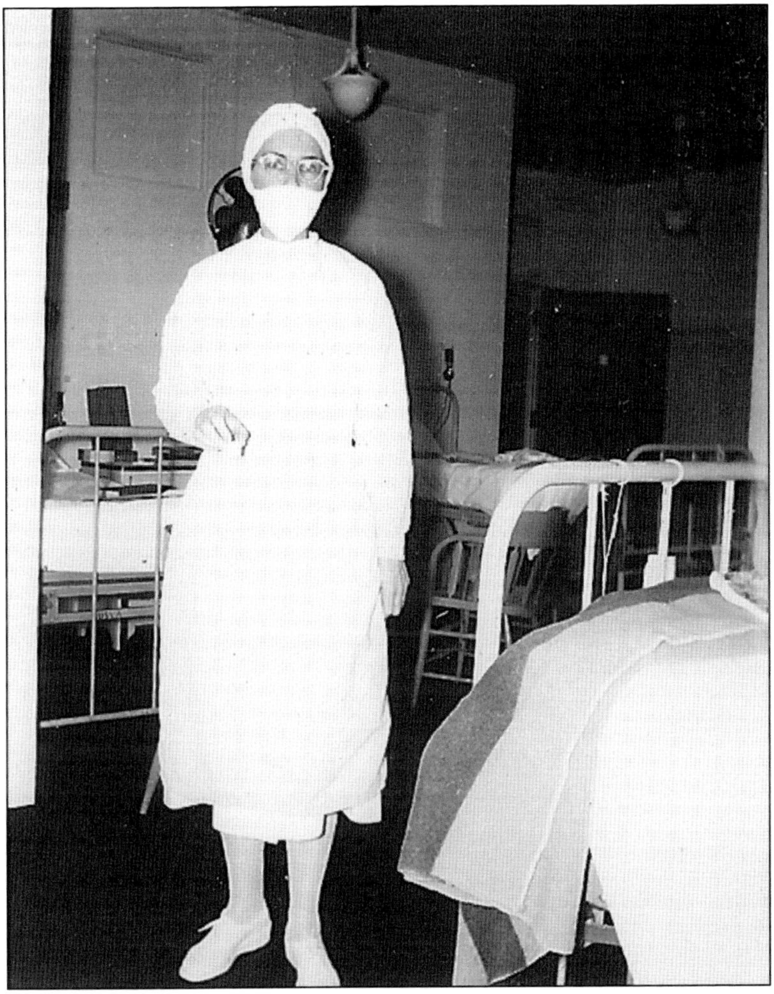

Raphael Rice, his wife, Helen, and four other nurses from the VA Hospital are pictured on a drive in 1917. (Courtesy of Rafe Rice Jr.)

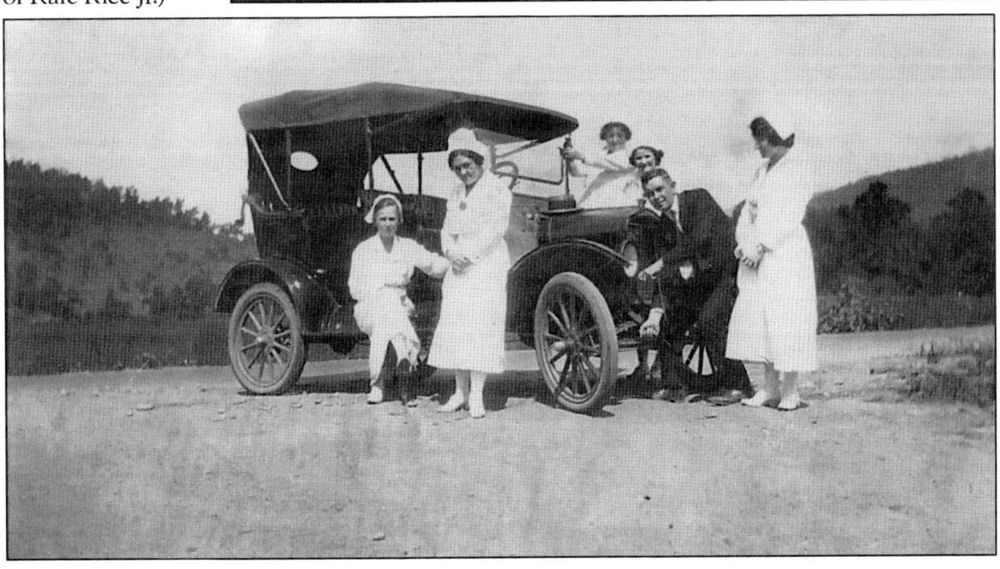

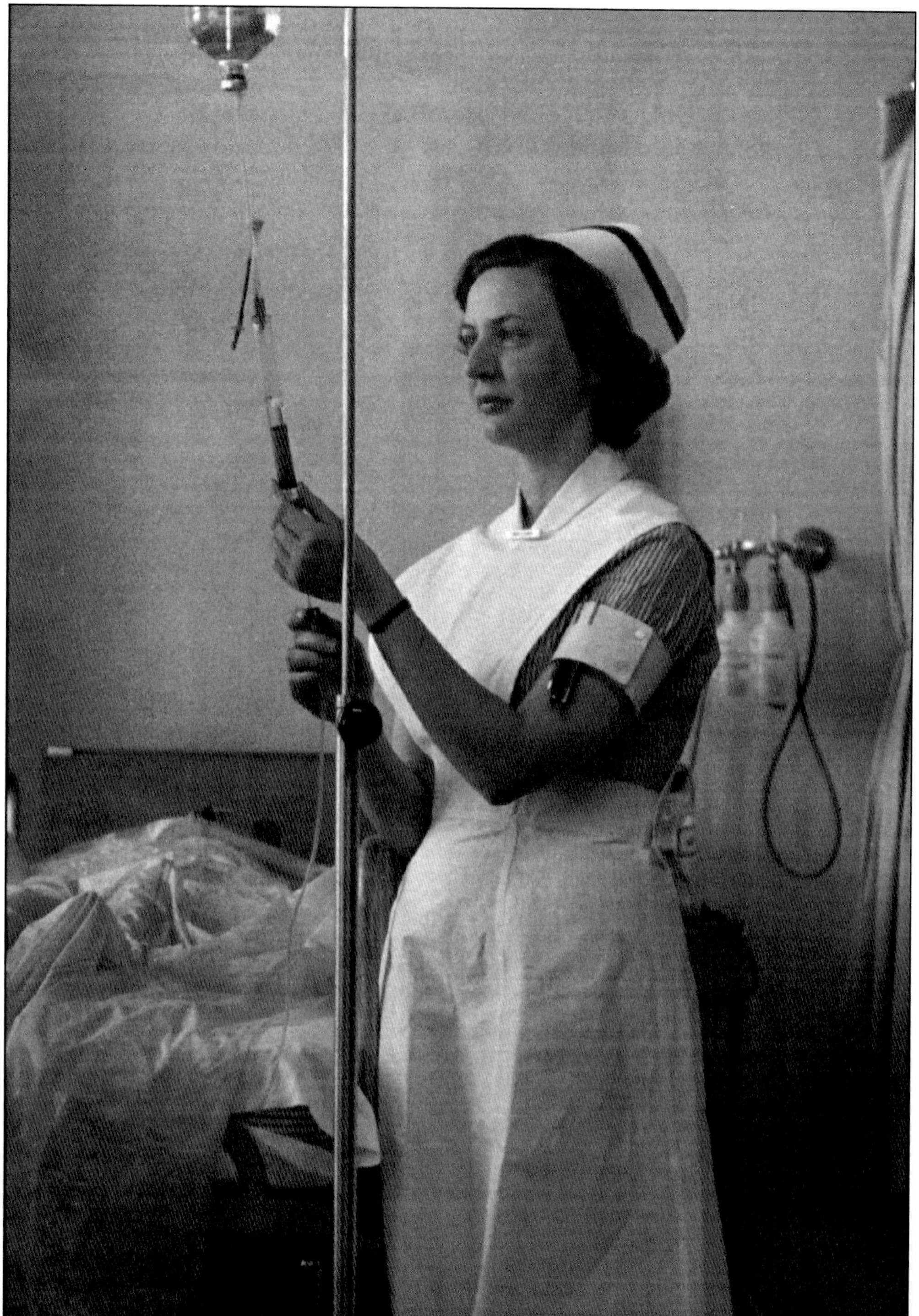

As time passed, more residents found work outside of the community. Isabel Duncan Reed, the wife of Jim Reed, worked as the supervisor of the cancer ward at Mission Hospital, located in Asheville. (Courtesy of Butch and Judy Reed.)

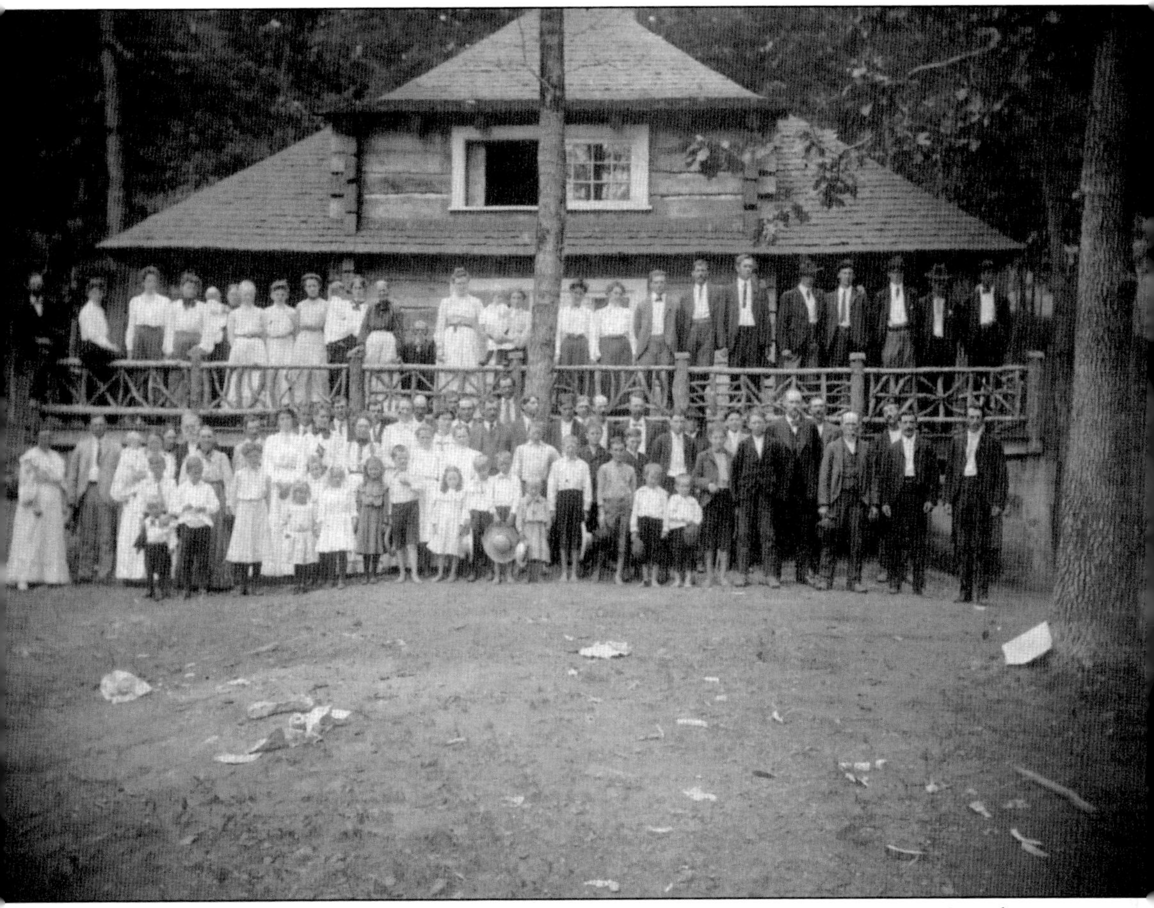

Residents from the Riceville community also worked over the mountain at Mountain Meadows Inn (1900–1954), which is located on 1,500 acres off Elk Mountain Scenic Highway, west of what is now Town Mountain Road. Several of the Reeds would walk around Kate Mountain (now Riceville Forest) to get to the inn, were they worked in the 1910s. (Courtesy of Butch and Judy Reed.)

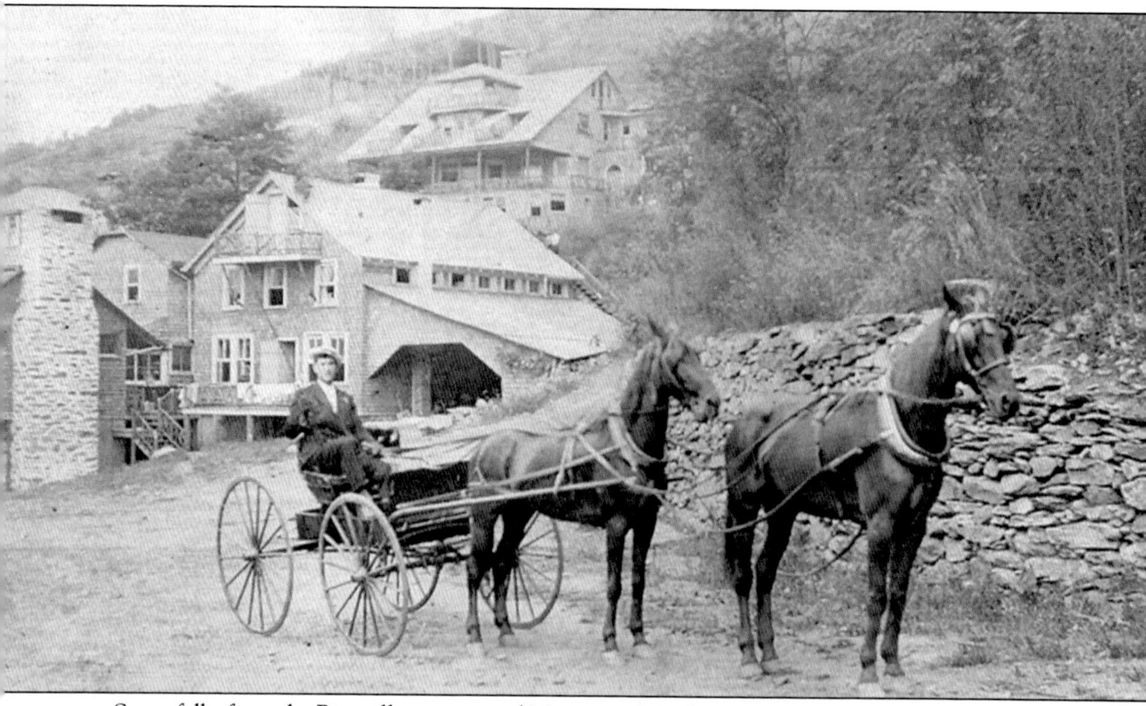

Some folks from the Riceville area visited Mountain Meadows Inn for a vacation retreat. According to the book *The State of Buncombe* by Mitzi Tessier, the inn was "built after George Douglas Miller bought the land from William R. Tice in 1902." Mountain Meadows Inn was originally one small building. Other rooms and buildings were added until the inn accommodated 100 guests. The old English-type inn included a "large main building, an annex with a long dining room, one cottage with 18 rooms, and another with two apartments." The old inn is privately owned now and can be found on Old Town Mountain Road, closer to the Blue Ridge Parkway end of the road. (Courtesy of Butch and Judy Reed.)

Four

RECREATION

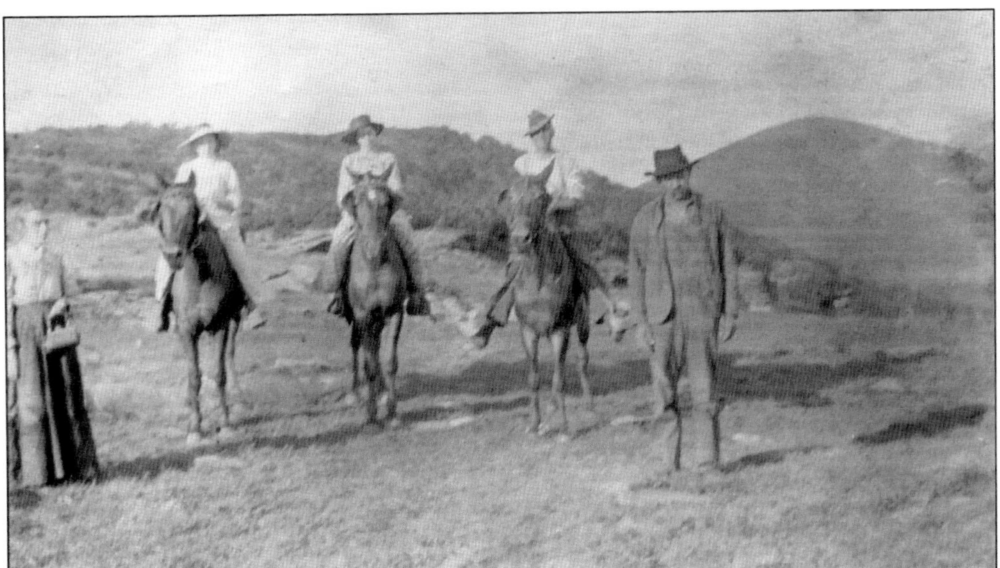

The Blue Ridge Parkway surrounds three sides of the valley and offers countless outdoor recreation opportunities to the Riceville community. Even before the parkway was built in the 1930s, Riceville residents would explore the surrounding wilderness on foot and on horseback. At Craggy Gardens in 1910 are, from left to right, mother Nancy "Nebraska" Glass Reed, children Loys, Elsie, and Walter, and father George Weldon Reed. (Courtesy of Butch and Judy Reed.)

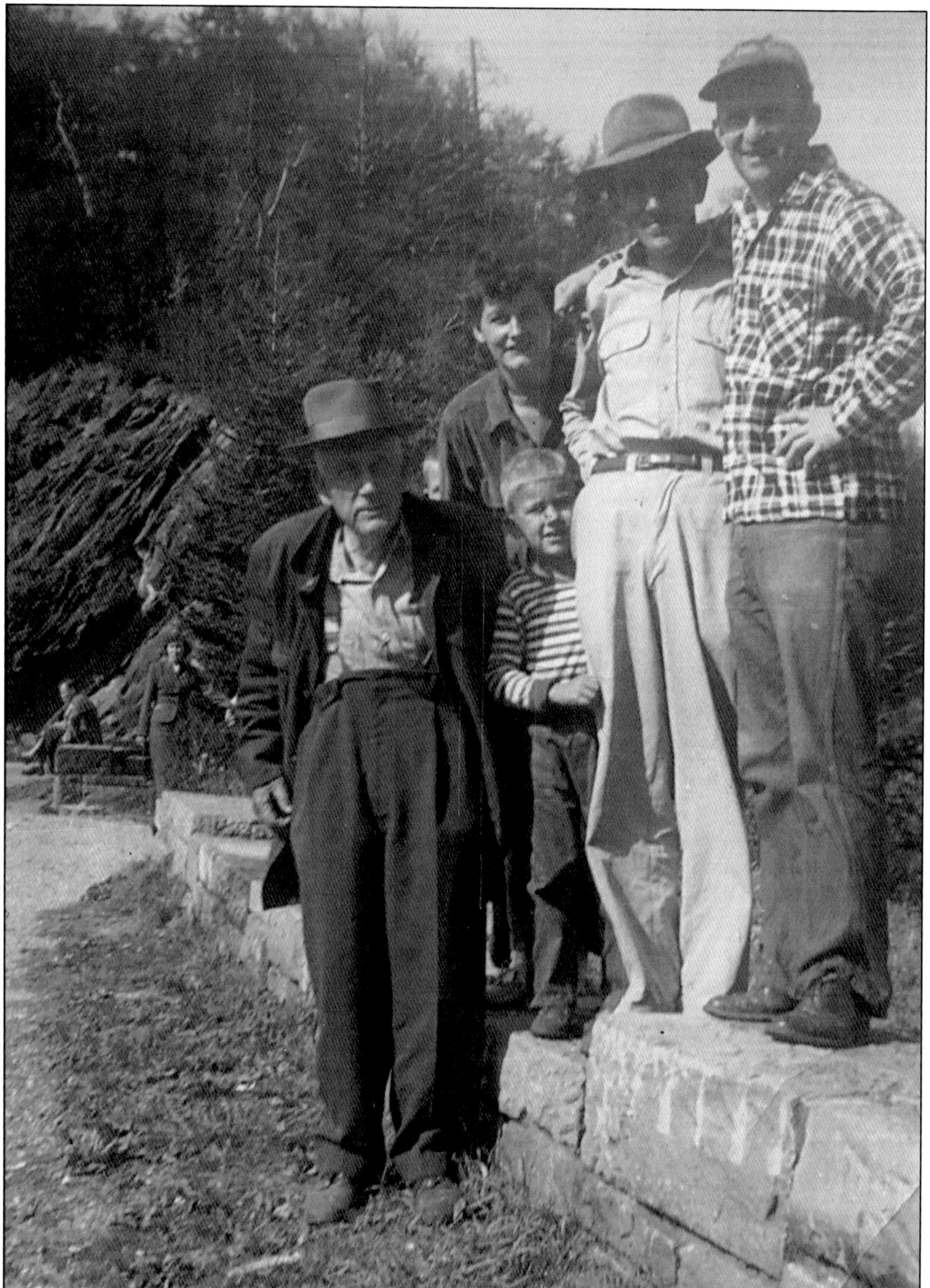

Once the Parkway was built, Riceville families would often take extended day trips with their relatives, sometimes packing as many as eight or nine people into one vehicle. Pictured at Newfound Gap in the 1950s are, from left to right, Charles Washington Shope, Willie Jenkins Shope, Steve Shope, Joe Shope, and Burgin Clinton Gregg. The woman is Willie Jenkins Shope. (Courtesy of Mr. and Mrs. Robin Gregg.)

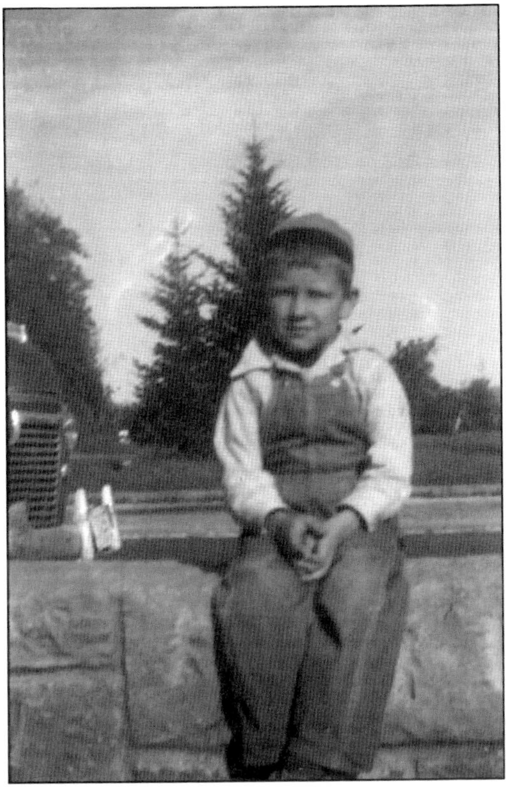

Steve Shope sits on top of the Blue Ridge Parkway underpass during a day trip out of the valley. (Courtesy of Mr. and Mrs. Robin Gregg.)

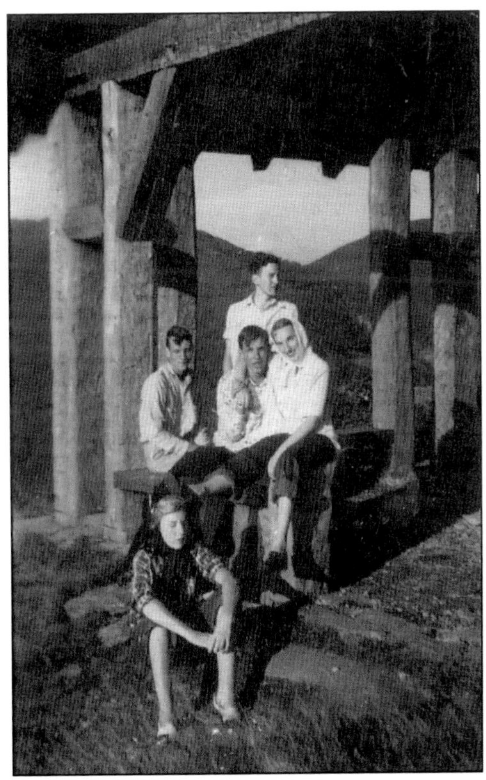

The Rice family poses in 1950 at the Craggy Garden's shed, looking back toward the Blue Ridge Parkway. Craggy Gardens was a popular destination for area families because it could be accessed by trails leading up the mountain from the Riceville valley. (Courtesy of Rafe Rice Jr.)

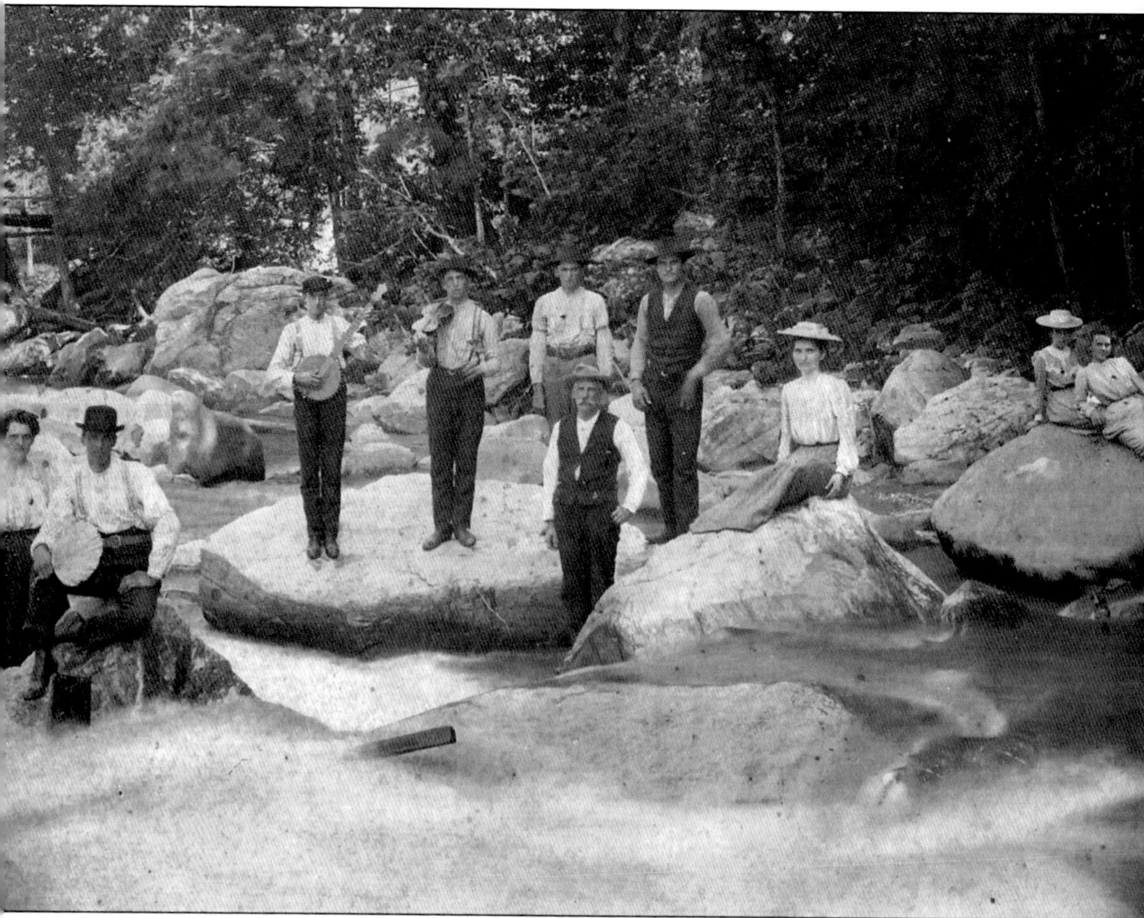

This photograph shows a Rice family gathering near Lake Lure. (Courtesy of Rafe Rice Jr.)

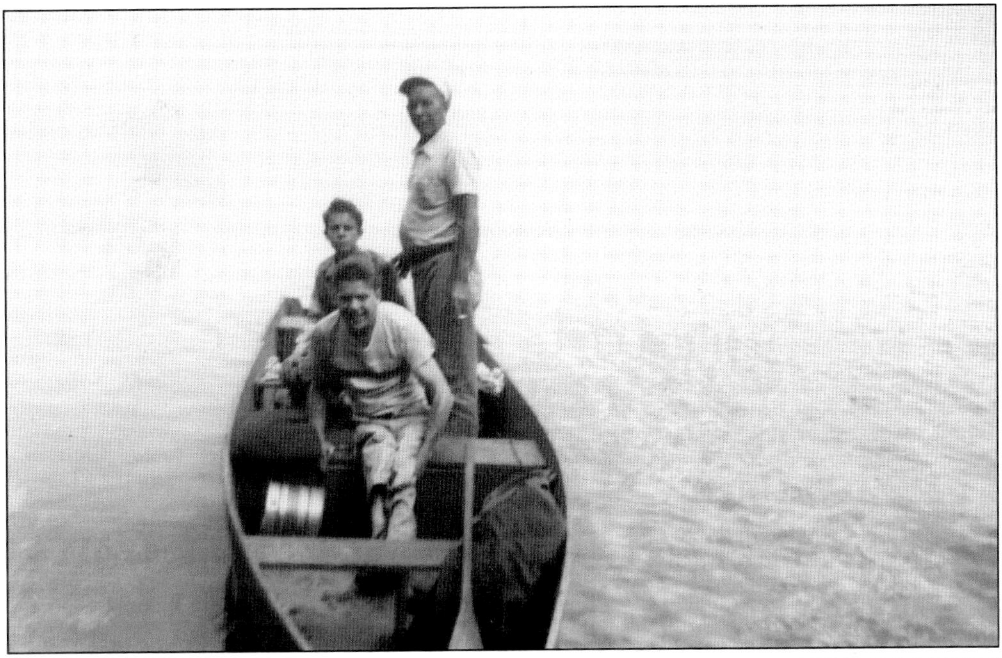

Another popular destination for Riceville residents was Lake James. Here, Horace Reed takes young relative George (front) and grandson Bruce boating in the early 1950s. (Courtesy of Butch and Judy Reed.)

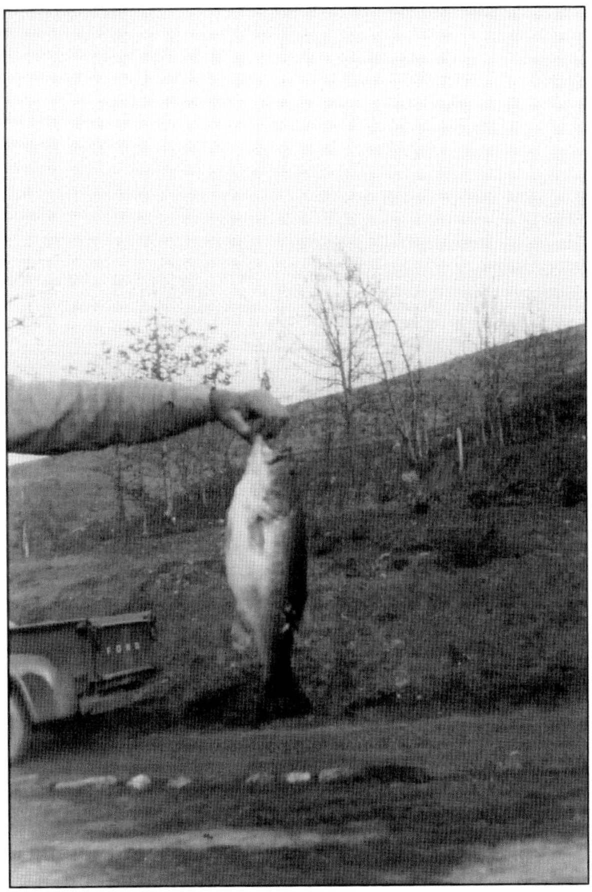

In the lakes and rivers in and near Riceville, fishing was a popular pastime. This photograph of an especially large catch was taken beside the Reed house. Reed Mountain, where the family's cattle grazed, can be seen in the background. (Courtesy of Butch and Judy Reed.)

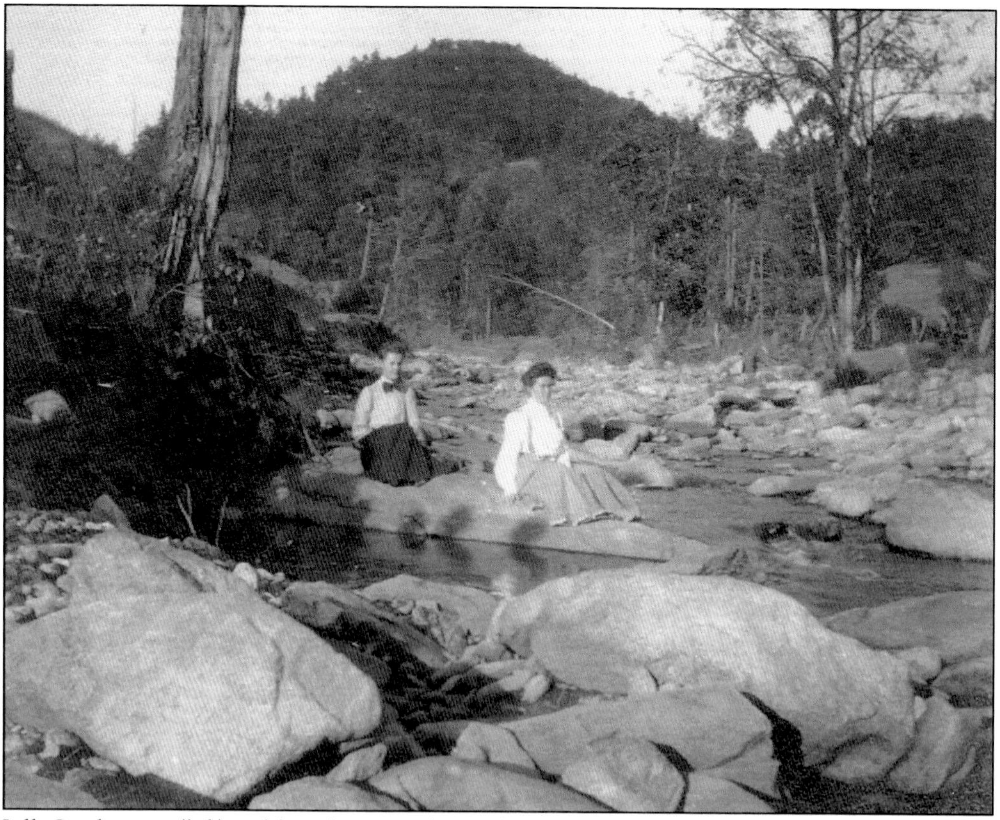

Lilly Stephenson (left) and friend pose on the creek near the Stephenson home on Bull Creek. Lilly was a lifelong member of the Riceville Presbyterian Church and taught the youth Sunday school for many years. When electricity came to the community, she contributed to the church to enable it to have lights, even before they were installed in her own home. (Courtesy of John Weakly.)

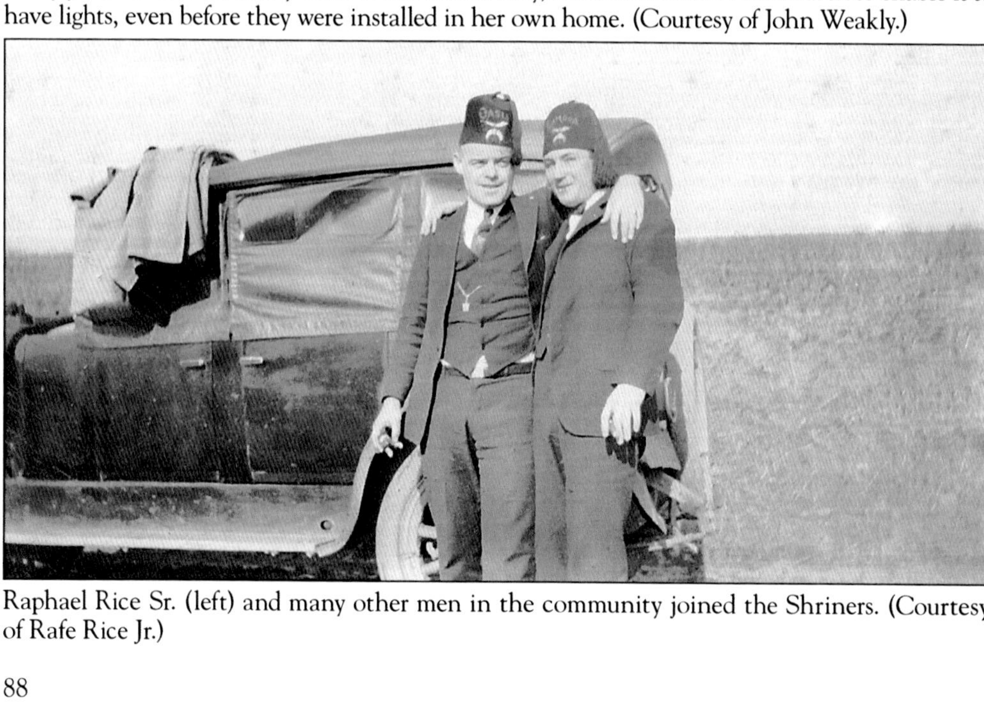

Raphael Rice Sr. (left) and many other men in the community joined the Shriners. (Courtesy of Rafe Rice Jr.)

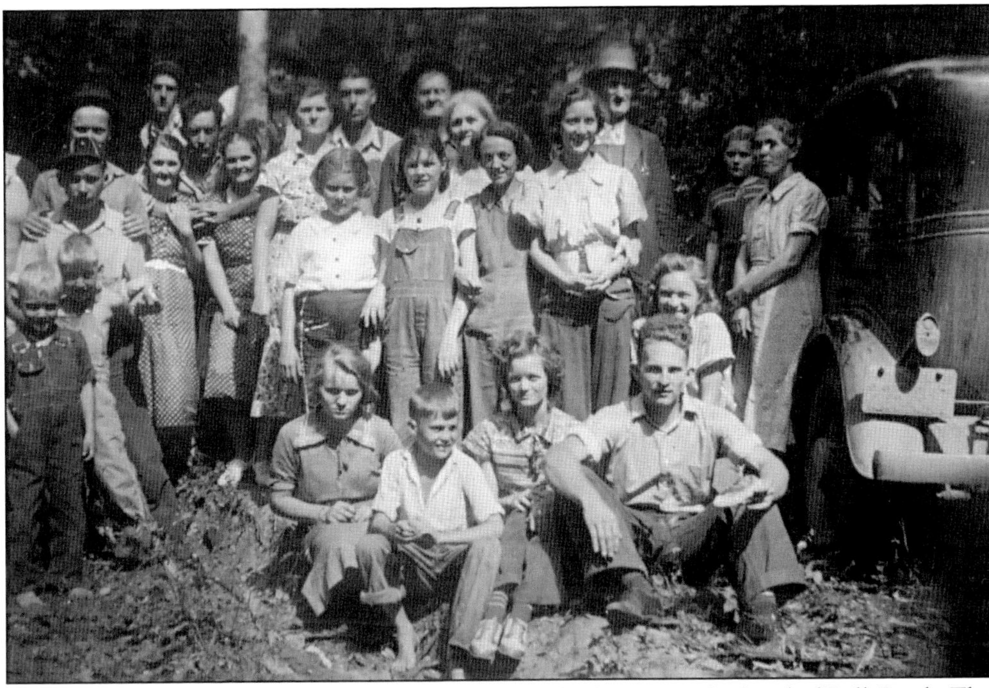

The Gragg family would often camp with friends and relatives on the head of Bull Creek. This photograph, taken on Sunday, October 16, 1938, includes Graggs, Greggs, Goodes, Smiths, Creasmans, and Buckners. (Courtesy of Mr. and Mrs. Robin Gregg.)

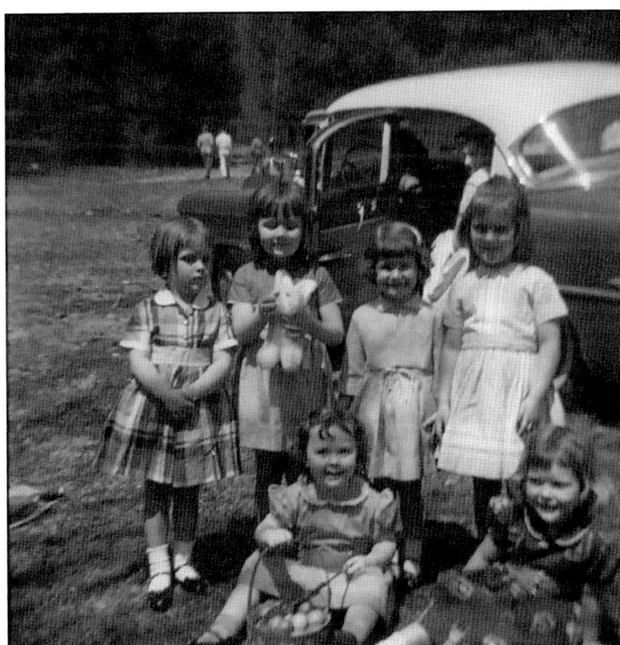

Shown from left to right are Jamie Fuller, Dawn Gregg, Teresa Gragg, Sherry Gregg, Linda Fuller, and Diane Messer. They are collecting Easter eggs in 1962 at the campsite near the head of Shope Creek. The area was a popular gathering and camping spot for locals. Riceville's residents would often hold camping parties for days at this location. (Courtesy of Mr. and Mrs. Robin Gregg.)

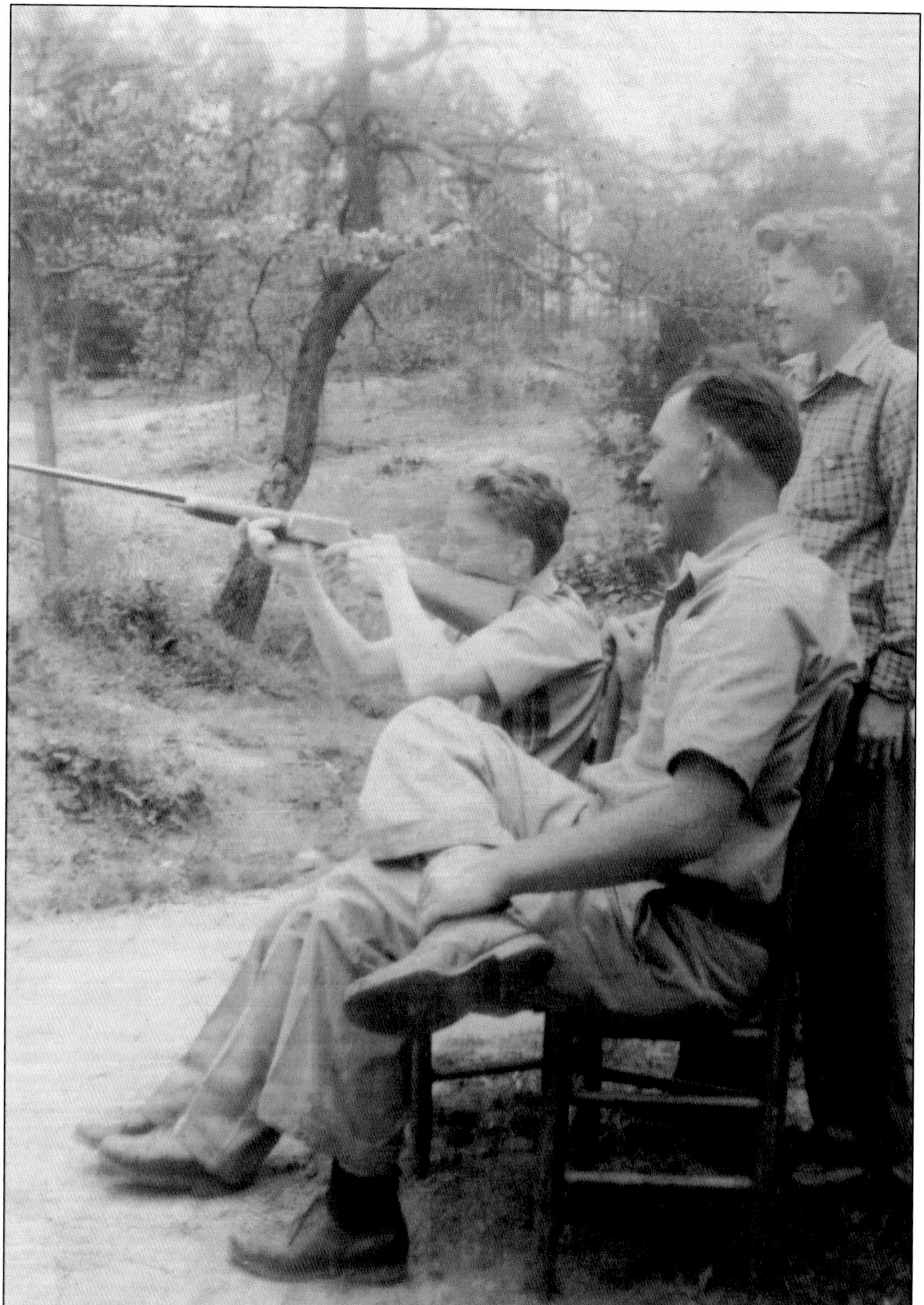

Learning to shoot was a rite of passage as well as a form of recreation for many young boys in the Riceville area. Father Horace, George (with gun), and Jim Reed practice up the hill from the Reed home place. George often made his relatives nervous because he tended to look a different way then where he was shooting. (Courtesy of Butch and Judy Reed.)

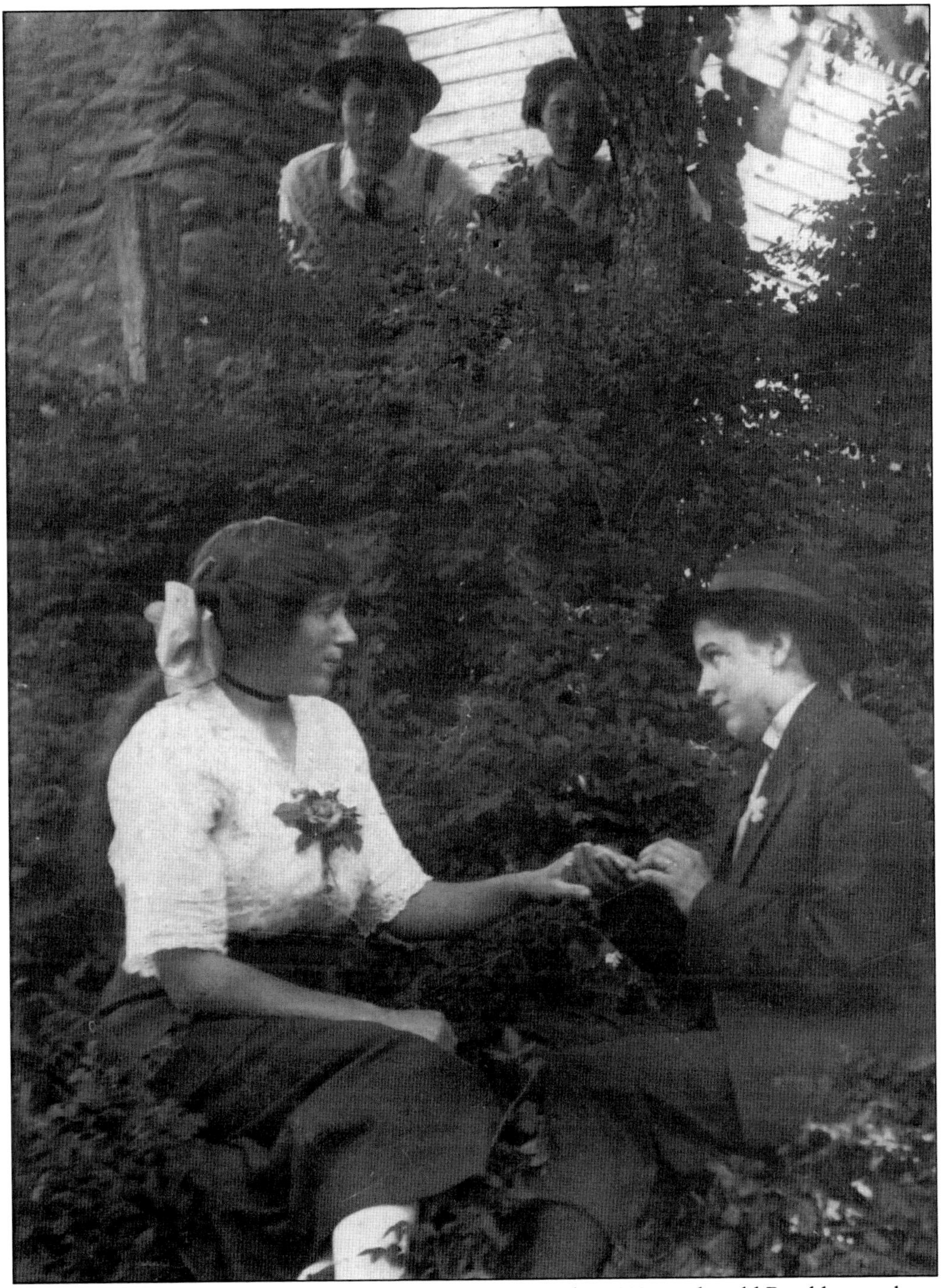

The Reed children stage an engagement photograph in the 1910s at the old Reed home place. Rheta Elevenia gives the ring to Loys while Walter and Elsie look on. The Reeds built a cabin near Craggy Gardens around this time because Rheta Elevenia, Altha Ada, Hetty Delener, and Willie Gertrude Reed all came down with tuberculosis. The girls could breathe better at the mountain cabin, and the family cared for them there. Still, all of them died between 1919 and 1925. (Courtesy of Butch and Judy Reed.)

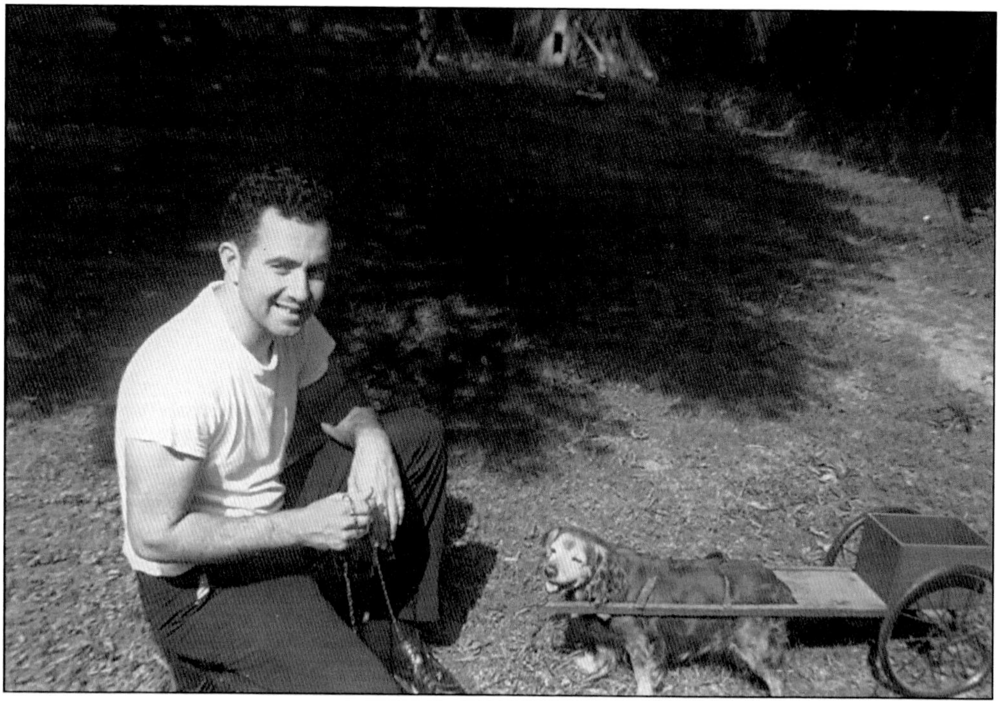

Rafe Rice Jr. teaches his dog Jiggs to pull a cart at his home just past Grassy Branch Baptist Church. Rafe built the cart when he was seven years old from some discarded wood and the wheels from his tricycle. And 50 years later, Tipper pulls Precious in the same cart. (Courtesy of Rafe Rice Jr.)

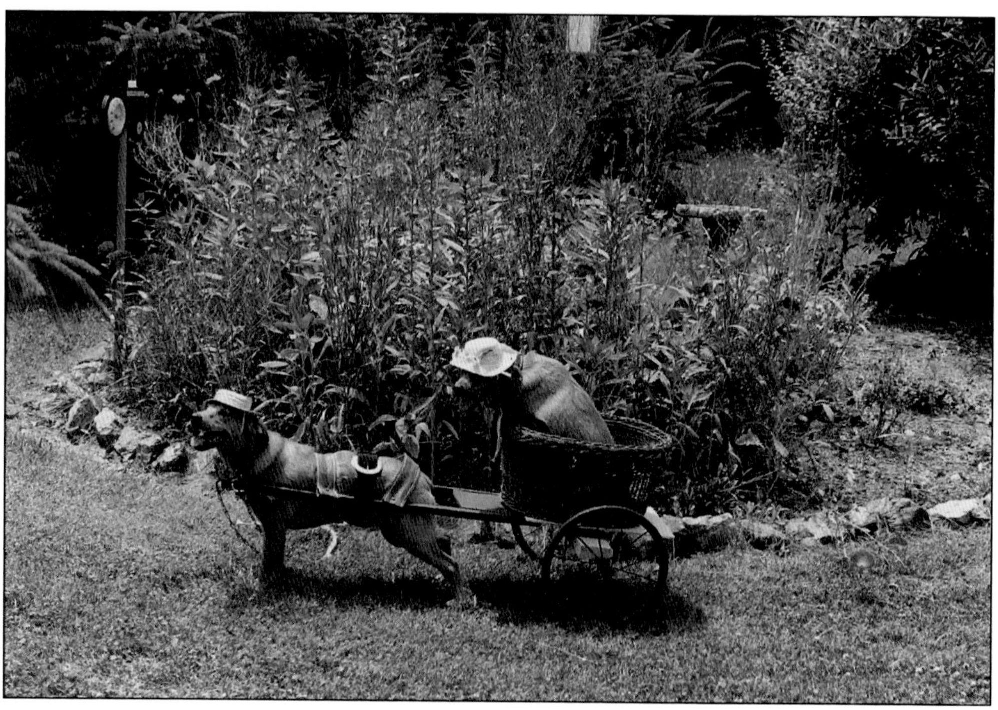

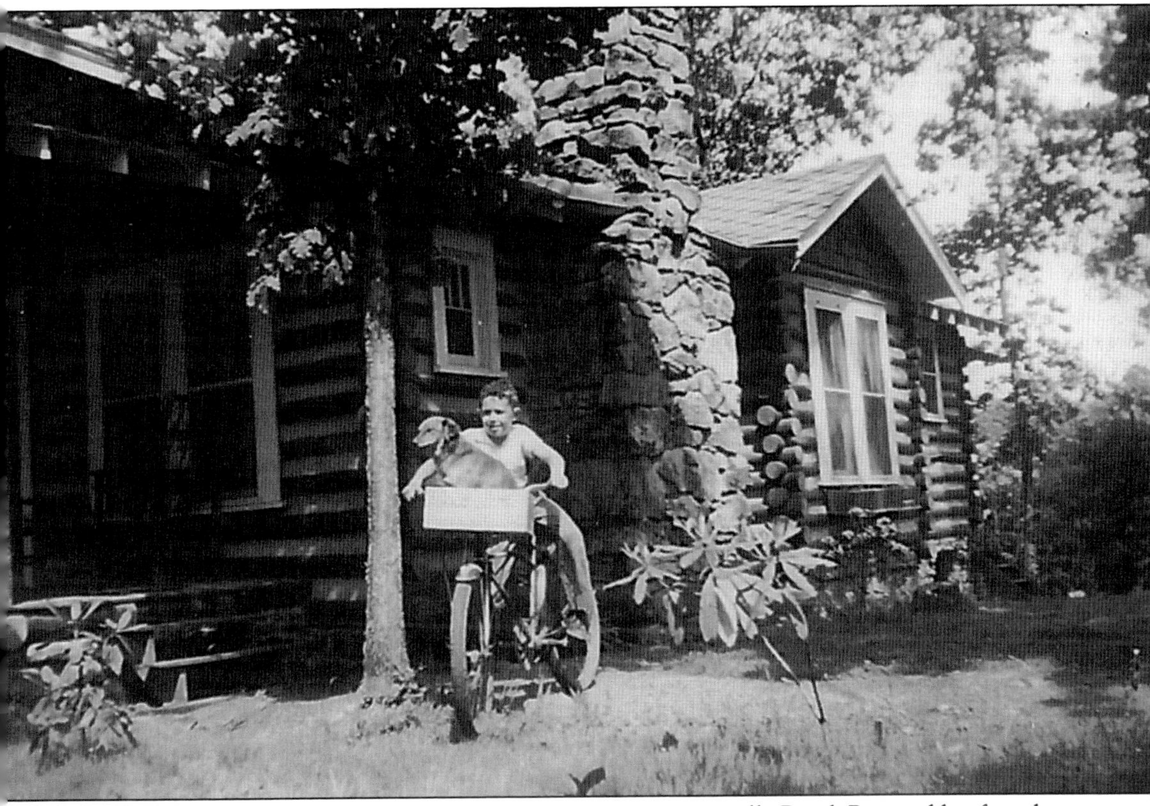

Rafe Rice Jr. rides his bike in front of his parents' home on Riceville Road. Ray and his friends would ride their bikes to Bull Creek to look for arrowheads. They would also carry their bikes up to the Blue Ridge Parkway when it was under construction and ride through the uncompleted tunnels near Rattlesnake Lodge. (Courtesy of Rafe Rice Jr.)

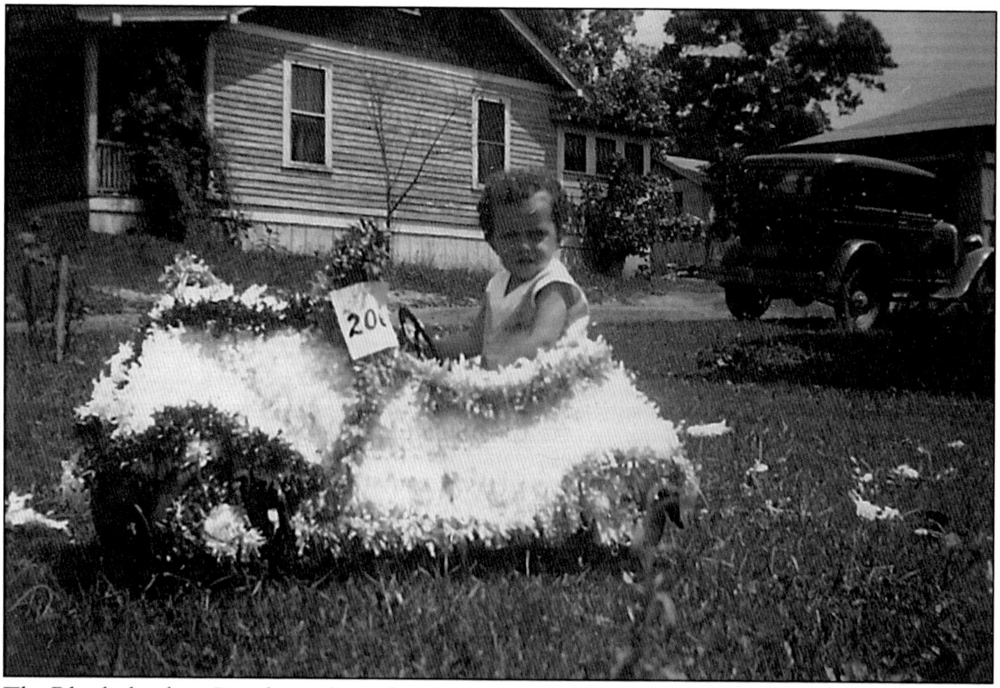

The Rhododendron Parade used to take place every year in Oteen, across from the VA Hospital. Rafe Rice Jr.'s parents built this float for their son to ride on in the 1930 parade. (Courtesy of Rafe Rice Jr.)

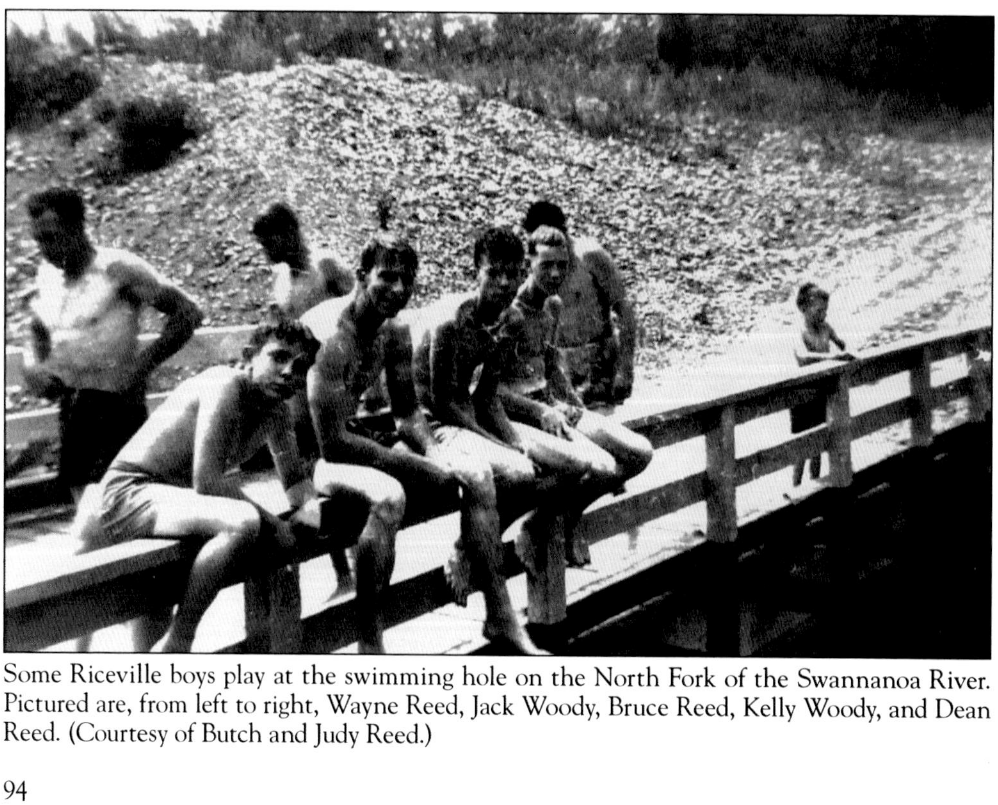

Some Riceville boys play at the swimming hole on the North Fork of the Swannanoa River. Pictured are, from left to right, Wayne Reed, Jack Woody, Bruce Reed, Kelly Woody, and Dean Reed. (Courtesy of Butch and Judy Reed.)

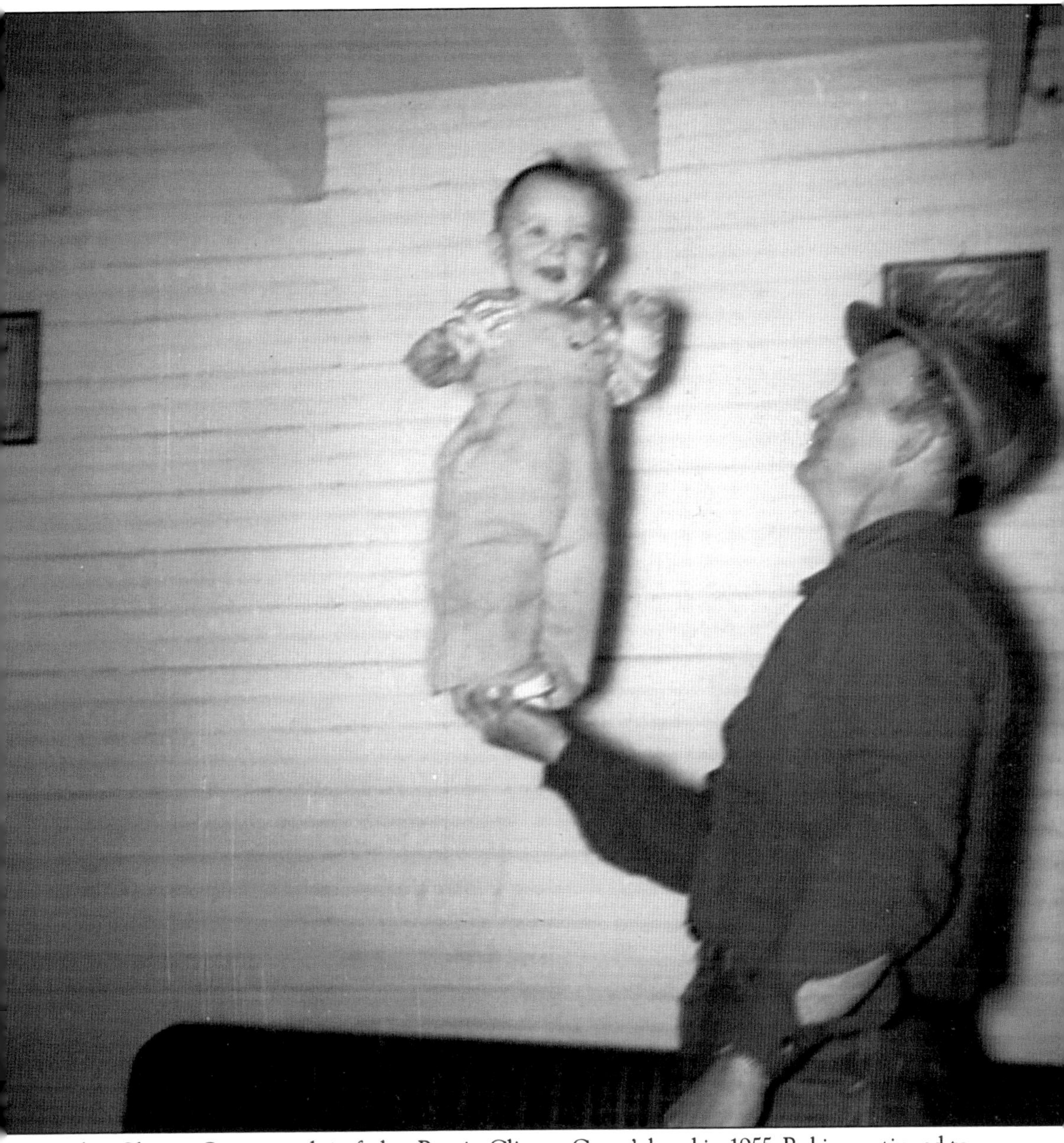

Robin Clinton Gregg stands in father Burgin Clinton Gregg's hand in 1955. Robin continued to stand in his father's hand until one day when he fell. Burgin attempted to catch Robin before he hit the ground, but he accidentally broke the boy's leg. Robin can still remember crawling around the house in a leg cast. (Courtesy of Mr. and Mrs. Robin Gregg.)

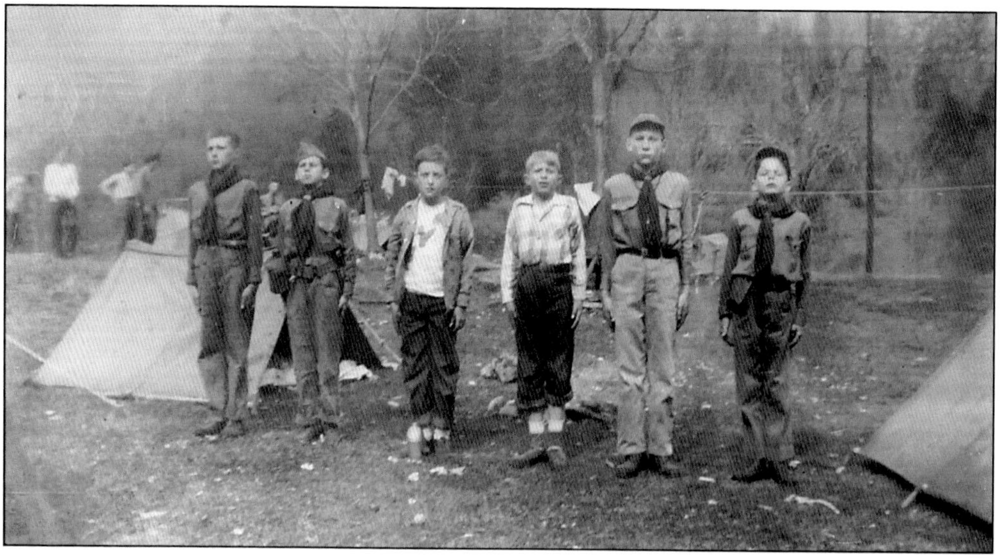

The first meeting to organize a Boy Scout troop was held April 22, 1949, at Bethel Methodist Church. On June 30, 1949, the group was chartered as Boy Scout Troop 30, Grassy Branch. By 1953, the troop had 62 boys, 26 active members, and the only Eagle Scout, Bobby Reed (bottom photograph, farthest left). The troop received awards for troop advancement for the years of 1949–1952, Boy's Life banners for the years 1949–1953, the national award for distribution of "Get Out and Vote" liberty bells, and the 1950 Veterans of Foreign Wars Scoutmaster Citizenship Award. Both photographs were taken at Camp Daniel Boone. (Courtesy of the Riceville Community Center.)

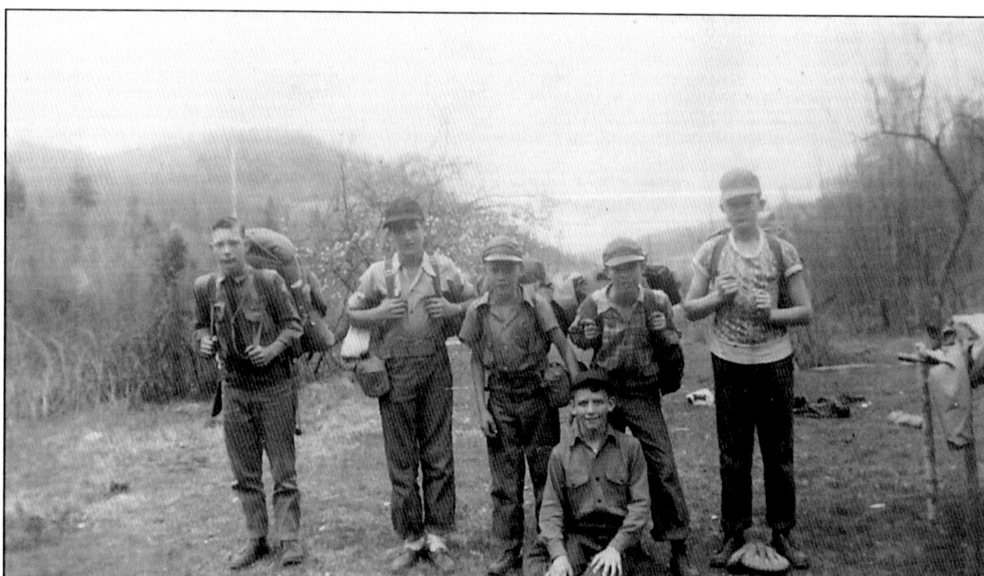

From left to right, Bruce Reed and Jim and Kelly Woody pose by the Reed house in their Boy Scout uniforms. (Courtesy of Butch and Judy Reed.)

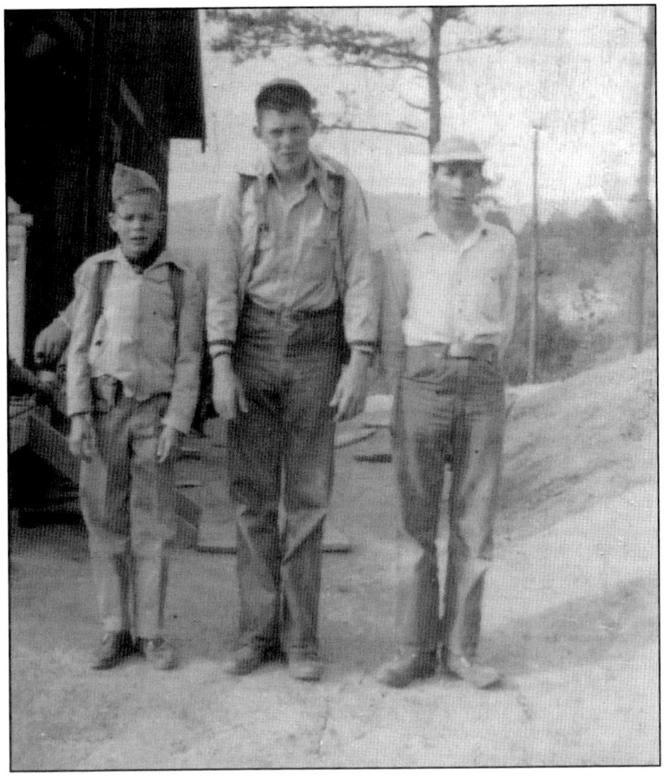

Cub Scout Den 5 plays a pickup football game. Mrs. Charlie Morris was made the den mother, and Rev. Keith Mitchell was the den dad. Den 5 met once a week, on Friday afternoons, at the home of the Den Mother. The meetings consisted of opening ceremonies, stories, handiwork, or work on projects, like collecting and mounting leaves, building soap-box cars, and making Indian costumes. (Courtesy of the Riceville Community Center.)

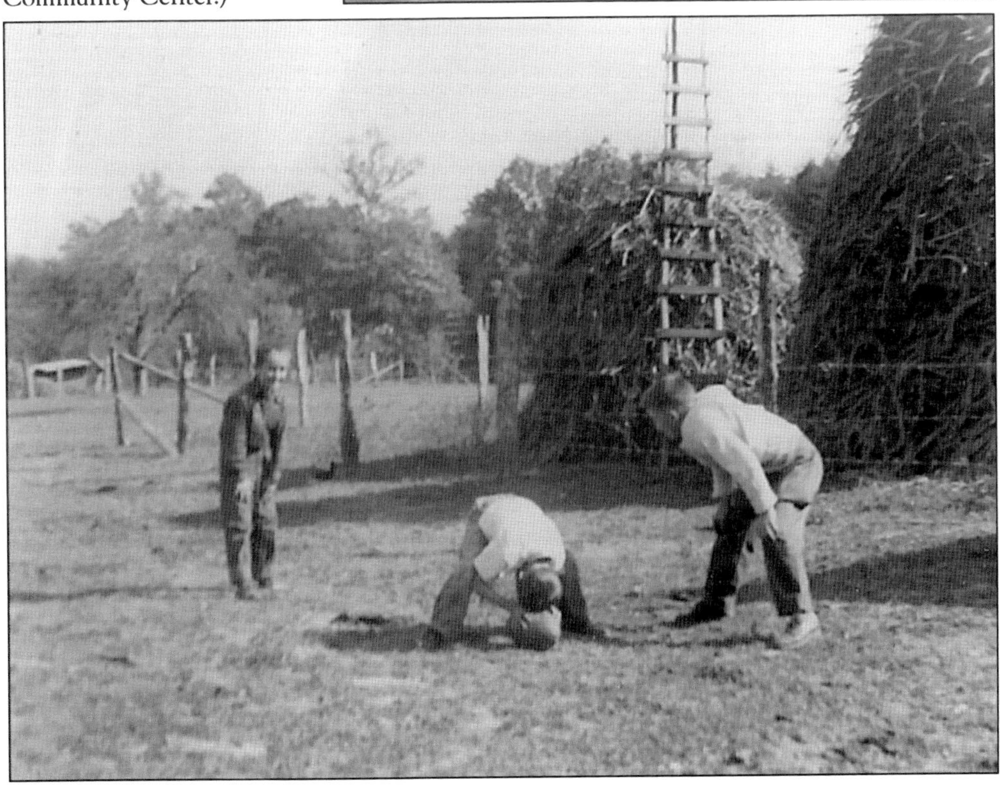

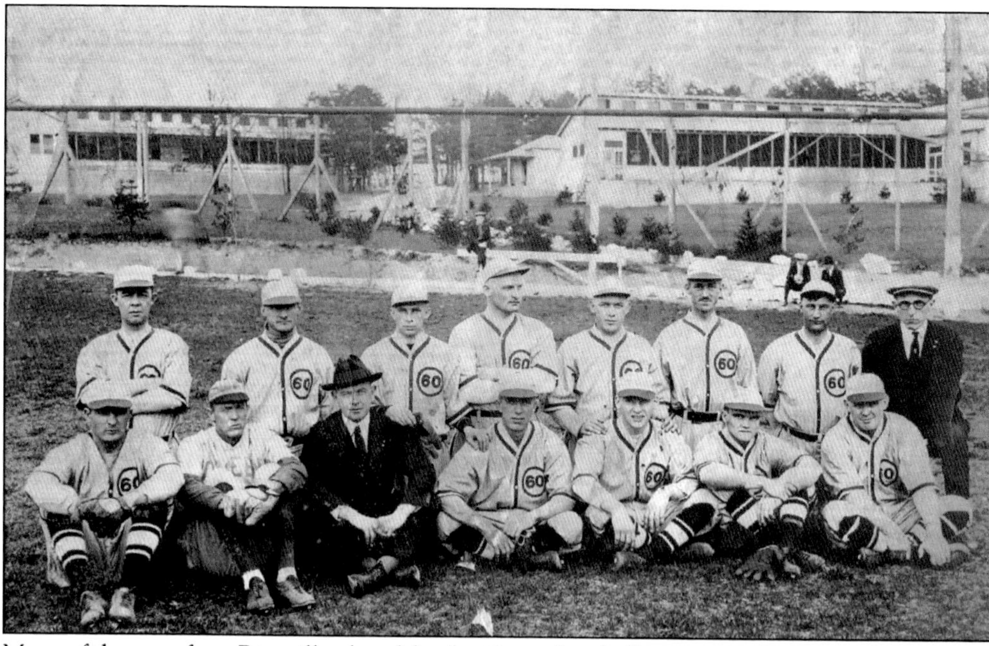

Many of the men from Riceville played for the Oteen baseball team, which practiced and played games at what is now the veterans affairs hospital. The old barracks can be seen behind the team in the photograph above. (Courtesy of Rafe Rice Jr.)

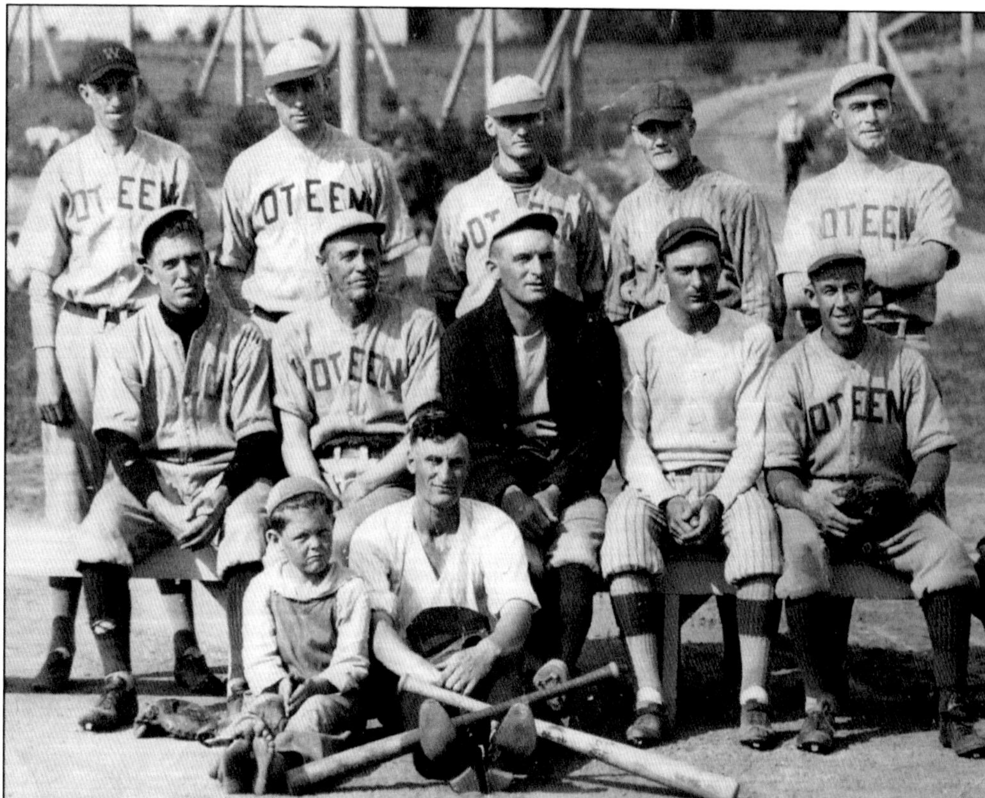

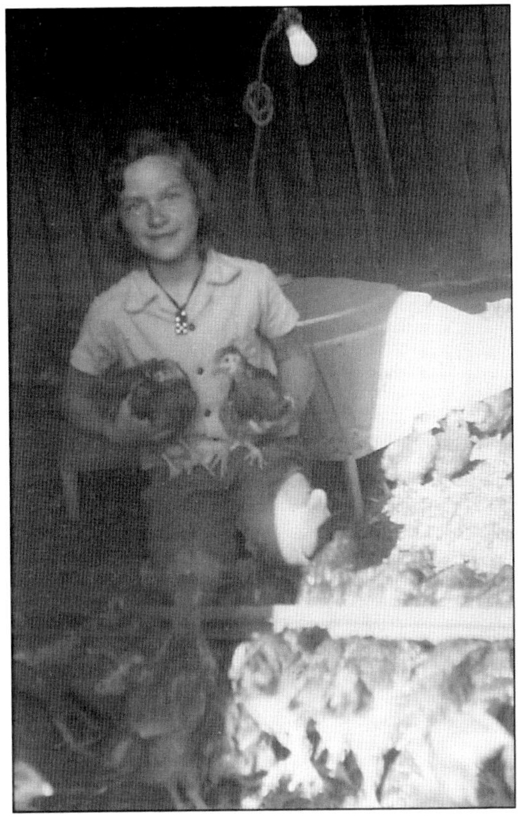

The Grassy Branch 4-H Club was organized in June 1953 and was sponsored by the Home Demonstration Club. The club motto and pledge gave Riceville's boys and girls inspiration to become better citizens by serving the community and country. Every year, each club member selected a project to work on. Linda Shuford selected poultry raising in 1953. The pullets she raised won a blue ribbon in the 4-H pullet show. Also, Marie Clark selected bean raising and canning as her project; her profit was $15.05. Some of the other girls did some nice work in Swedish darning. (Courtesy of the Riceville Community Center.)

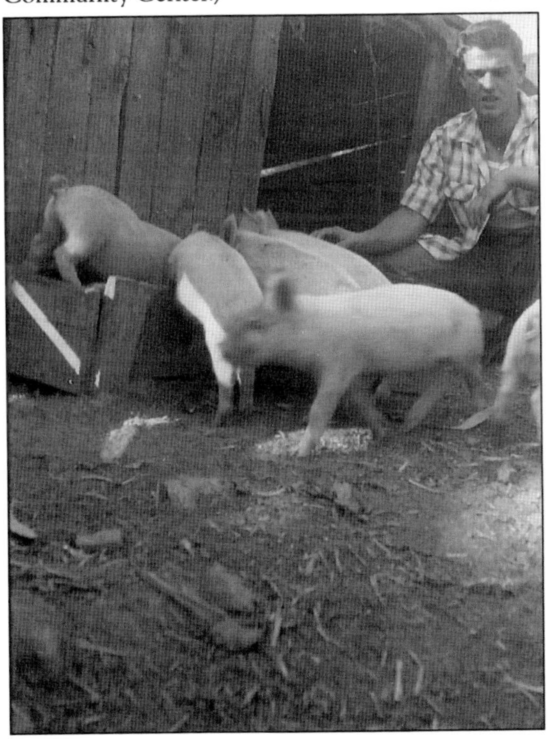

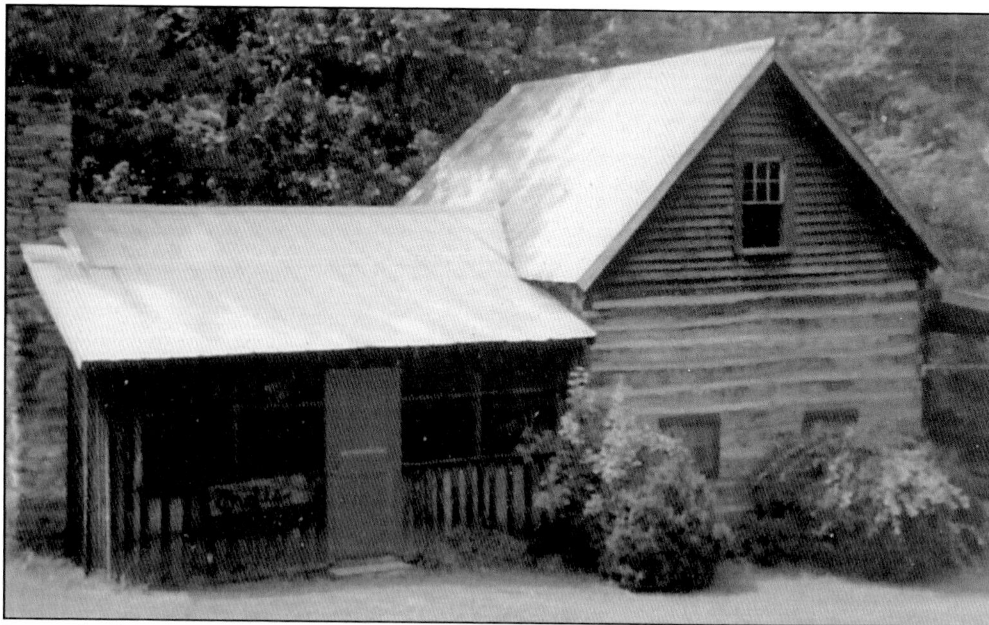

Located off Jones Cove Road, Camp Awa-Niko for Girls was founded in 1951 by Ruth White and Nancy Wrenn after their return from serving with the American National Red Cross in Okinawa, Japan. Camp Awa-Niko (Okinawa spelled backwards) covered more than 400 acres of wooded and cleared land in a sheltered mountain cove and the surrounding ridges. The activities offered by the camp included—horseback riding, swimming, canoeing, hiking, badminton, overnight trips, nature study, music, dramatics, arts and crafts, archery, riflery, dancing, photography, outdoor cooking, field games, and indoor games. Nancy and Ruth ran the camp together until 1972. Pictured is the craft house, built by Nancy and Ruth, that was constructed onto the back of the Joseph Hasque Rice cabin and the lake. Below, the porch of the cabin can be seen overlooking the camp lake. (Courtesy of Nancy Wrenn.)

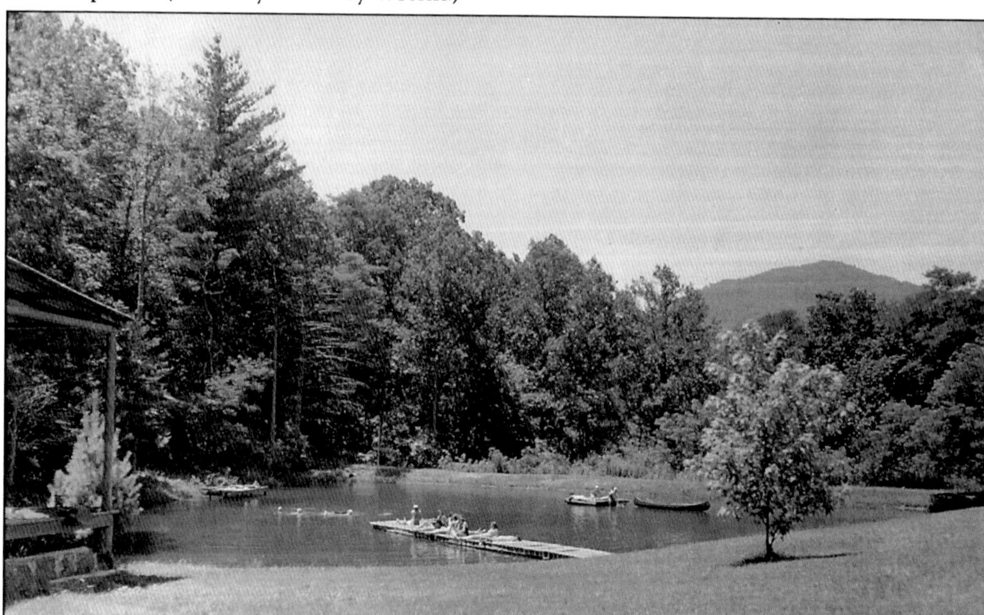

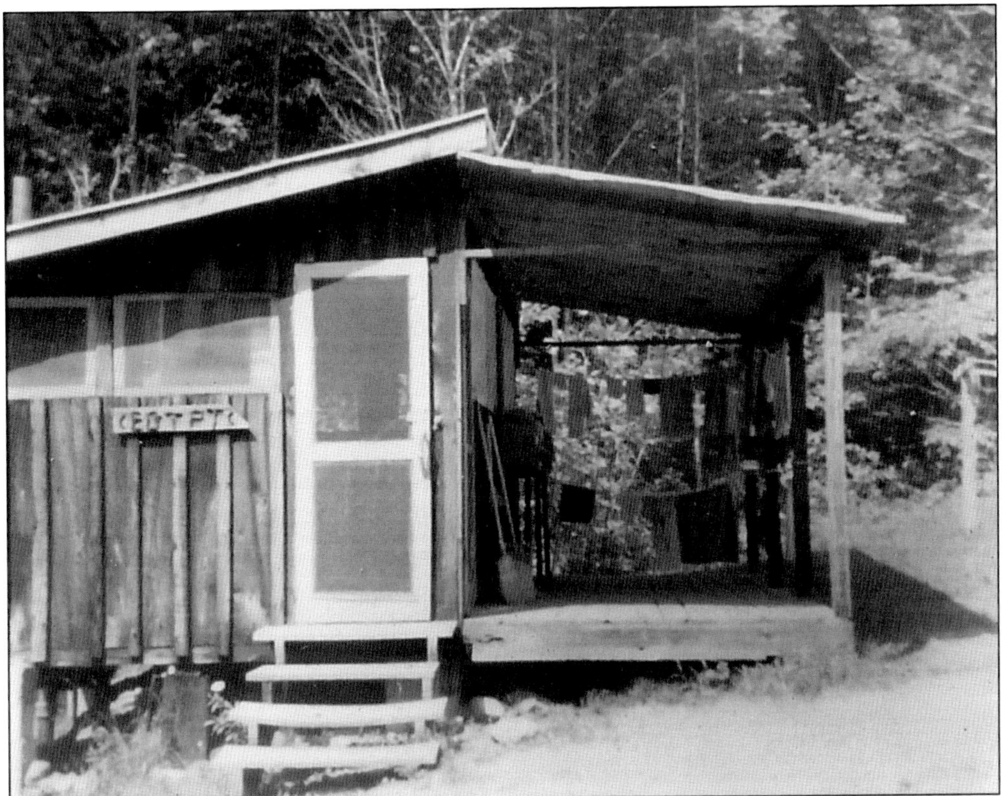

The bathhouse at Camp Awa-Niko was referred to as "Egypt." It had three commodes, a shower, and a big trough for brushing teeth. During the first summer, Nancy Wrenn and Ruth White used their bedroom as the camp kitchen. They had four campers and four adult counselors, and they all slept in the craft house. The camp girls were aged nine through 15. (Courtesy of Nancy Wrenn.)

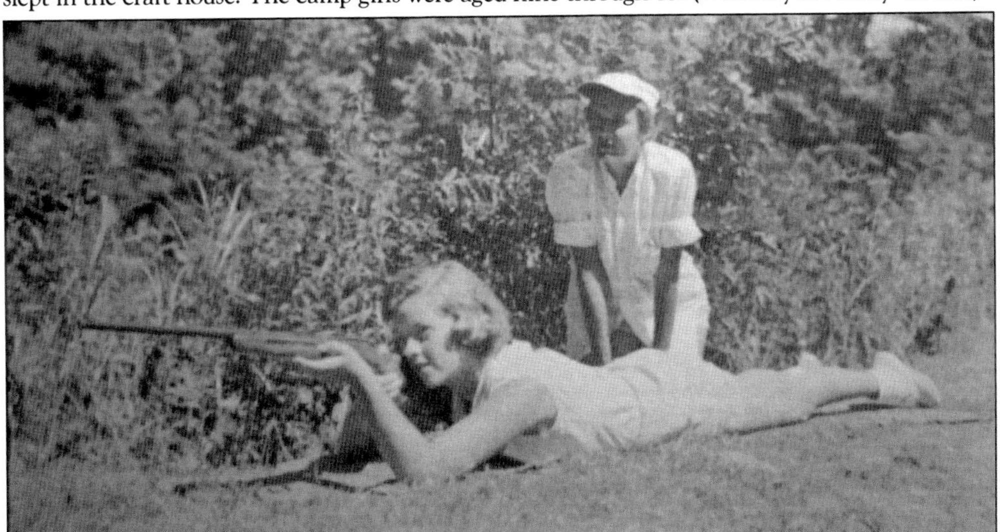

Ruth White teaches a camper how to shoot. During the off-season, Nancy Wrenn and Ruth taught school and built new structures for the camp. After a couple of years, they had expanded to having 12 campers and two cabins. (Courtesy of Nancy Wrenn.)

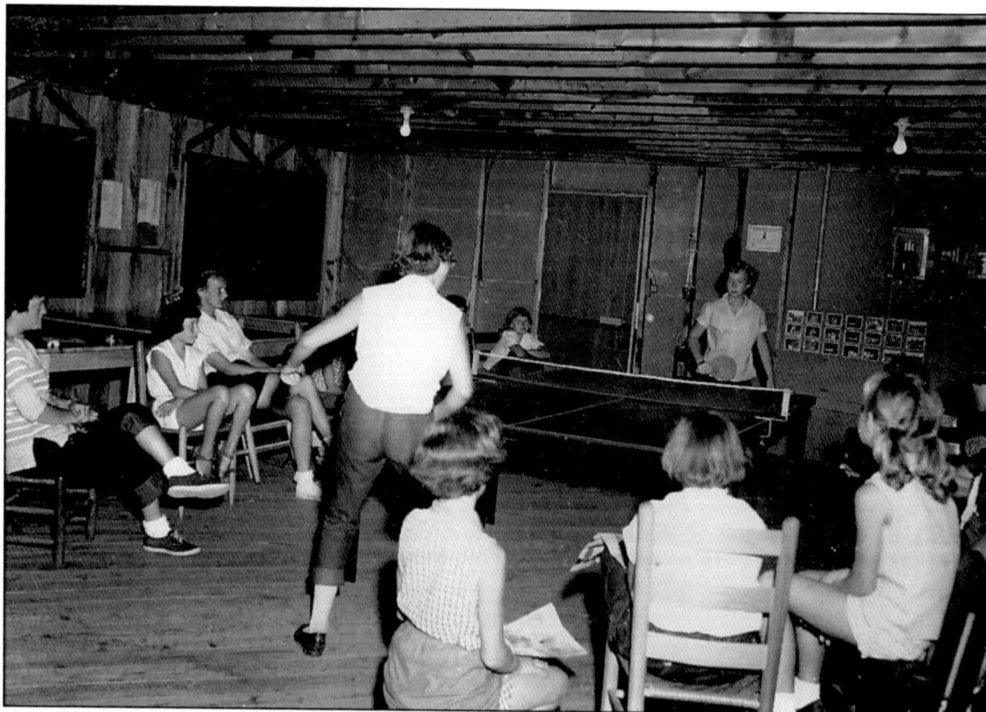

The girls play ping-pong in the game room. By 1955, the camp was going at full strength and had 25 campers and five cabins. The camp season lasted for 28 days. (Courtesy of Nancy Wrenn.)

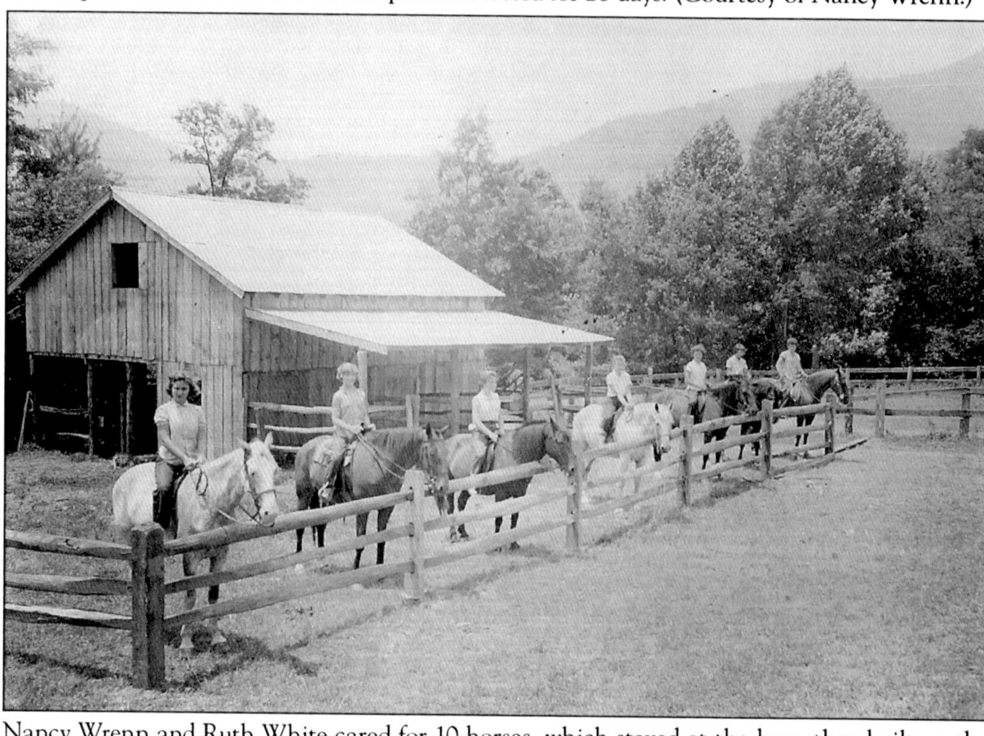

Nancy Wrenn and Ruth White cared for 10 horses, which stayed at the barn they built on the old Trantham property. The barn still stands today. (Courtesy of Nancy Wrenn.)

Five

CREATING COMMUNITY

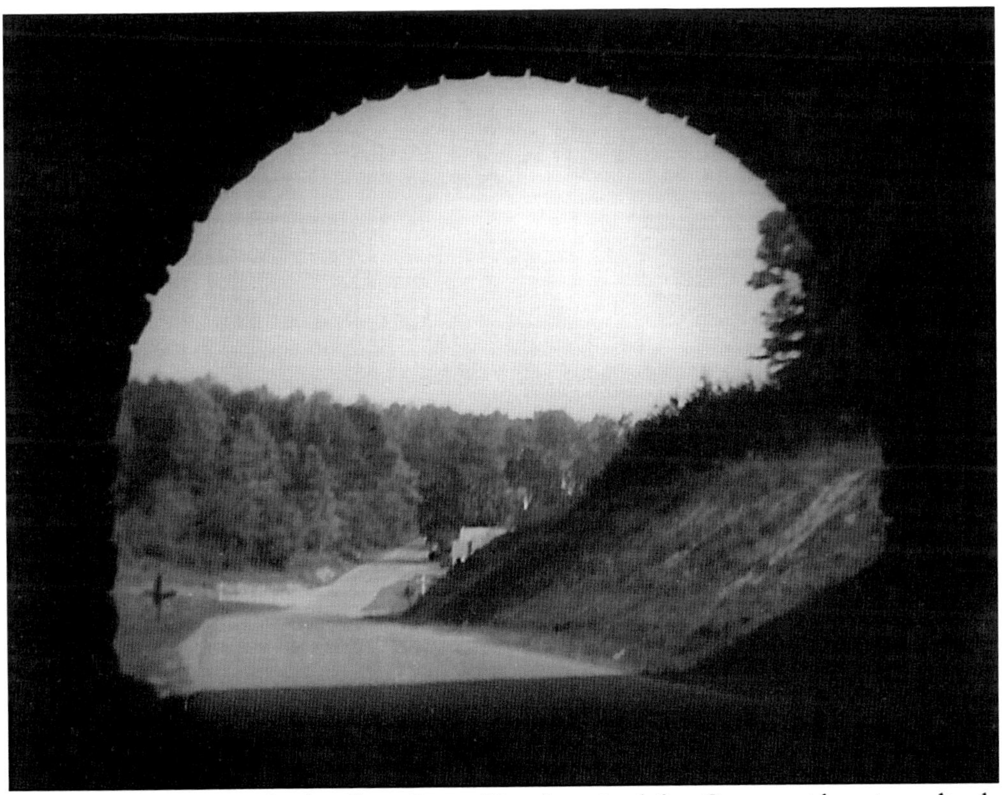

Traveling five miles out of Asheville on Route 70 and turning left at Oteen, residents immediately drive through the lovely grounds of the veterans hospital and enter the underpass, over which is the beginning of the well-known Blue Ridge Parkway. Coming out of the underpass is the entrance to the Riceville community. The community stretches seven miles in length, lying along the curving Riceville Road, and ambling out via five adjoining roads: Parker, Bull Creek, Jones Cove, Shope Creek, and Dillingham Circle. (Courtesy of the Riceville Community Center.)

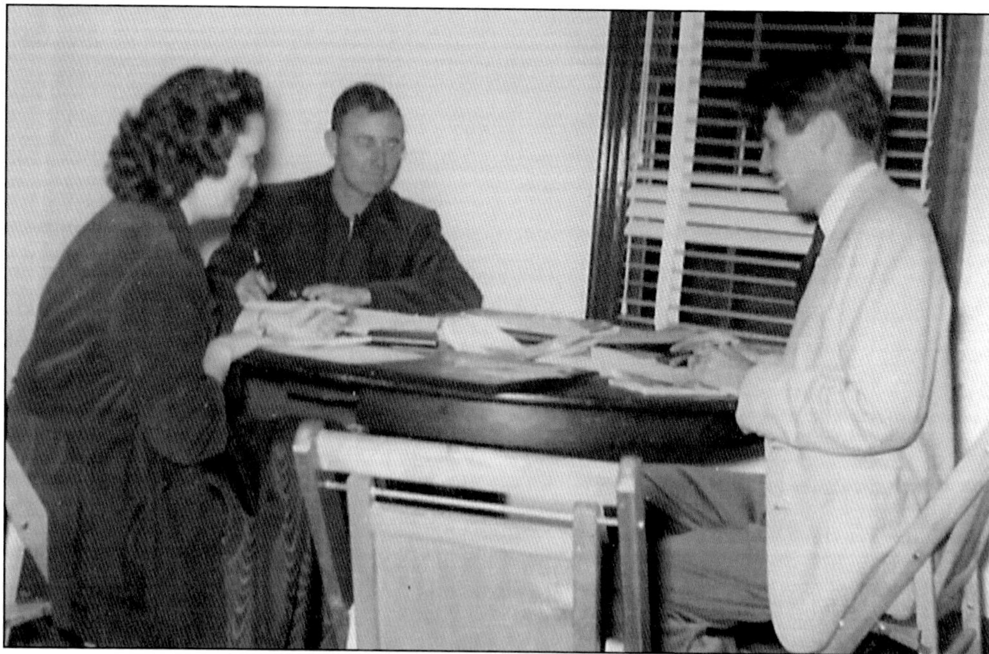

Riceville's residents have always been active in the community. The period from the 1950s through the 1970s, however, was one of the more active times of community development. The Riceville Community Development Council (pictured putting together a community scrapbook) was founded in the 1950s with the question, "How are we working together now?" To answer this question, the group identified seven community organizations: the Riceville Men's Club, the Home Demonstration Club, Boy Scout Troop 30, Cub Scout Den 5, the 4-H Club, the Riceville Community Club, and the Birthday Club. (Courtesy of the Riceville Community Center.)

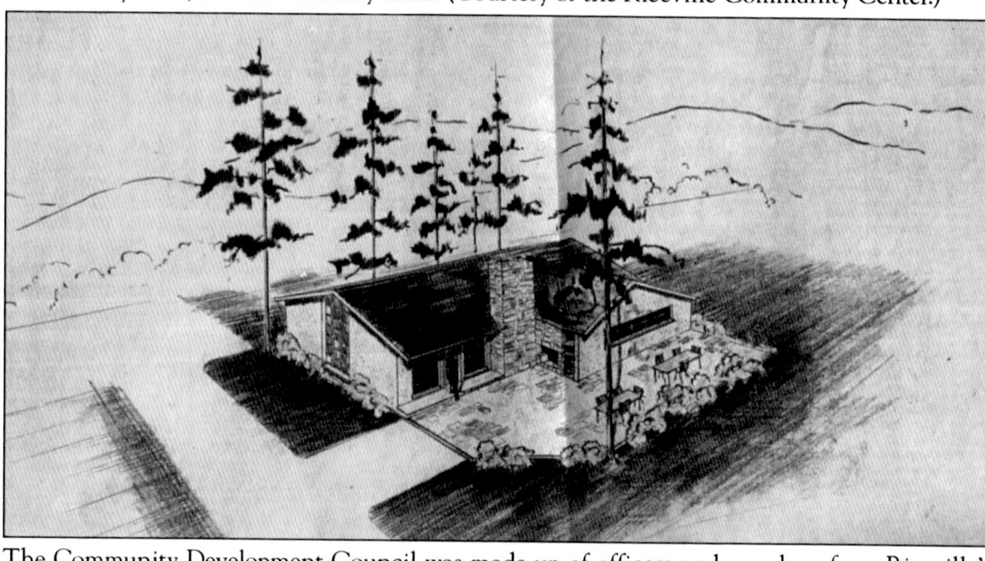

The Community Development Council was made up of officers and members from Riceville's churches and other community organizations. The overall mission of the council was to help coordinate and support the existing organizations through aiding in the development of the Riceville Community Center. Pictured is the sketch of the original Riceville Community Center, off Parker Road. (Courtesy of the Riceville Community Center.)

The land and layout for the original Community Center was referred to by the members of the Riceville Community Development Council as "Riceville's Dream." The building committee members were Hillard Shope, Rev. A.D. Smith, C.V. Shope, and Cecil McMillian. The building committee and many of the other members of the club gave many hours of work on the building. Once it was completed, there was a large meeting hall, or dining room, with a stage, a large fireplace, and an adjoined kitchen with stoves, a refrigerator, large sinks, cabinets, and a serving window. The basement contained restrooms, storage and furnace rooms, and a large recreation room. The building was put into use as soon as it was finished. The churches came together for community Christmas programs and on other special occasions. It was used by both adults and youth as a meeting place for the men's club, Home Demonstration Club, Scout troops, and other such organizations. (Courtesy of the Riceville Community Center.)

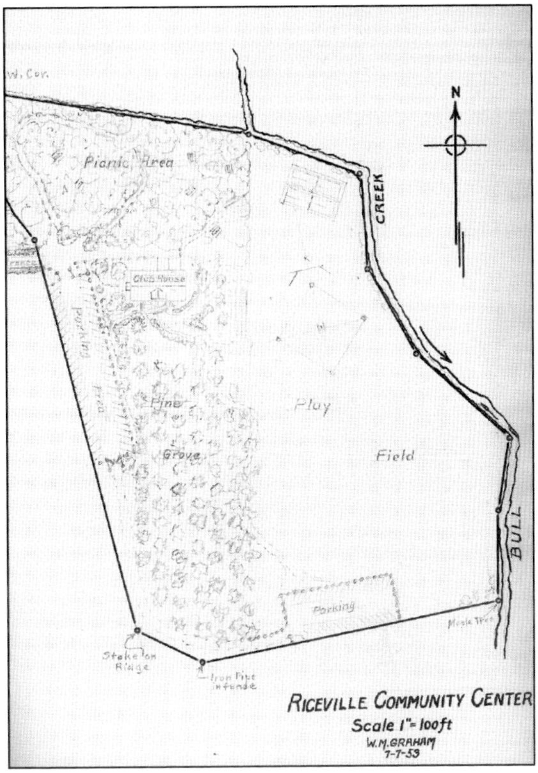

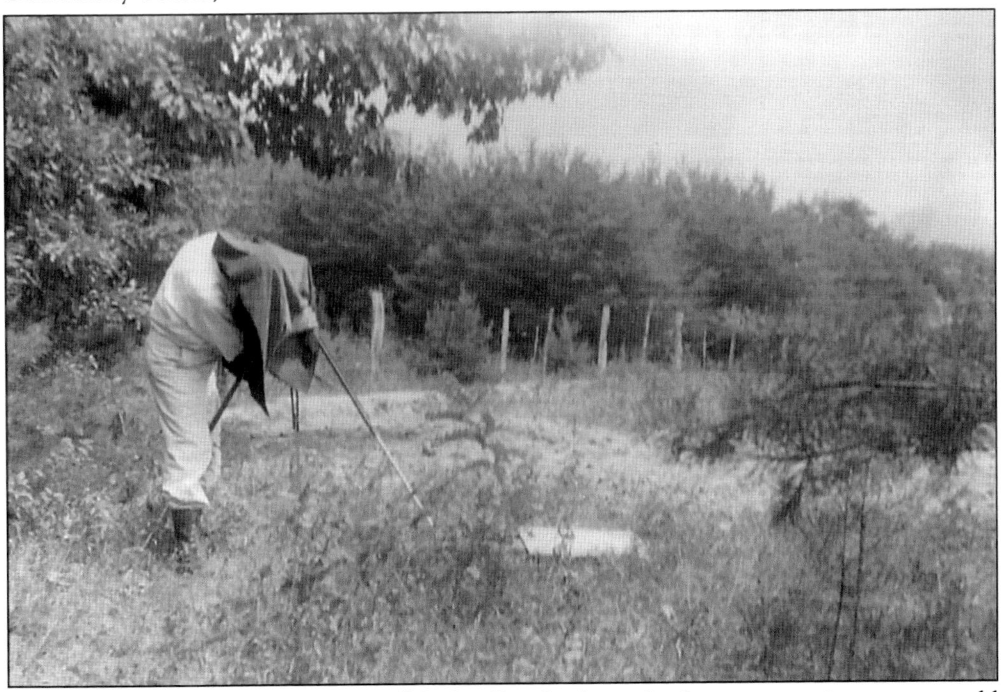

A surveyor measures the property off Parker Road, where the first community center would eventually be built. In 1953, the Riceville Men's Club bought nine acres from the Tolly Parker Estate. (Courtesy of the Riceville Community Center.)

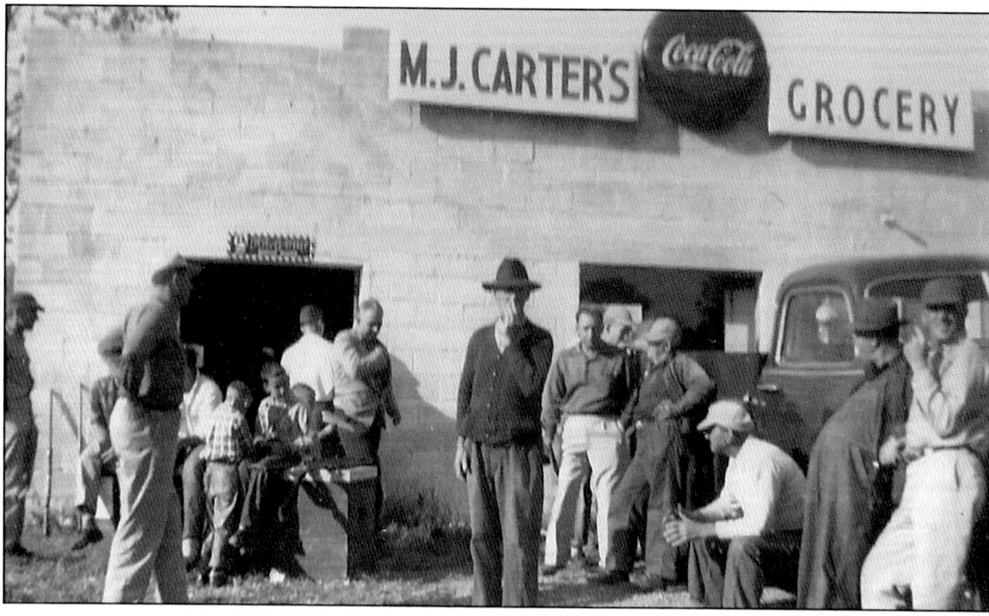

The Riceville Men's Club was composed of men from the Riceville community, which begins at Warren Wilson College and goes to the Blue Ridge Parkway underpass at Oteen. Most of the men were members of Berea Baptist, Riceville Presbyterian, Bethel Methodist, and Grassy Branch Baptist Churches. The men's club and the Home Demonstration Club worked to raise money to build the community center by holding country-style steak suppers, bake sales, and three turkey shoots; families in the community also made donations. Above, community members wait for the start of the turkey shoot in front of Carter's grocery, and below, they also wait in a field just across the street from the old store. (Courtesy of the Riceville Community Center.)

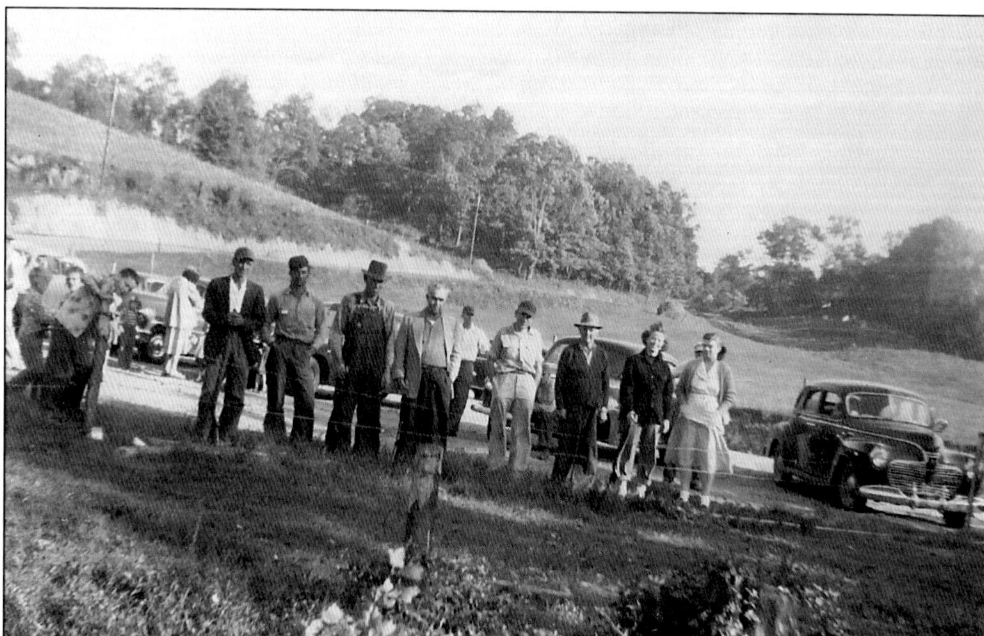

Shown is an original flyer for one of the Riceville turkey shoots. (Courtesy of the Riceville Community Center.)

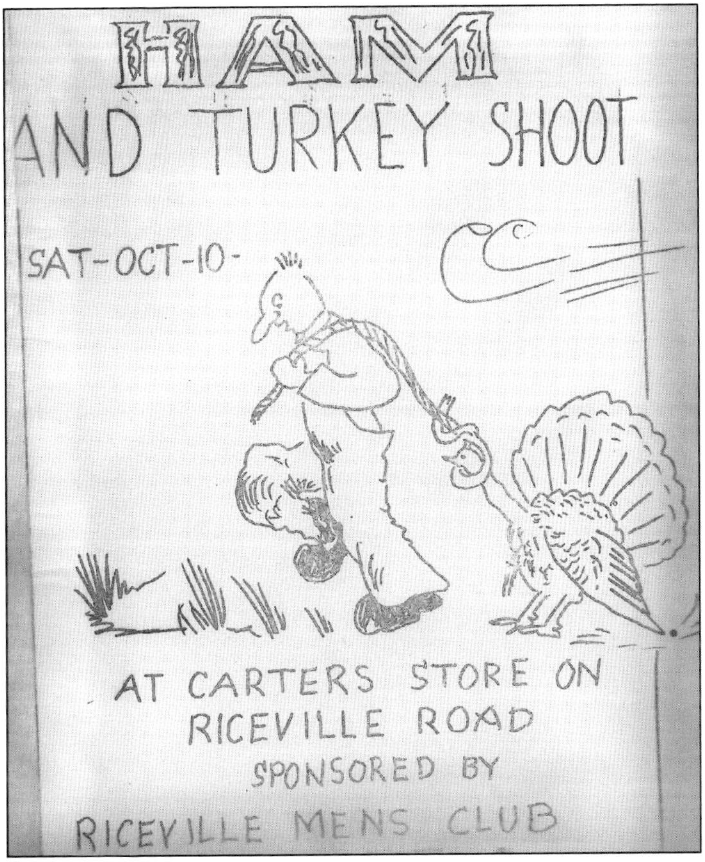

In August 1953, a community-wide picnic was held on the site of the new community center. A variety of games were offered, and a supper was spread out on long tables under the trees. Well over 100 people attended, most of them seeing the actual site for the first time. (Courtesy of the Riceville Community Center.)

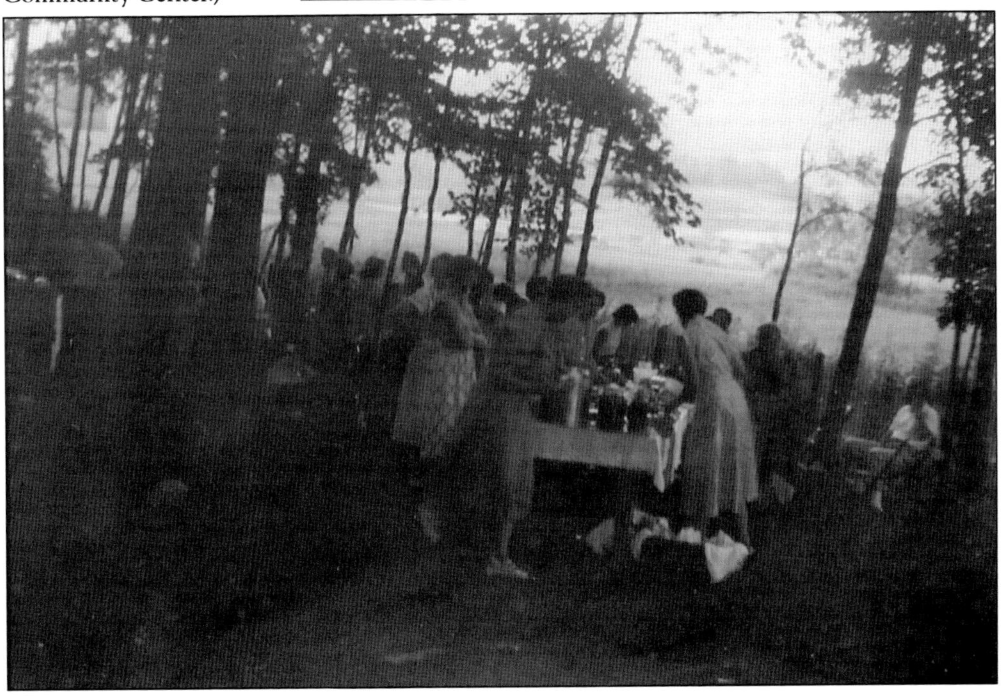

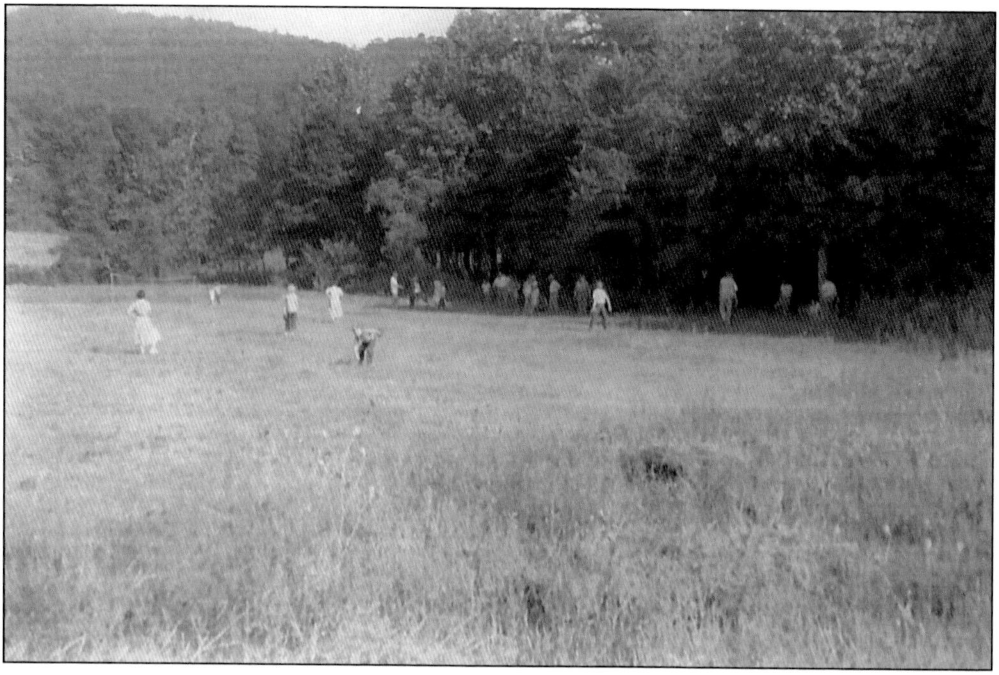

The community played horseshoes and sponsored a pickup baseball game at a community picnic on the site of the envisioned community center. An unfortunate accident occurred when Helen Clark and Helen Shope were struck by a baseball bat, which slipped from a batter's hand. It was a serious injury for Clark, who needed hospitalization. Out of concern, a community purse was collected through the men's club to share the expenses with Clark. The purse amounted to nearly $100. Clark made a full recovery. (Courtesy of the Riceville Community Center.)

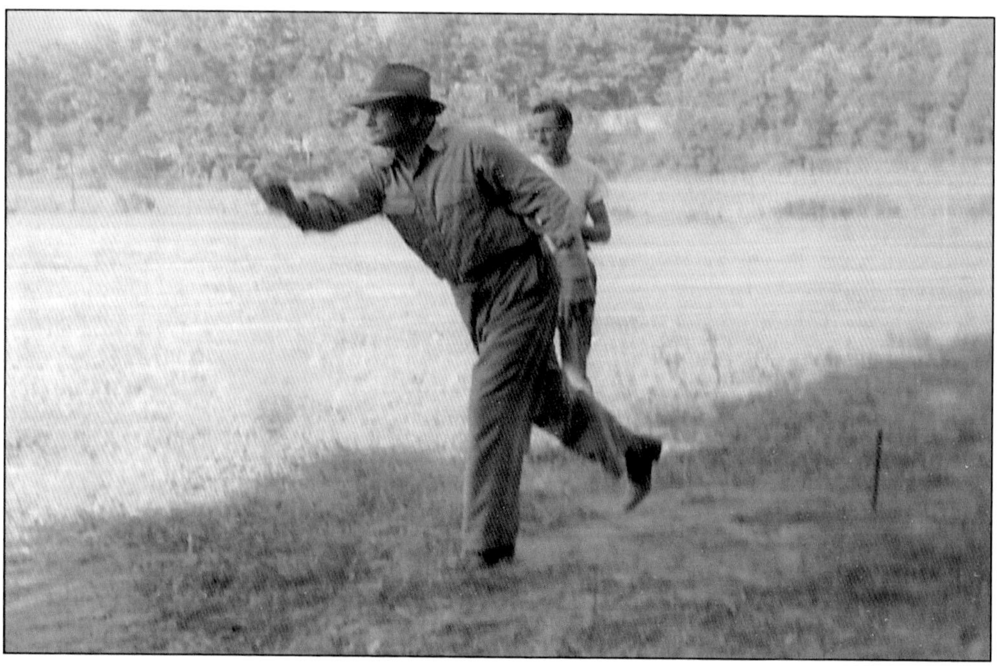

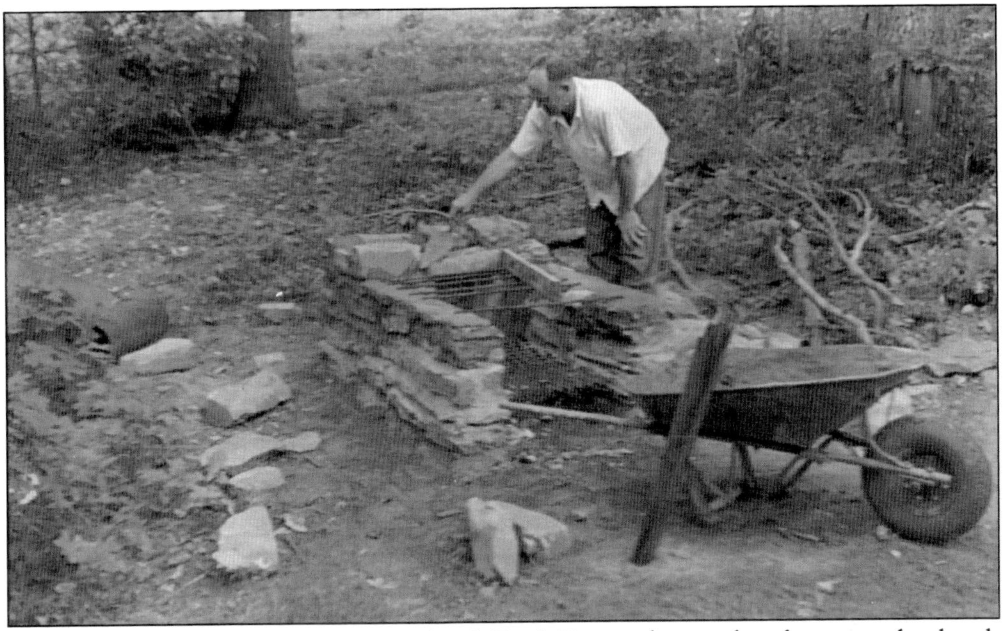

Members of the Riceville Presbyterian Church Triple F erected an outdoor furnace at the church in the summer of 1953. The Triple F hosted community gatherings at the church, including a scavenger hunt, spelling bee, and old-time box supper. That summer, prizes for the best speller were awarded to Rev. Keith Mitchell and Linda Shuford. Edith Stone's box won first prize. Tip and Sara Sawyer were in charge of the scavenger hunt. (Courtesy of the Riceville Community Center.)

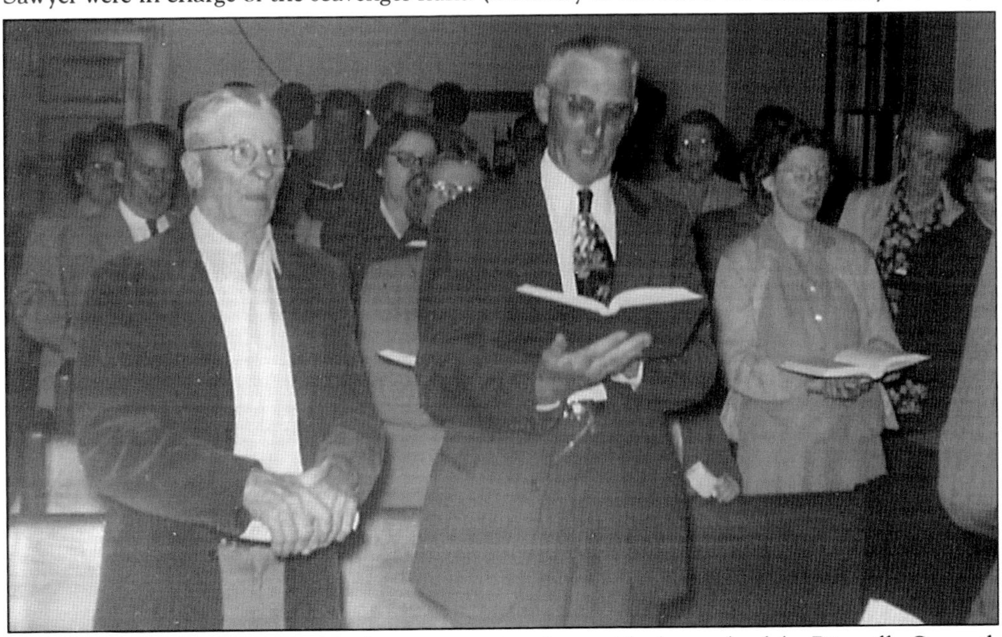

In the 1950s, to bring people together, to acquaint them with the work of the Riceville Council, and to create interest in the community center, an old Riceville tradition of "Community Sings" was revived. Anywhere from 60 to 100 people generally attended, and the gatherings were greatly enjoyed by those who came. Various people from each of the churches took turns in leading the songs. (Courtesy of the Riceville Community Center.)

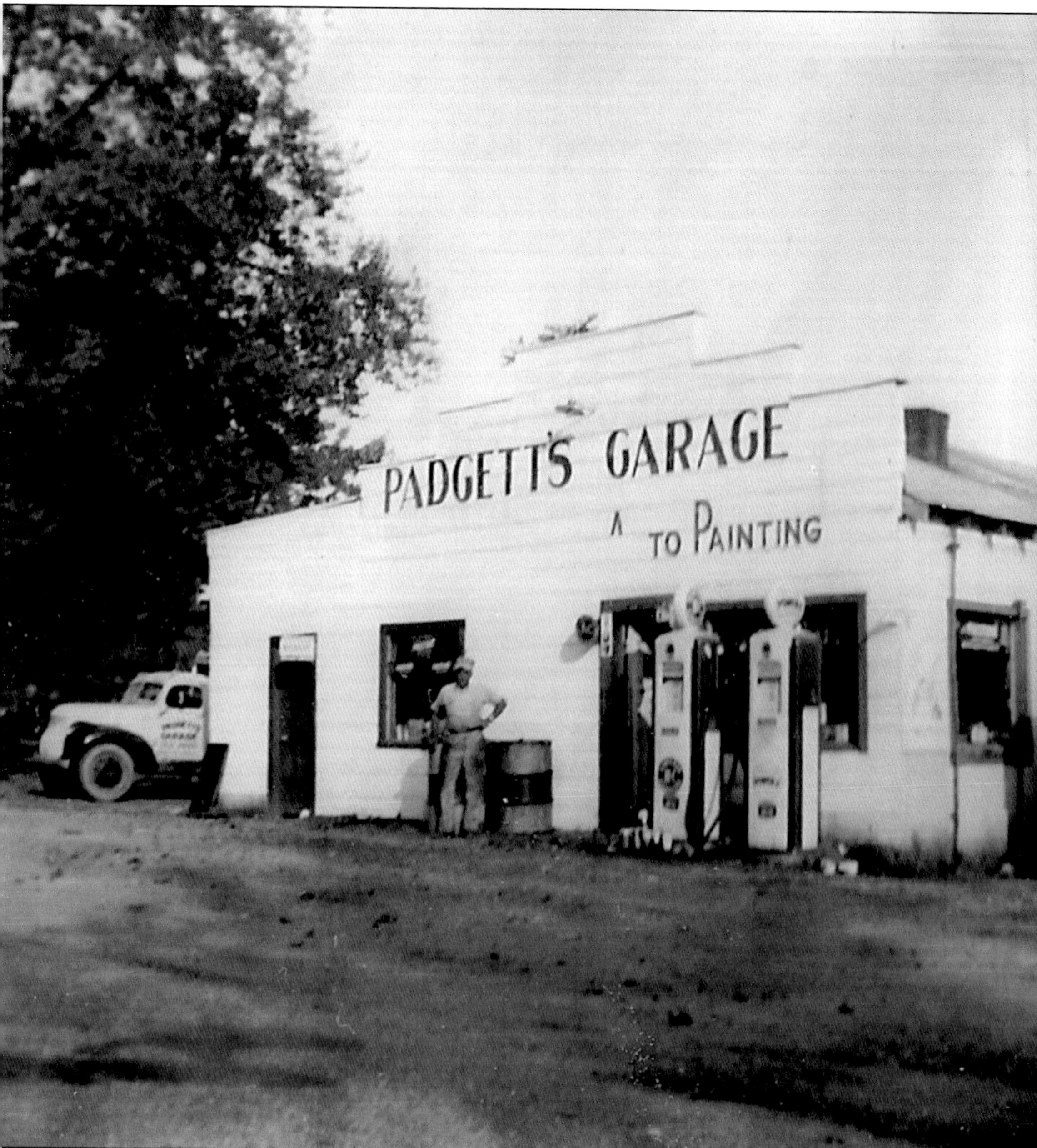

Though Riceville's post offices and schools had closed by the 1950s, Riceville's residents were still able to purchase many of their everyday necessities in the community at one of many country stores. Near the Blue Ridge Parkway tunnel was Padgett's Garage, owned and operated by Bill Padgett, one of the past members of Riceville's Board of Directors. (Courtesy of the Riceville Community Center.)

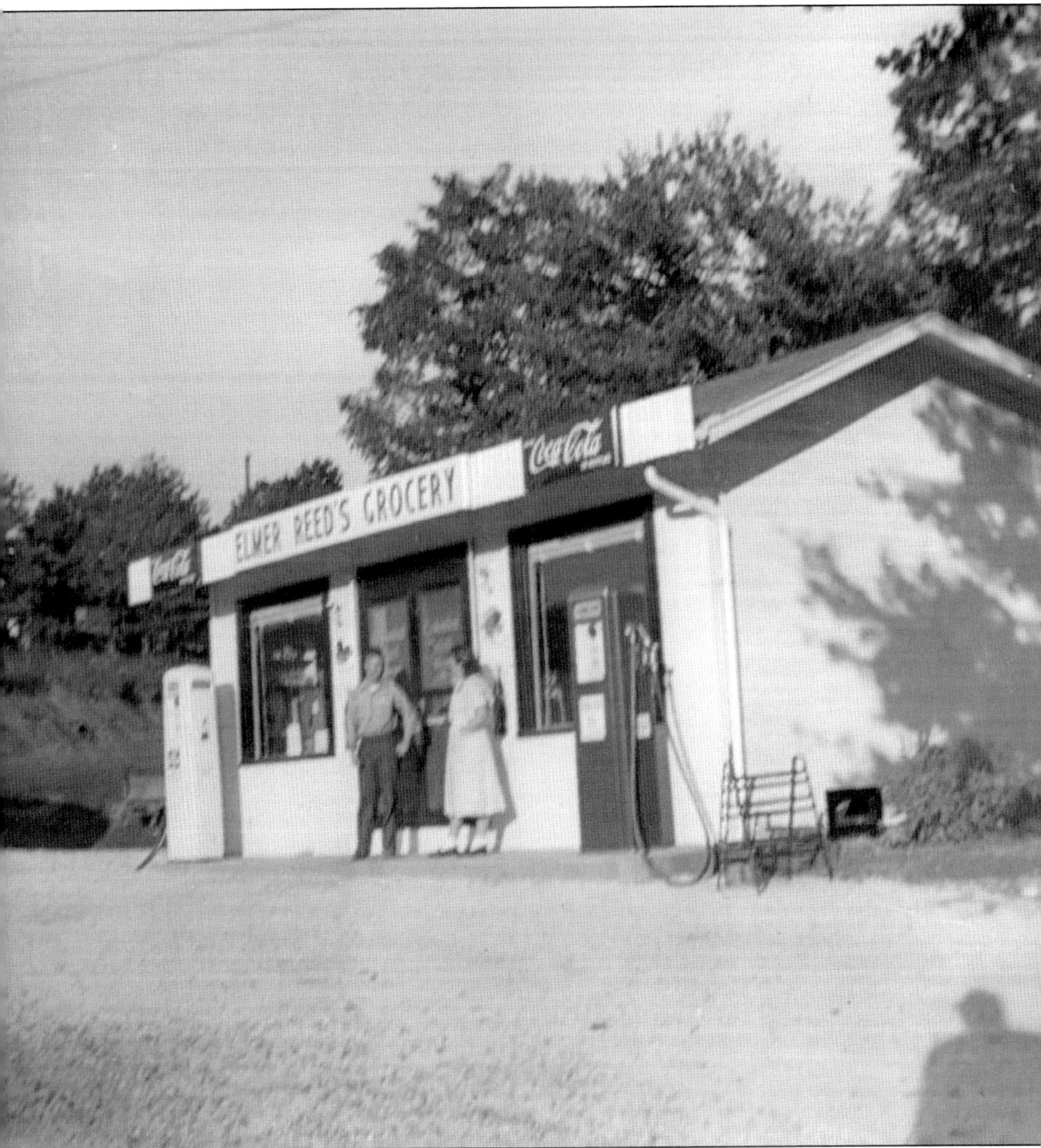

Between Grassy Branch and Bethel Methodist Church was Elmer Reed's Grocery. Reed sold gas, oil, and food to the community. The building has since been renovated into a home. For fun, he glued a dime to the steps of the store and would watch people try to pick it up. Reed also owned a chicken farm nearby with a chicken house more than 200 feet long. He invented one of the earliest chicken feeding and lighting systems. (Courtesy of the Riceville Community Center.)

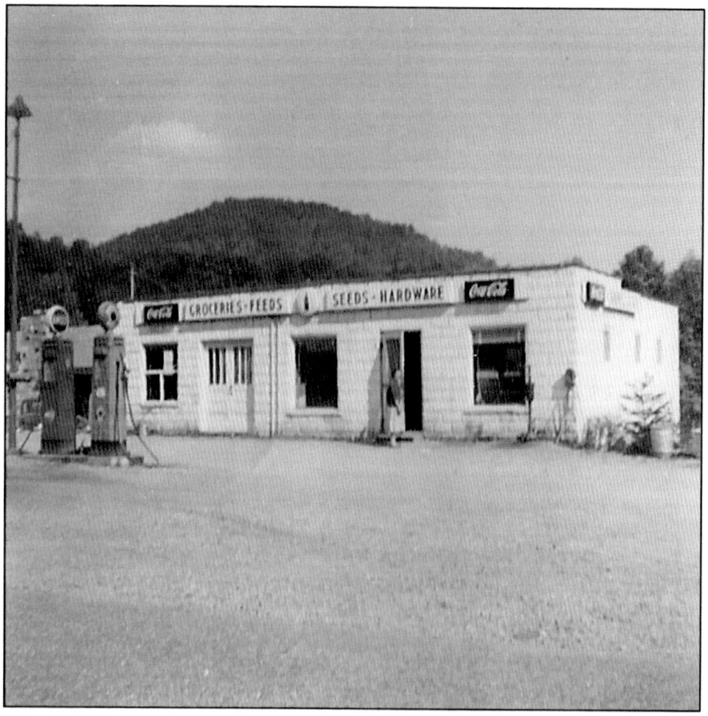

The brick-front building near the current fire station was Tal Shope's store, which carried a variety of goods. For a short time after the store closed, Mrs. Shandler operated a white-tablecloth tearoom in the building. Then Norman Ayers ran a grocery store and gas station there. The store had to be closed when the Environmental Protection Agency discovered the gas tanks were leaking. Neighbors tried to raise money to fund repair, but the store still closed. (Courtesy of the Riceville Community Center.)

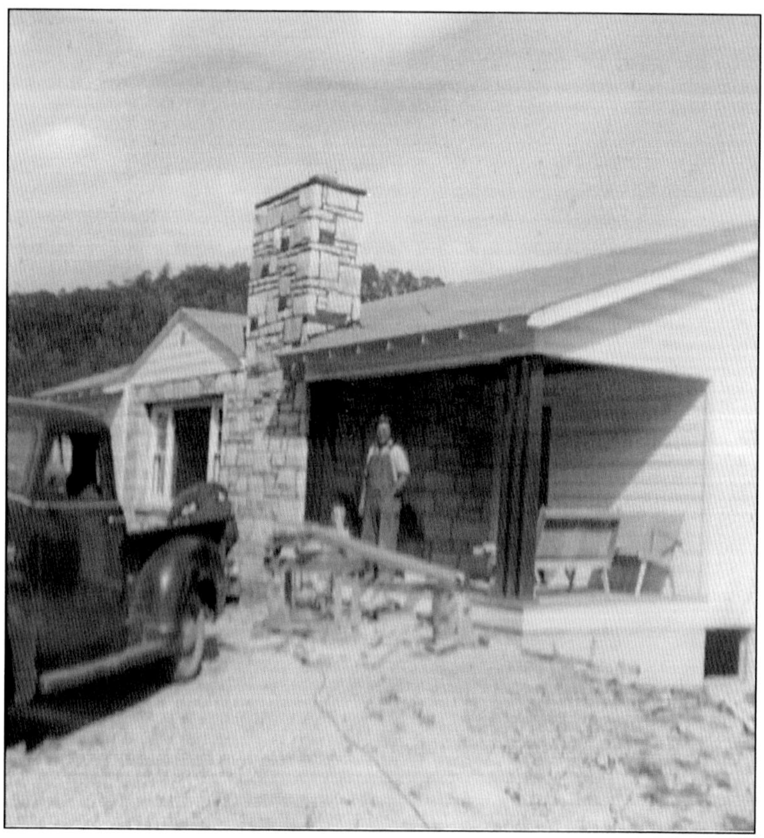

Tal Shope completed a home, built largely by his own labor, adjacent to his store. Tal stands on the front porch of his new home. (Courtesy of the Riceville Community Center.)

Tip and Sara Shope Sawyer's home, located off Riceville Road, is shown just after it was completed in the 1950s. They built the home just above where Sara was born, in a farmhouse built by her father in the early part of the 20th century. (Courtesy of the Riceville Community Center.)

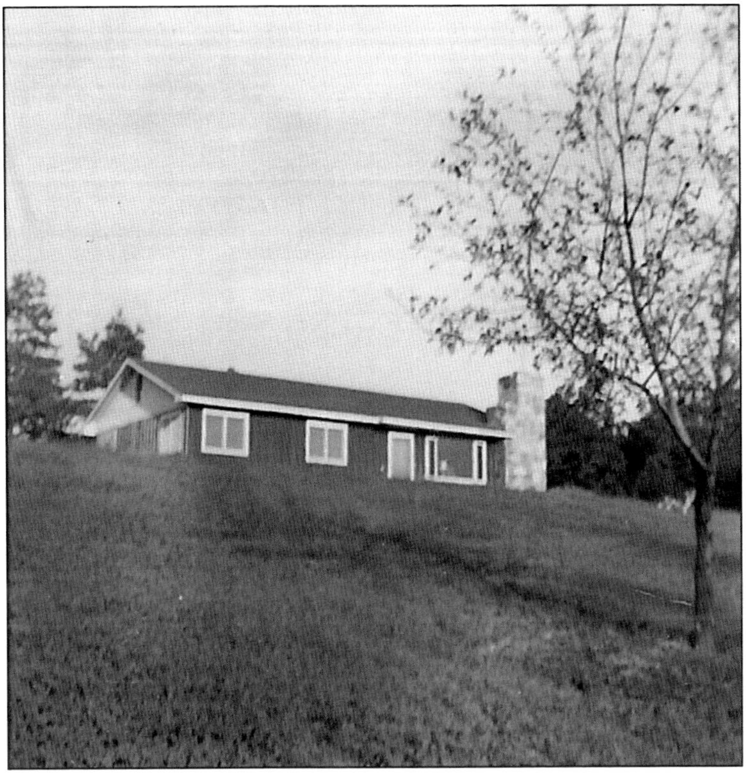

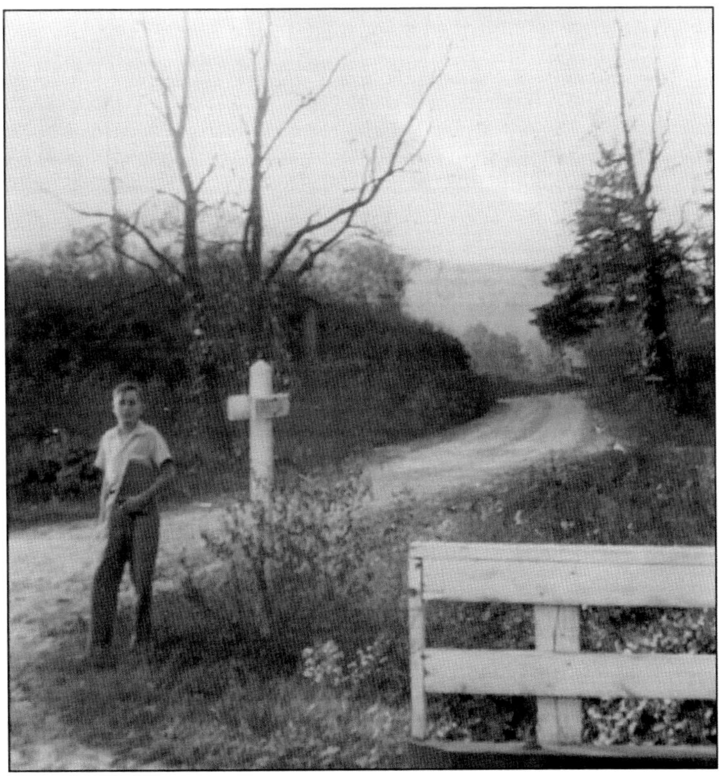

Road improvements were another goal of the Riceville Community Development Council, as better roads would continue to support and grow the community. Here, a boy stands at the intersection of Parker and Riceville Roads. (Courtesy of the Riceville Community Center.)

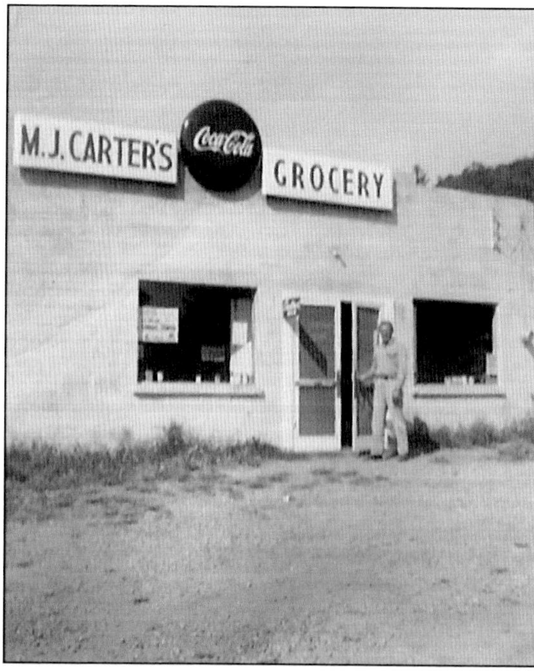

Just before the intersection of Bull Creek Road and Riceville Road was Carter's grocery. Nancy Wrenn still remembers the store before it became the cinder block building it is today: "It was a wooden building then, it had a little community store; it carried soup and coffee. It had a front porch that came out almost into Riceville Road and chairs, and people would sit there and watch whoever was going by. Every once in a while you'd go down there and start taking with people. It wasn't really a social occasion. It was just happenstance that they were there and you were there, and you caught up with one another's news. Our friend Bearden used to tell us that he was sorry he couldn't help us get in hay on Saturdays because he had to walk down to the store and help direct traffic." (Courtesy of the Riceville Community Center.)

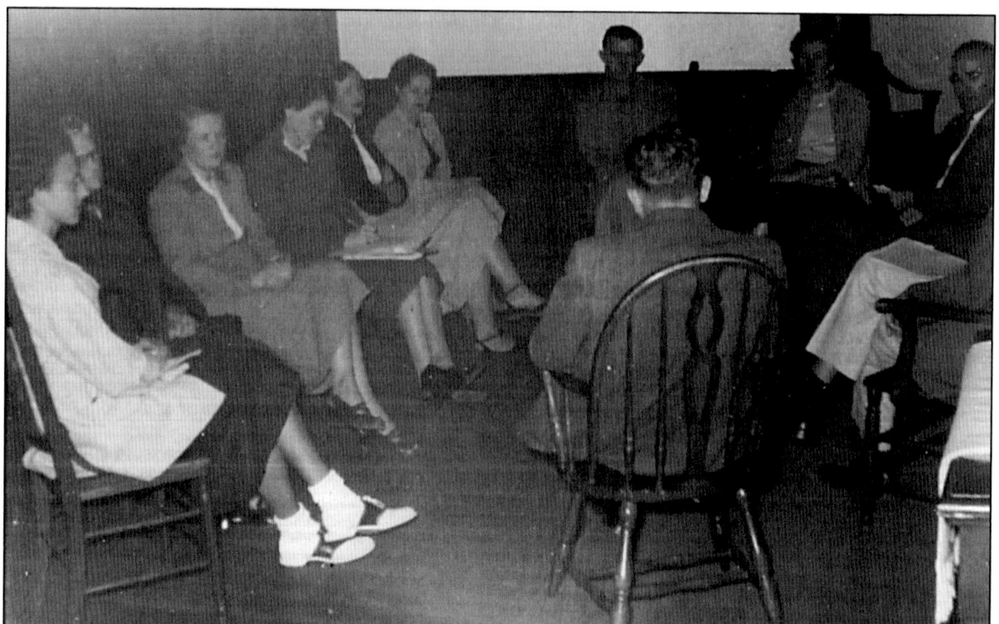

The Swannanoa Valley Inter-Church Association included some of the seven or eight churches between Riceville and Swannanoa. Some of its activities included Fifth Sunday Night Meetings, which took turns meeting in the various member churches; special meetings for the community, such as Easter sunrise service, Thanksgiving service, special World Day of Prayer meetings, and the annual Week of Revival; youth association meetings, which brought the young people of the community together every other month for supper, special programs, and a social; and a fieldwork program through Warren Wilson College, which provided help for the community and gave practical training to students. (Courtesy of the Riceville Community Center.)

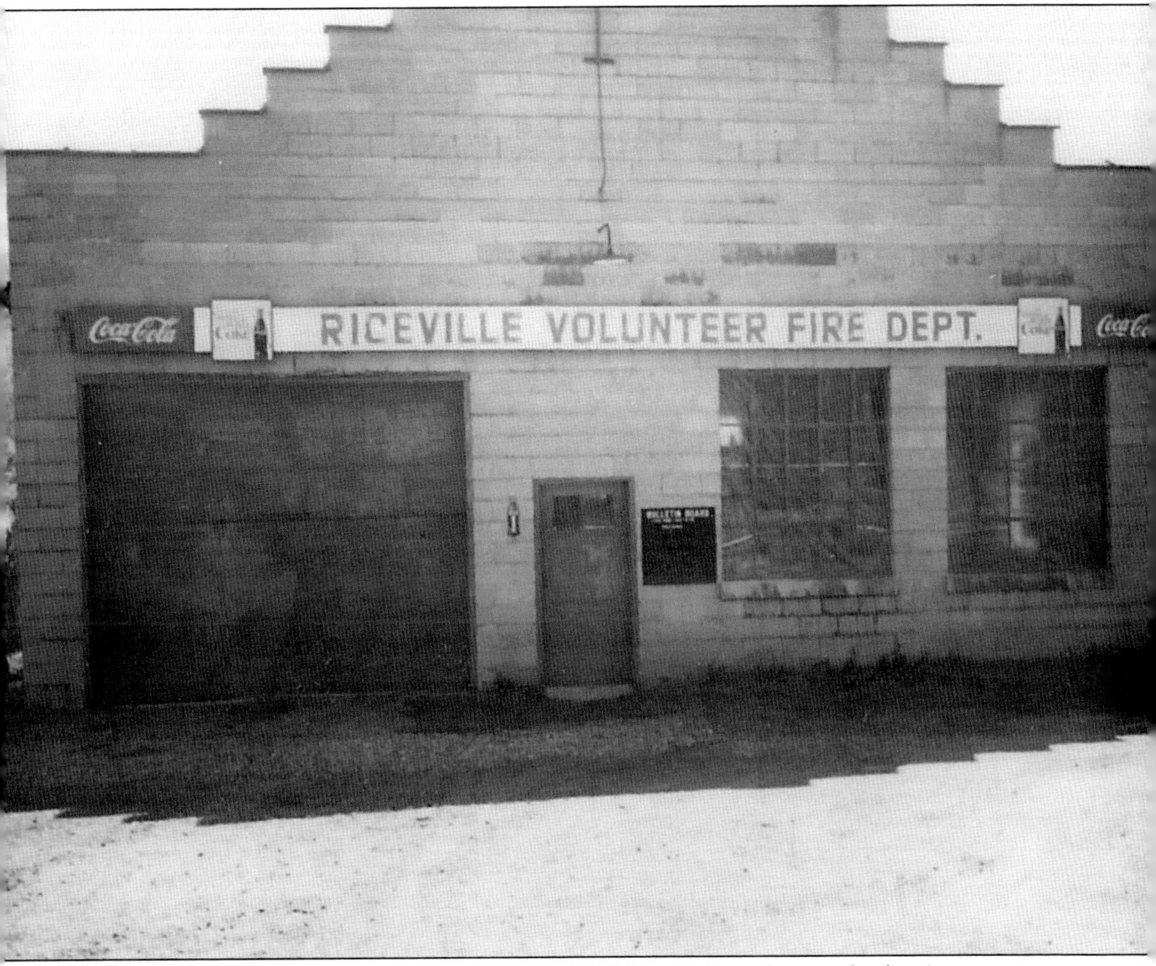

Near the current fire station was once Dooley Clark's workshop (currently the Automotive Volkswagen Hobby Shop), which had previously been a factory that manufactured metal spiral staircases. This garage was also used as the first community fire station for about four years. On October 19, 1964, the Riceville Board of Directors met and started making plans for a volunteer fire department. A letter was sent to every home in the area telling of the organization and requesting support. Each Monday night was set aside as the meeting night of the volunteer fire department, and anyone who wanted to become a firefighter was invited to attend the meetings. After attending three consecutive meetings, residents were eligible to become a volunteer firefighter. The weekly meetings were held in the community building each Monday night until February 1965, when a building on Riceville Road was rented from Viola Clark. At this time, Riceville had approximately 30 volunteer firemen. The first officers were fire chief G.R. Robertson, assistant chief Harry Byas, treasurer Francis Keenan, and secretary Douglas Allison. (Courtesy of the Riceville Community Center.)

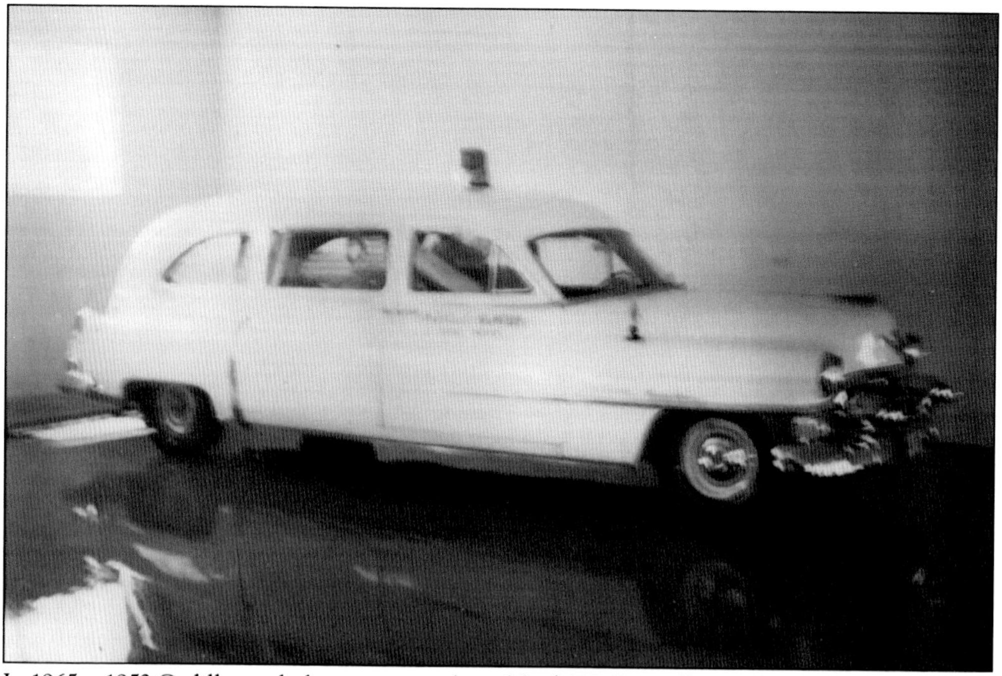

In 1965, a 1953 Cadillac ambulance was purchased for $609. Riceville was the first fire department in Buncombe County to have an ambulance. (Courtesy of the Riceville Fire Department.)

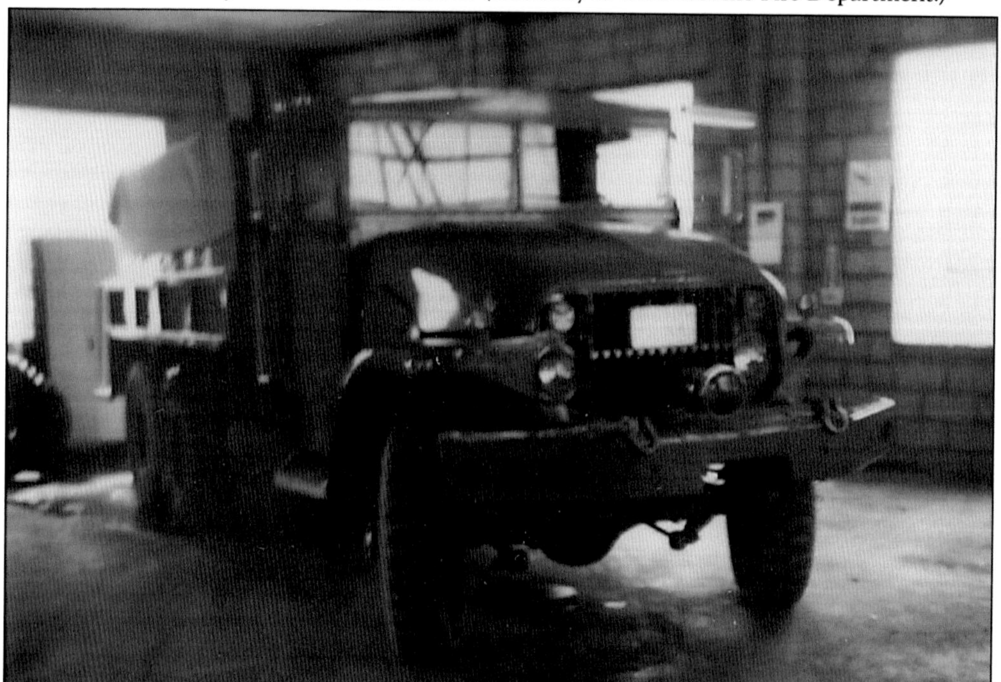

In 1966, an Army Six Cargo Truck was bought for $250. The men at the fire department built a 2200-gallon tank to go on top of the truck. This tanker was used by both the county and the city to fight house and wood fires. It was of great value in fighting fire where the water supply was limited. (Courtesy of the Riceville Fire Department.)

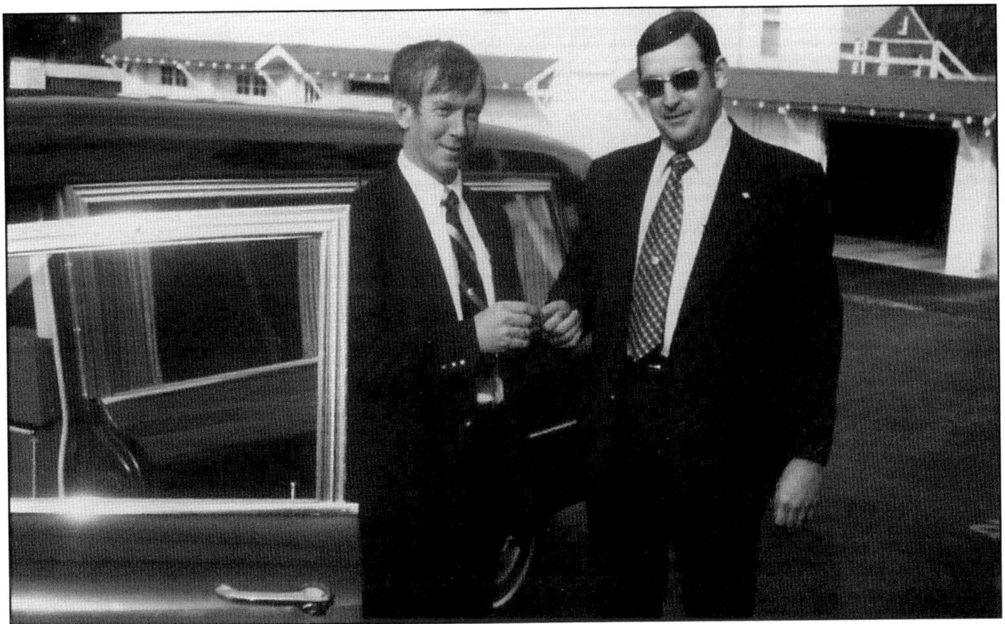

Bob Miller, of Miller Funeral Home in Black Mountain, donated one of his hearses to the Riceville Volunteer Fire Department. Roy Creasman, chief of the Riceville Volunteer Fire Department and patrol chief for the Buncombe County Sheriff Department, helped convert the 1964 Cadillac into an ambulance to join the other already in use by the department. (Courtesy of the Riceville Fire Department.)

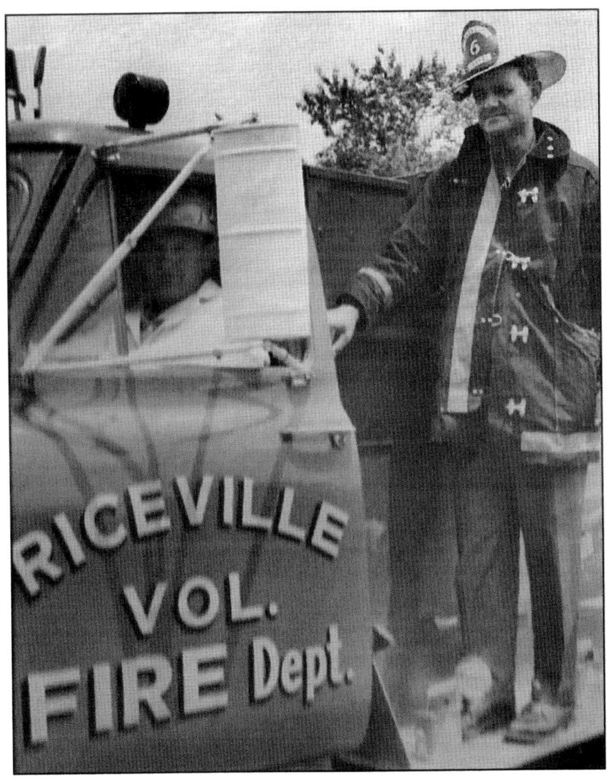

The first pumper truck was bought from Union Road Volunteer Fire Department on March 13, 1965. This pumper cost $1,200 and stayed in service until 1971. In April 1971, Roy and Wilbur Creasman flew to the American La France Factory in Allentown, Pennsylvania, to pick up the new 1970 Ford Pumper. They arrived at the fire station at the time most men were getting home from work. Phones rang, sirens blew, and the air horn sounded to let everyone know the new truck, which had been a dream for six years, had arrived. Many people came to see and inspect the new truck. (Courtesy of the Riceville Fire Department.)

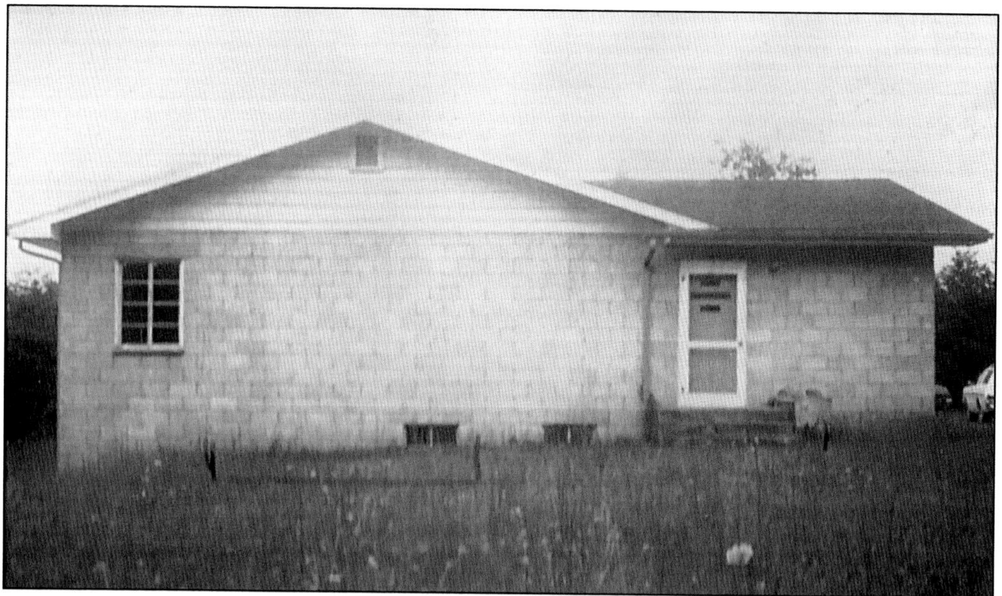

In July 1972, the original community building was sold to Dr. Joseph Schandler for $25,000. This money was to be applied to the new community center and fire department. Plans for the new building were drawn by Henry Gaines and approved by the building committee in June 1972. Bids were let, and the contract was approved and awarded to H.M. Rice and Son, contractors from Weaverville, North Carolina. A loan of $60,000 was obtained from Clyde Savings and Loan Association of Clyde, North Carolina. (Courtesy of the Riceville Fire Department.)

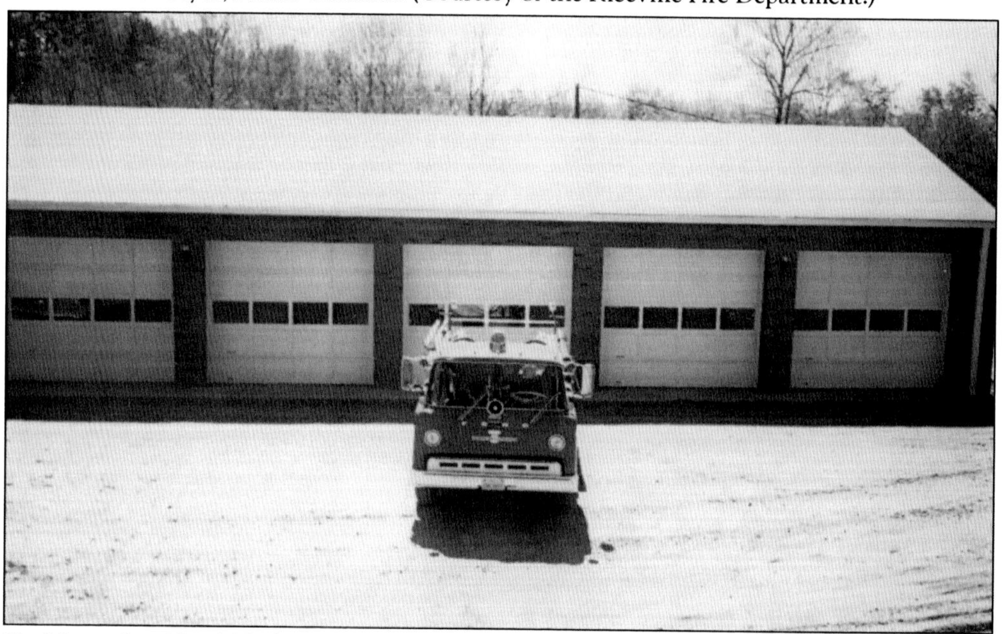

On November 20, 1965, three acres of land between Shope's store and Bull Creek Bridge on Riceville Road was purchased from Carl V. Almond of Greenville, Tennessee, for $3,990. This property was transferred to the Riceville Community Center on June 19, 1972, and became the site of the Riceville Community Center and Volunteer Fire Department. (Courtesy of the Riceville Community Center.)

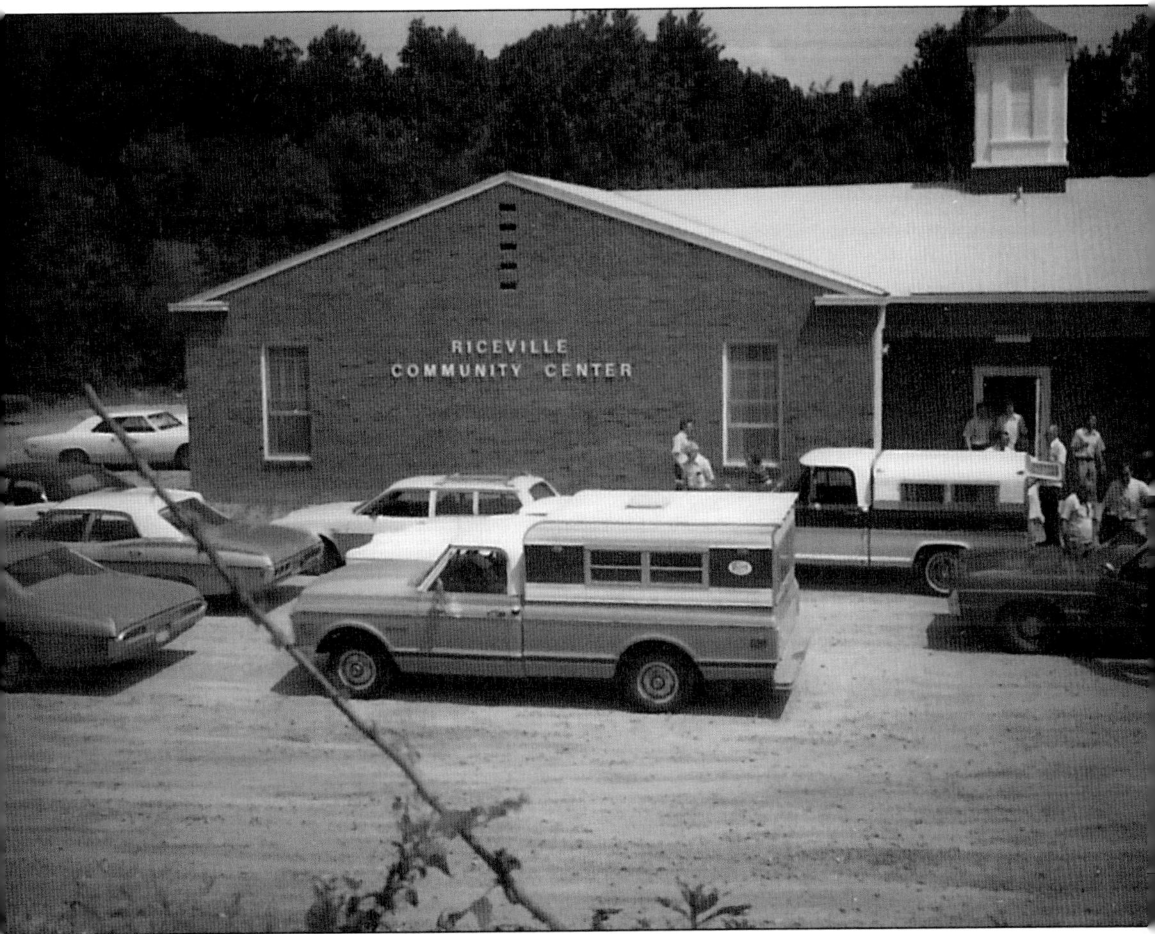

During the last week of October 1972, grading began, and construction was started for the new community building and fire department. Everyone watched with much interest as the construction advanced. The building was accepted, and the final payment to the contractor was made April 6, 1973, at a total cost of $82,775. (Courtesy of the Riceville Community Center.)

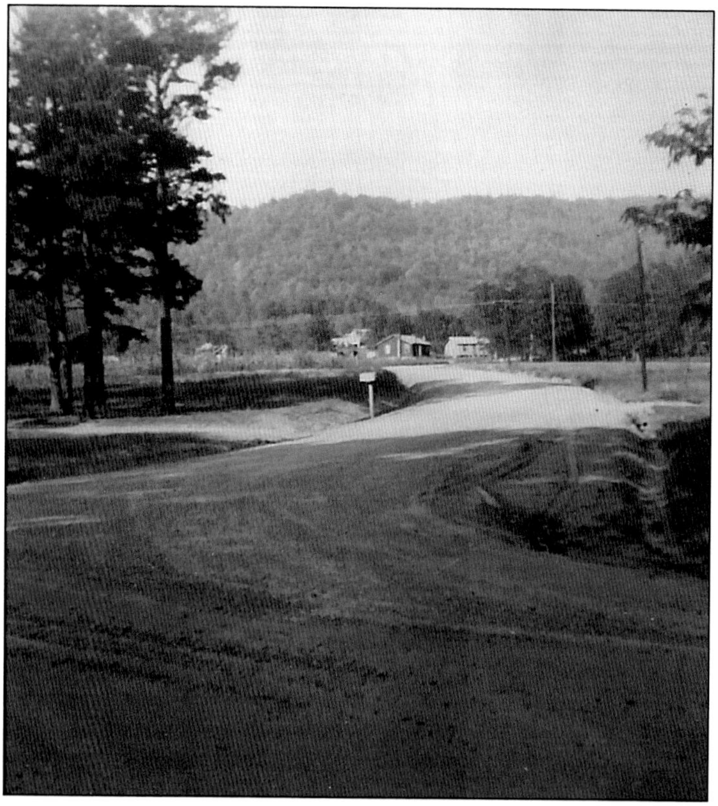

During the 1950s, the upper end of Bull Creek Road was widened and greatly improved. (Courtesy of the Riceville Community Center.)

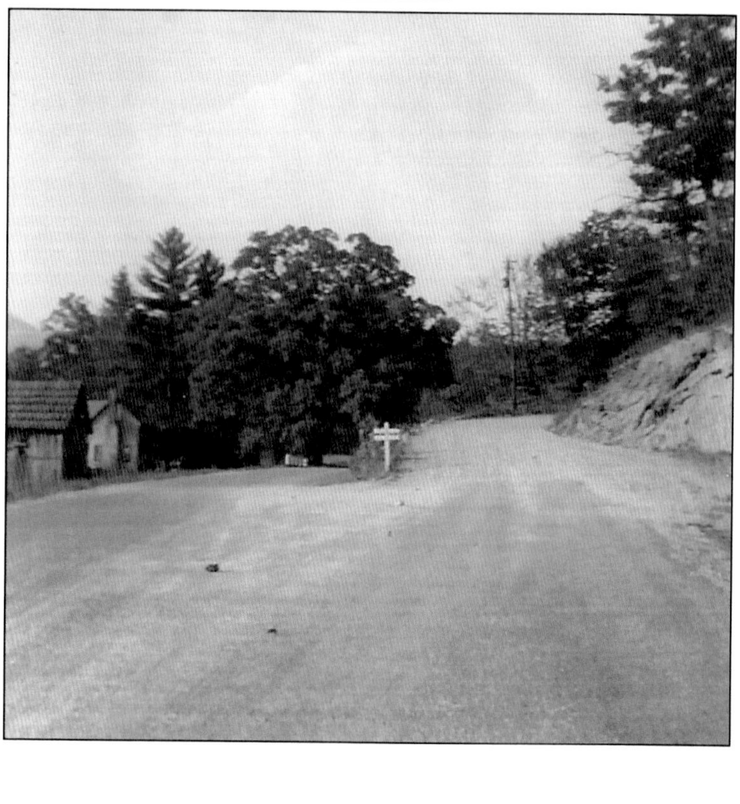

Here, Shope Creek Road branches right, off Bull Creek Road. Other road improvements during the 1950s included the paving of a half-mile stretch of Dillingham Circle, and an unsuccessful petition circulated among the landowners of Parker, Bull Creek, and Jones Cove Roads who sought to join the roads. (Courtesy of the Riceville Community Center.)

This view shows the valley, from the Riceville Presbyterian Church cemetery, in the 1950s. Carter's store can be seen in the distance. (Courtesy of the Riceville Community Center.)

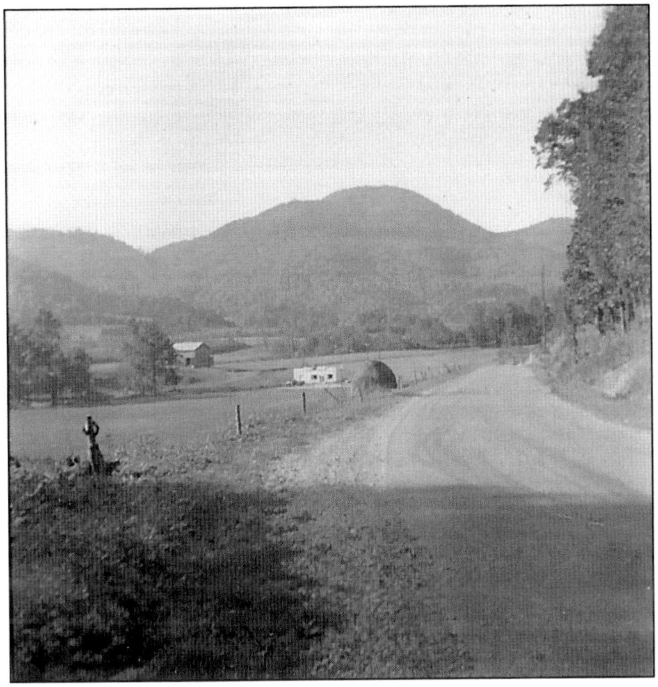

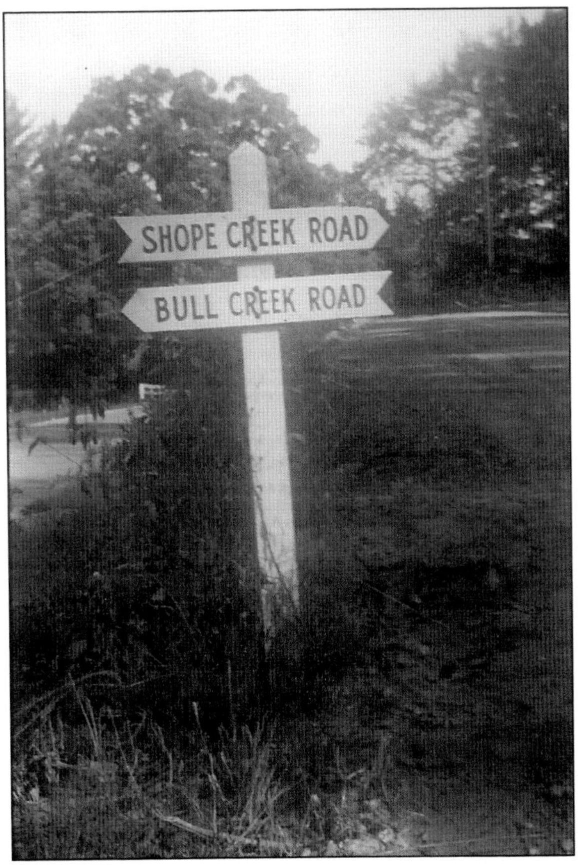

The intersection of Bull Creek and Shope Creek Roads is pictured in the 1950s. The Riceville Men's Club undertook many projects to improve the overall look of the Riceville community. In 1953, H.M. Creasman was the president of the club, which had 63 members at that time. One of the successful projects was erecting road signs throughout the valley. (Courtesy of the Riceville Community Center.)

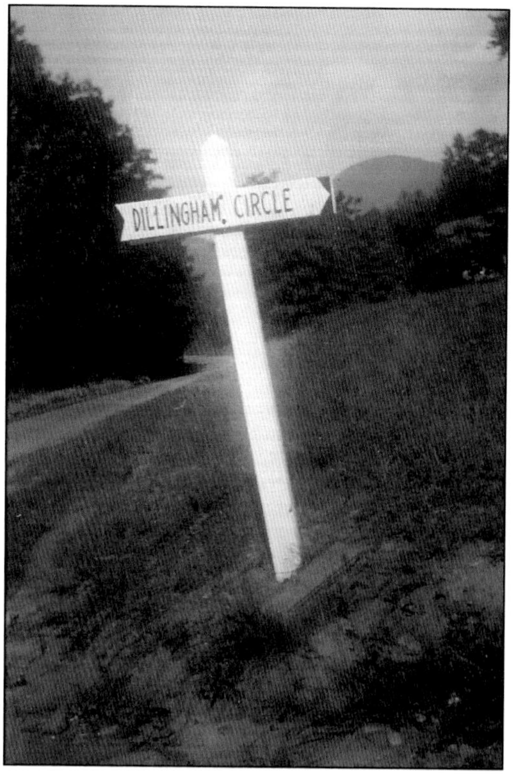

Shown in the 1950s is the entrance to one end of Dillingham Circle. Riceville Road can be seen winding through the background. (Courtesy of the Riceville Community Center.)

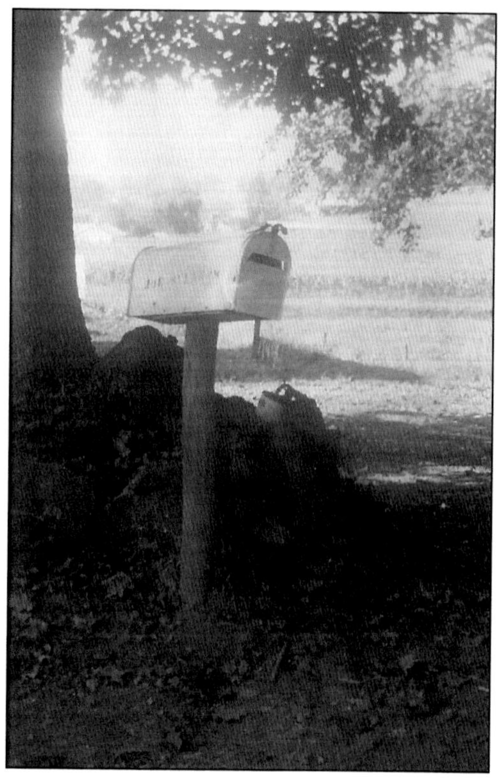

Another project of the Riceville Men's Club was mailbox improvement. The Grassy Branch Home Demonstration Club cooperated with the men's club on this project. Joe Sellers's mailbox was one of the many slated for improvement. (Courtesy of the Riceville Community Center.)

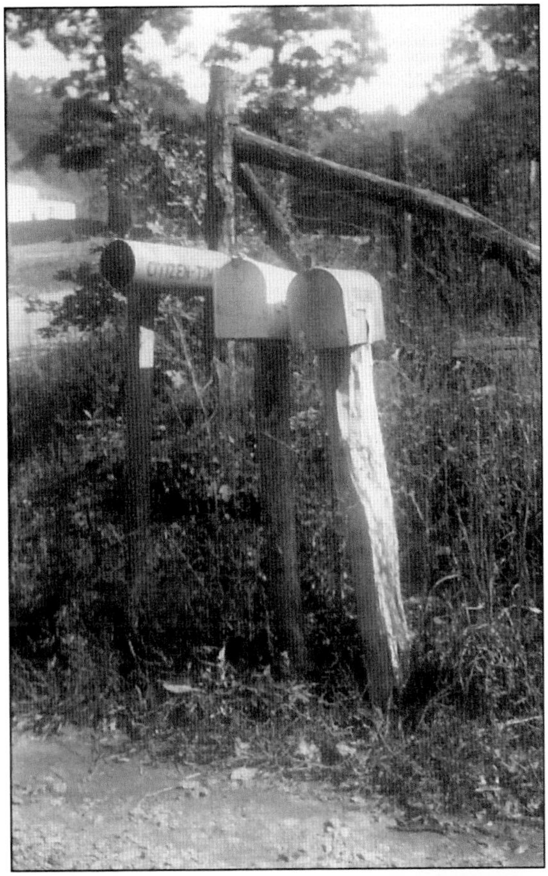

The change from the old mailboxes (right) to the new mailboxes (below) was meant to establish a uniform and aesthetically pleasing look for Riceville's roads and to create a sense of community. (Courtesy of the Riceville Community Center.)

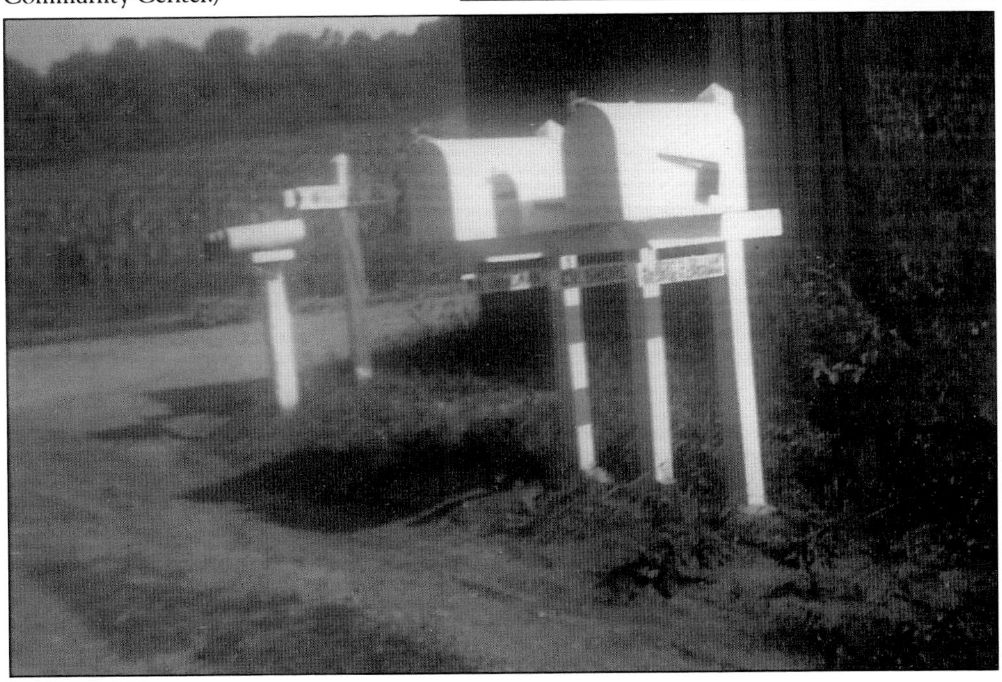

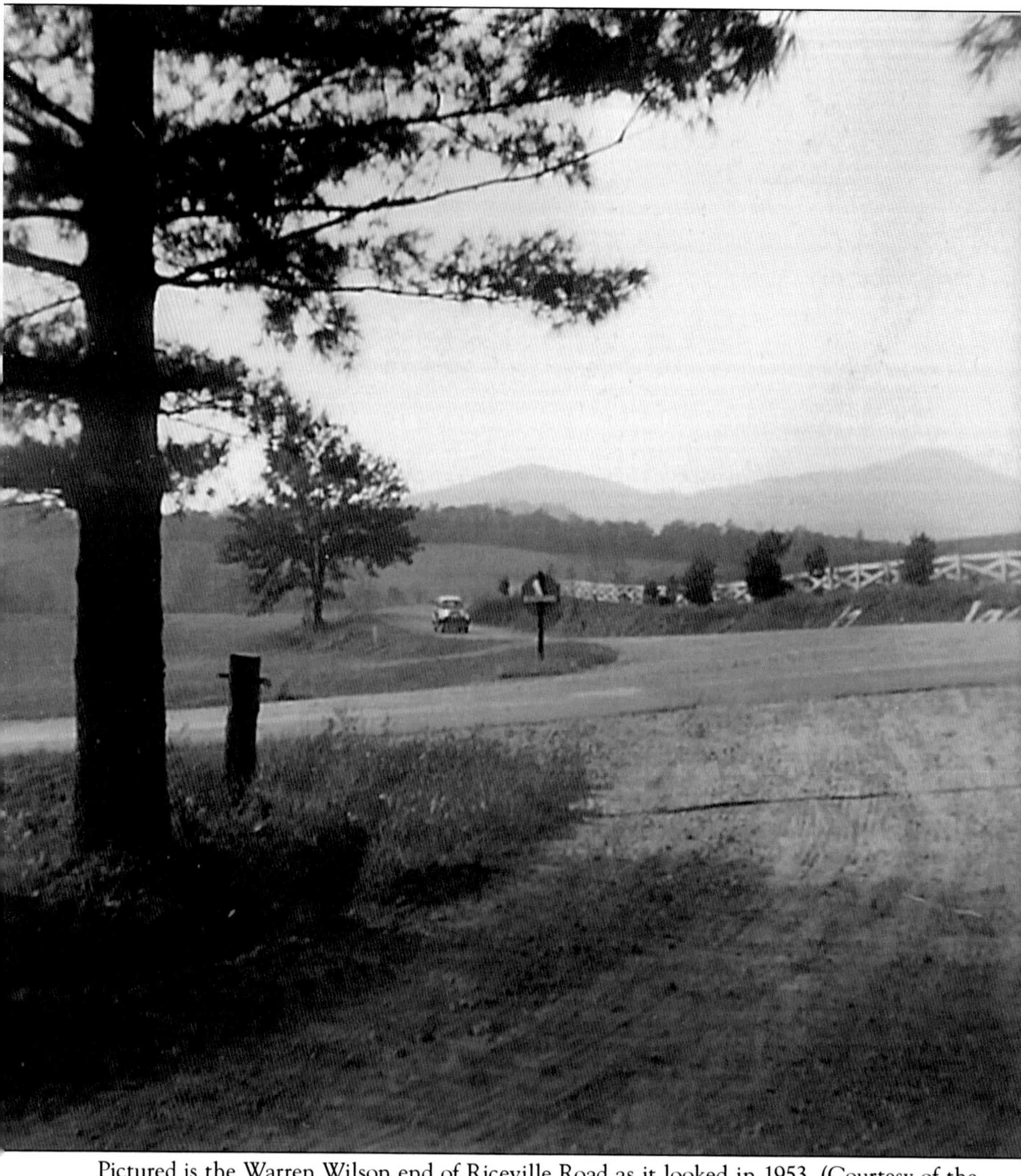

Pictured is the Warren Wilson end of Riceville Road as it looked in 1953. (Courtesy of the Riceville Community Center.)

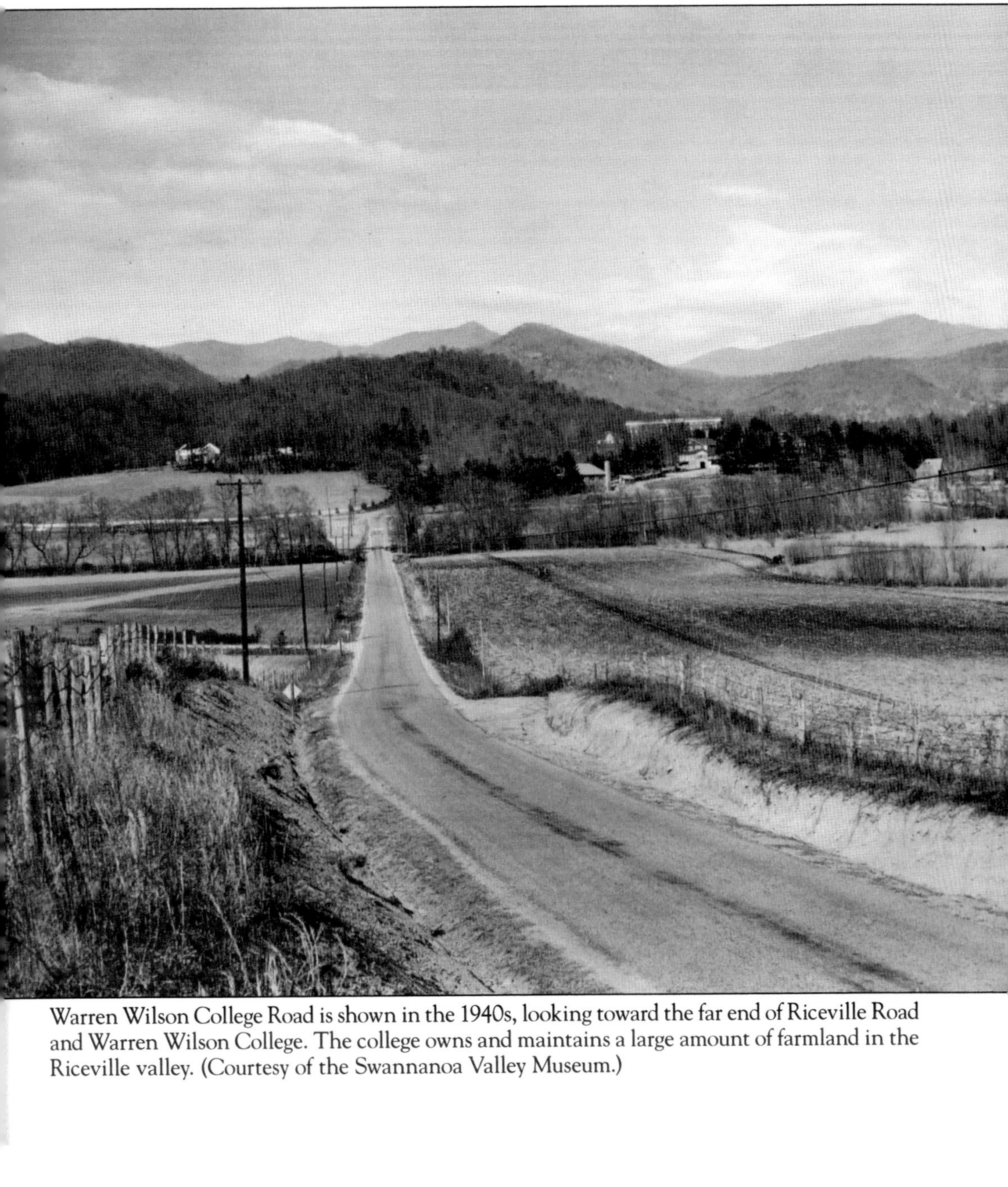

Warren Wilson College Road is shown in the 1940s, looking toward the far end of Riceville Road and Warren Wilson College. The college owns and maintains a large amount of farmland in the Riceville valley. (Courtesy of the Swannanoa Valley Museum.)

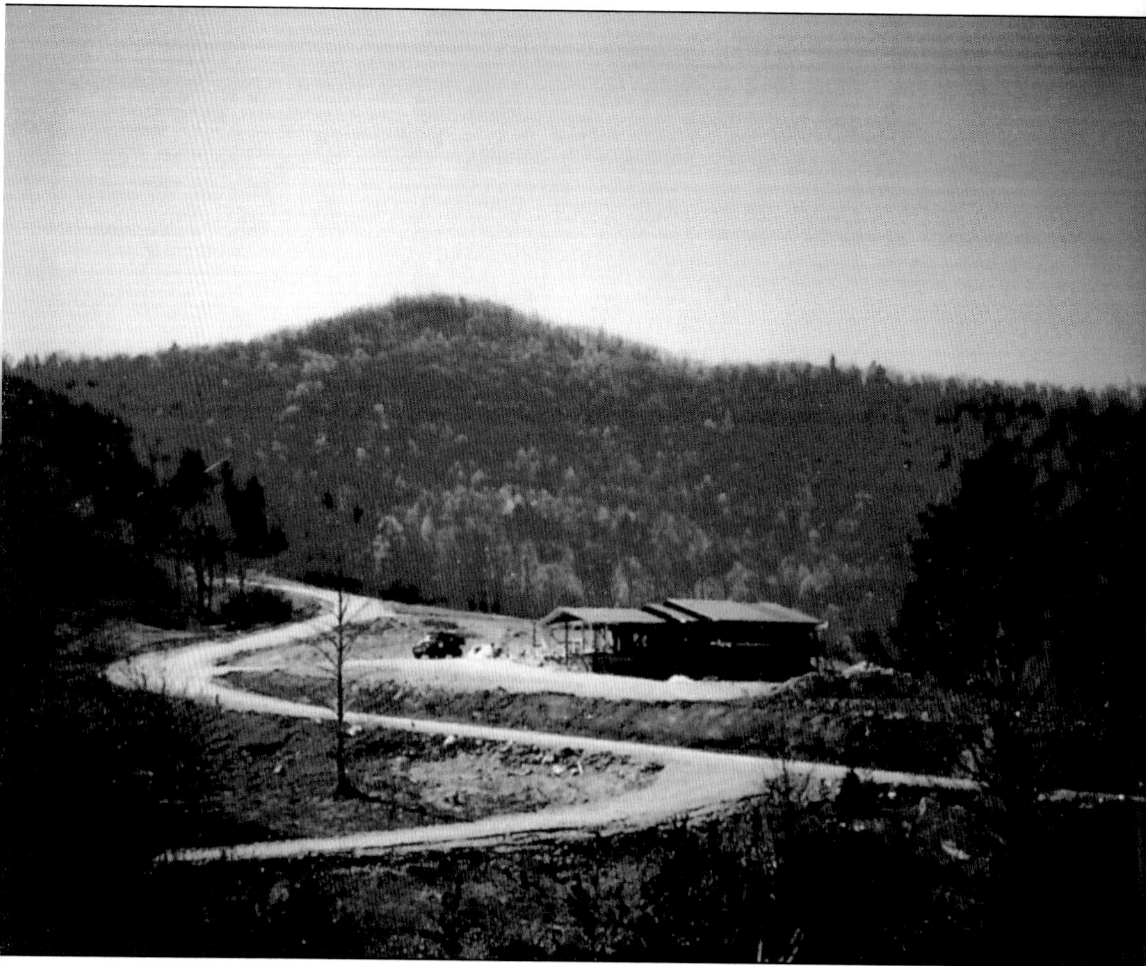

Jewell Acres was one of the first subdivisions in Riceville. Pictured is the first house built in part of the subdivision, as it looked during construction in 1972. (Courtesy of Kevin and Jennifer Hefner.)

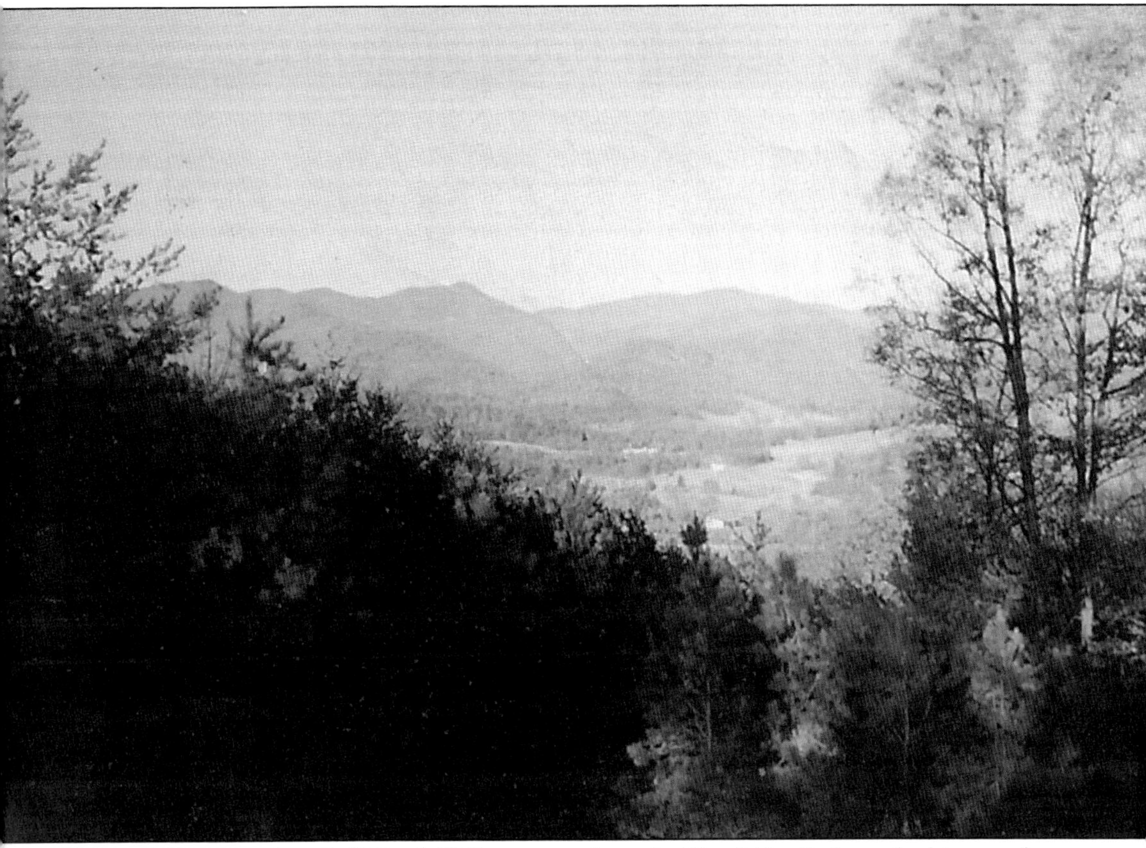

This is a 1970s view of the Bull Creek Valley, as seen from the Blue Ridge Parkway, looking north. (Courtesy of Rafe Rice Jr.)

www.arcadiapublishing.com

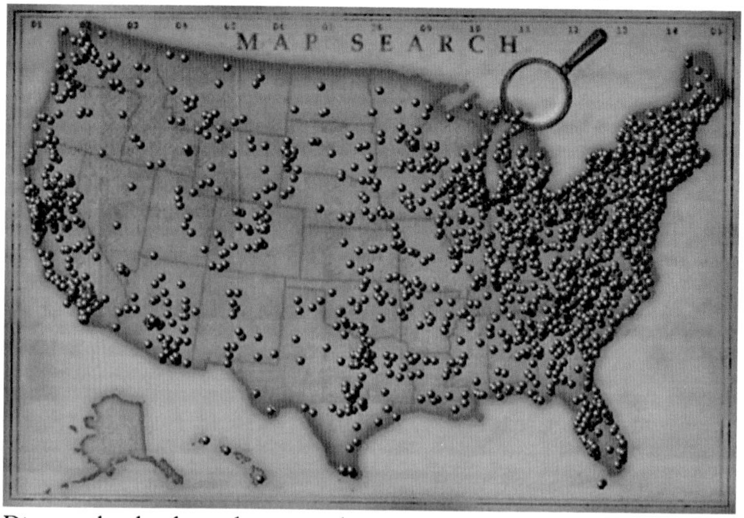

Discover books about the town where you grew up, the cities where your friends and families live, the town where your parents met, or even that retirement spot you've been dreaming about. Our Web site provides history lovers with exclusive deals, advanced notification about new titles, e-mail alerts of author events, and much more.

MADE IN THE USA

Arcadia Publishing, the leading local history publisher in the United States, is committed to making history accessible and meaningful through publishing books that celebrate and preserve the heritage of America's people and places. Consistent with our mission to preserve history on a local level, this book was printed in South Carolina on American-made paper and manufactured entirely in the United States.

This book carries the accredited Forest Stewardship Council (FSC) label and is printed on 100 percent FSC-certified paper. Products carrying the FSC label are independently certified to assure consumers that they come from forests that are managed to meet the social, economic, and ecological needs of present and future generations.

FSC
Mixed Sources
Product group from well-managed forests and other controlled sources

Cert no. SW-COC-001530
www.fsc.org
© 1996 Forest Stewardship Council

Find *Your* Place in History.